The *Sams Teach Yourself in 24 H*

Sams Teach Yourself in 24 Hours books provide quick and e
proven step-by-step approach that works for you. In just 24
hour or less, you will tackle every task you need to get the results you want.
Let our experienced authors present the most accurate information to get
you reliable answers—fast!

Terms Used Throughout the Book

ActiveX   A technology developed by Microsoft to allow components to be created, primarily for Windows computers. ActiveX components, or controls, can be embedded in Web pages.

applet   A Java program that is designed to be embedded in a Web page.

argument   A parameter that is passed to a function when it is called. Arguments are specified within parentheses in the function call.

array   A set of variables that can be referred to with the same name and a number, called an index.

Boolean   A type of variable that can store only two values: true and false.

concatenate   The act of combining two strings into a single, longer string.

conditional   A JavaScript statement that performs an action if a particular condition is true, usually using the if statement.

decrement   To decrease the value of a variable by one. In JavaScript, this can be done with the decrement operator, --.

debug   Finding and removing errors, or bugs, in a program or script.

element   A single member of an array, referred to with an index.

event   A condition, often the result of a user's action, that can be detected by a script.

expression   A combination of variables, constants, and operators that can be evaluated to a single value.

function   A group of JavaScript statements that can be referred to using a function name and arguments.

Hypertext Markup Language (HTML)   The language used in Web documents. JavaScript statements are not HTML, but can be included within an HTML document.

increment   To increase the value of a variable by one. In JavaScript, this is done with the increment operator, ++.

interpreter   The browser component that interprets JavaScript statements and acts on them.

Java   An object-oriented language developed by Sun Microsystems. Java applets can be embedded within a Web page. JavaScript has similar syntax, but is not the same as Java.

Teach Yourself JavaScript 1.3

in 24 Hours

JavaScript   A scripting language for Web documents, loosely based on Java's syntax, developed by Netscape. JavaScript is now supported by the most popular browsers.

loop   A set of JavaScript statements that is executed a number of times or until a certain condition is met.

method   A specialized type of function that can be stored in an object and acts on the object's properties.

Navigator   A browser developed by Netscape, and the first to support JavaScript.

object   A type of variable that can store multiple values, called properties, and functions, called methods.

operator   A character used to divide variables or constants used in an expression.

parameter   A variable sent to a function when it is called, also known as an argument.

Property   A variable that is stored as part of an object. Each object can have any number of properties.

scope   The part of a JavaScript program that a variable was declared in and is available to.

statement   A single line of a script or program.

string   A group of text characters that can be stored in a variable.

variable   A container, referred to with a name, that can store a number, a string, or an object.

VBScript   A scripting language developed by Microsoft, with syntax based on Visual Basic. VBScript is supported only by Microsoft Internet Explorer.

Michael Moncur

SAMS
Teach Yourself

JavaScript 1.3
in 24 Hours

SAMS
201 West 103rd St., Indianapolis, Indiana 46290 USA

Sams Teach Yourself JavaScript 1.3 in 24 Hours

Copyright © 1999 by Sams Publishing

International Standard Book Number: 0-672-31407-x

Library of Congress Catalog Card Number: 98-86224

Printed in the United States of America

First Printing: January 1999

01   00   10 9 8 7 6

Trademarks

Warning and Disclaimer

EXECUTIVE EDITOR
Mark Taber

AQUISITIONS EDITOR
Scott D. Meyers

DEVELOPMENT EDITOR
Scott D. Meyers

MANAGING EDITOR
Lisa Wilson

PRODUCTION EDITOR
Carol Bowers

COPY EDITOR
Sean Medlock

INDEXER
Heather Goens

PROOFREADER
Gene Redding

TECHNICAL EDITOR
Michelle Wyner

INTERIOR DESIGNER
Gary Adair

COVER DESIGNER
Aren Howell

LAYOUT TECHNICIANS
Brian Borders
Amy Parker
Susan Geiselman

Overview

Introduction

Contents

Dedication

To my grandmothers, Alice Moncur and Edna Tippets. They've been my biggest fans since I started writing, and I'm thankful for their love and support.

Acknowledgments

I'd like to thank everyone at Sams for their help with this book and for the opportunity to write it. In particular, David Mayhew, Scott Meyers, and Mark Taber helped me get started and kept things moving along. The editor, Sean Medlock, helped keep the writing clear and consistent. Michelle Wyner, the technical reviewer, was extremely vigilant in testing the scripts and double-checking my writing, and this book owes much to her.

I'd also like to thank everyone at the Studio B agency, especially David and Sherry Rogelberg, for their help throughout this project.

Finally, personal thanks go to my wife, Laura, my parents, Gary and Susan Moncur, and the rest of my family and my friends, particularly Chuck Perkins, Matt Strebe, Cory Storm, Robert Parsons, Dylan Winslow, Scott Durbin, Ray Jones, James Chellis, Curt Siffert, and Henry J. Tillman. I couldn't have done it without your support.

About the Author

MICHAEL MONCUR is a freelance Webmaster and author and has worked with the Internet since Gopher was still a cool thing. He previously wrote *Laura Lemay's Web Workshop: JavaScript* for Sams.net and contributed to *JavaScript Unleashed* and *Sams Teach Yourself CGI Programming with Perl 5 in a Week*. He has also written several best-selling books about networking and the CNE and MCSE programs. In his spare time (about an hour per year), he composes music and builds model rockets.

Tell Us What You Think!

As the reader of this book, *you* are our most important critic and commentator. We value your opinion and want to know what we're doing right, what we could do better, what areas you'd like to see us publish in, and any other words of wisdom you're willing to pass our way.

As the Executive Editor for the Web development team at Macmillan Computer Publishing, I welcome your comments. You can fax, email, or write me directly to let me know what you did or didn't like about this book—as well as what we can do to make our books stronger.

Please note that I cannot help you with technical problems related to the topic of this book, and that due to the high volume of mail I receive, I might not be able to reply to every message.

When you write, please be sure to include this book's title and author, as well as your name and phone or fax number. I will carefully review your comments and share them with the author and editors who worked on the book.

Fax: 317-817-7070
Email: webdev@mcp.com
Mail: Mark Taber
Web Development Team
Macmillan Computer Publishing
201 West 103rd Street
Indianapolis, IN 46290 USA

Introduction

The World Wide Web began as a simple repository for information, but it has grown into much more—it entertains, teaches, advertises, and communicates. As the Web has evolved, the tools also have evolved. Simple markup tools such as HTML have been joined by true programming languages—including JavaScript.

Now, don't let the word "programming" scare you. For many, the term conjures up images of long nights staring at the screen, trying to remember which sequence of punctuation marks will produce the effect you need. (Don't get me wrong. Some of us enjoy that sort of thing.)

Although JavaScript is a programming language, it's a very simple one. As a matter of fact, it makes a great introduction to programming if you haven't done it before. It requires very little knowledge to start programming with JavaScript—you'll write your first program in Hour 2, "Creating a Simple Script."

If you can create a Web page with HTML, you can easily use JavaScript to improve a page. JavaScript programs can range from a single line to a full-scale application. In this book, you'll start with simple scripts and proceed to complex applications, such as a card game and a shopping cart script.

If you've spent much time developing pages for the Web, you know that the Web is constantly changing, and it can be hard to keep up with the latest languages and tools. This book will help you add JavaScript to your Web development toolbox, and I think you'll enjoy learning it.

I really had fun writing this book—and believe it or not, writing isn't always fun. I hope you'll have as much fun as you experiment with JavaScript and its capabilities.

How to Use This Book

This book is divided into 24 lessons. Each one covers a single JavaScript topic and should take about an hour to complete. The lessons start with the basics of JavaScript and continue with more advanced topics. You can study an hour a day, or at whatever pace suits you. (If you choose to forego sleep and do your studying in a single 24-hour period, you may have what it takes to be a computer book author.)

Q&A, Quiz, and Exercises

At the end of each hour's lesson, you'll find three final sections. The Q&A section answers a few of the most common questions about the hour's topic. The Quiz section includes three questions to test your knowledge, and the Exercises section offers ways for you to gain more experience with the techniques the hour covers.

This Book's Web Site

Because JavaScript and the Web are constantly changing, you'll need to stay up to date after reading this book. This book's Web site, maintained by author Michael Moncur, includes the latest updates, as well as downloadable versions of the listings and graphics for the examples in this book. Here's the address:

`http://www.jsworkshop.com/`

If you have questions or comments about this book, notice an error, or can't get one of the scripts to work, you can also reach the author by email at `tyjs@starlingtech.com`. (Please check the Web site first to see if your question has been answered.)

PART I
Getting Started

Hour

HOUR 1

Understanding JavaScript

The World Wide Web (WWW) began as a text-only medium—the first version of the HTML specification didn't even have the capability to include graphics on a page. Although it's still not quite ready to give television a run for its money, the Web has come a long way.

Today's Web sites can include a wealth of features: graphics, sounds, animation, video, and sometimes even useful content. Web scripting languages, such as JavaScript, are one of the easiest ways to spice up a Web page and to interact with users in new ways.

The first hour of this book introduces the concept of Web scripting and the JavaScript language. It also describes how JavaScript, Java, and other Web languages fit into the scheme of things. The following topics will be covered in this hour:

- What Web scripting is, and what it's good for
- How scripting and programming are different (and similar)

- What JavaScript is
- The differences between JavaScript and Java
- How to include JavaScript commands in a Web page
- How different Web browsers handle JavaScript
- Choosing between JavaScript and alternative languages

Learning Web Scripting Basics

In the world of science fiction movies (and many other movies that have no excuse), computers are often seen obeying commands in English. While this may indeed happen in the near future, computers currently find it easier to understand languages like BASIC, C, and Java.

If you know how to use HTML to create a Web document, you've already worked with one computer language. You use HTML tags to describe how you want your document formatted, and the browser obeys your commands and shows the formatted document to the user.

Since HTML is a simple text markup language, it can't respond to the user, make decisions, or automate repetitive tasks. Interactive tasks like these require a more complex language: a programming language, or a *scripting* language.

While many programming languages are complex, scripting languages are generally simple. They have a simple syntax, can perform tasks with a minimum of commands, and are easy to learn. Web scripting languages allow you to combine scripting with HTML to create interactive Web pages.

Scripts and Programs

A movie or play follows a script—a list of actions (or lines) for the actors to perform. A Web script provides the same type of instructions for the browser. A script in JavaScript can range from a single line to a full-scale application. (In either case, JavaScript programs always run within a browser or other JavaScript-enabled applications.)

Some programming languages must be *compiled*, or translated into machine code, before they can be executed. JavaScript, on the other hand, is an *interpreted* language: The browser executes each line of script as it comes to it.

There is one main advantage to interpreted languages: Writing or changing a script is very simple. Changing a JavaScript script is as easy as changing a typical HTML document, and the change is enacted as soon as you reload the document in the browser.

So what's the difference between scripting and programming? It depends on who you ask. We'll refer to scripting throughout this book, but feel free to include JavaScript Programming on your resume after you've finished this book.

Introducing JavaScript

JavaScript was developed by Netscape Communications Corporation, the makers of the popular Netscape Navigator Web browser. JavaScript was the first Web scripting language to be introduced, and it is by far the most popular.

JavaScript was originally called LiveScript and was first introduced in Netscape Navigator 2.0 in 1995. It was later renamed JavaScript to indicate its relationship with Java.

JavaScript is almost as easy to learn as HTML, and it can be included directly in HTML documents. Here are a few of the things you can do with JavaScript:

- Add scrolling or changing messages to the browser's status line.
- Validate the contents of a form and make calculations. (For example, an order form can automatically display a running total as you enter item quantities.)
- Display messages to the user, either as part of a Web page or in alert boxes.
- Animate images or create images that change when you move the mouse over them.
- Detect the browser in use and display different content for different browsers.
- Detect installed plug-ins and notify the user if a plug-in is required.

This is just a quick sample of what JavaScript can do. You can do much more with JavaScript, including creating entire applications. We'll explore the uses of JavaScript throughout this book.

JavaScript vs. Java

Before we delve into JavaScript, let's take a quick look at its namesake, Java. Java is a programming language developed by Sun Microsystems that can be used to create *applets*, or programs that execute within a Web page.

Java is also a densely populated island in Indonesia and a slang term for coffee. This has resulted in a widespread invasion of coffee-related terms in computer literature, such as the title of this note.

Java is a compiled language, but the compiler produces code for a *virtual machine* rather than a real computer. The virtual machine code is then interpreted by a Web browser. This allows the same Java applet to execute the same way on PCs, Macintoshes, and UNIX machines, and on different browsers—at least in theory.

At this point, we need to make one thing clear: Java is a fine language, but you won't be learning it in this book. Although their names and some of their commands are similar, JavaScript and Java are entirely different languages. Here are a few of the most glaring differences:

- Java applets are compiled into *class files* to be used on a Web page; JavaScript uses simple text commands, which can be included in the HTML document itself.
- Java applets are generally displayed in a box within the Web document; JavaScript scripts can affect any part of the Web document itself.
- While JavaScript is best suited to simple applications and adding interactive features to Web pages, Java can be used for incredibly complex applications. For example, Corel's WordPerfect word processing suite is available in a Java version; this is a project JavaScript definitely couldn't handle.

There are many other differences (and a similarity or two), but the important thing to remember is that JavaScript and Java are separate languages. They're both useful for different things; in fact, they can be used together to combine their advantages.

How JavaScript Fits into a Web Page

As you hopefully already know, HTML (Hypertext Markup Language) is the language you use to create Web documents. To refresh your memory, Listing 1.1 shows a short but sadly typical Web document.

LISTING **1.1** A SIMPLE HTML DOCUMENT.

```
1:  <HTML>
2:  <HEAD>
3:  <TITLE>Our Home Page</TITLE>
4:  </HEAD>
5:  <BODY>
```

```
 6: <H1>The American Eggplant Society</H1>
 7: <P>Welcome to our Web page. Unfortunately,
 8: it's still under construction.</P>
 9: </BODY>
10: </HTML>
```

This document consists of a header within the <HEAD> tags and the body of the page within the <BODY> tags. To add JavaScript to a page, you'll use a similar tag: <SCRIPT>.

The <SCRIPT> tag tells the browser to start treating the text as a script, and the </SCRIPT> tag returns to the regularly scheduled HTML. In most cases, you can't use JavaScript statements except within <SCRIPT> tags. The exception is event handlers, described later in this chapter.

Using the <SCRIPT> tag, we can add a short script (in this case, just one line) to the Web document, as shown in Listing 1.2. If you try this or other examples in this book yourself, don't type the line numbers—they're just for your convenience in referring to the script.

If you want to try this example in a browser but don't want to type it, the HTML document is available on this book's Web site, http://www.jswork-shop.com/ (as are all of the other listings).

LISTING 1.2   A SIMPLE HTML DOCUMENT WITH A SIMPLE SCRIPT.

```
 1: <HTML>
 2: <HEAD>
 3: <TITLE>Our Home Page</TITLE>
 4: </HEAD>
 5: <BODY>
 6: <H1>The American Eggplant Society</H1>
 7: <P>Welcome to our Web page. Unfortunately,
 8: it's still under construction.
 9: We last worked on it on this date:</P>
10: <SCRIPT LANGUAGE="JavaScript">
11: document.write(document.lastModified);
12: </SCRIPT>
13: </BODY>
14: </HTML>
```

The document.write statement, which you'll learn more about later, sends output as part of the Web document. In this case, it displays the modification date of the document.

Notice that the <SCRIPT> tag in Listing 1.2 includes a parameter: Language="JavaScript". This specifies the scripting language to the browser. You can also specify a JavaScript version, as you'll learn later in this hour.

In this example, we placed the script within the body of the HTML document. There are actually four different places where you might use scripts:

- In the body of the page. In this case, the output of the script is displayed as part of the HTML document when the browser loads the page.

- In the header of the page, between the <HEAD> tags. Scripts in the header aren't executed immediately, but can be referred to by other scripts. The header is often used for functions—groups of JavaScript statements that can be used as a group.

- Within an HTML tag. This is called an *event handler* and allows the script to work with HTML elements. Event handlers are the one type of script where you don't need to use the <SCRIPT> tag. You'll learn more about event handlers in Hour 4, "How JavaScript Programs Work."

- In a separate file entirely. JavaScript supports the use of files with the .js extension containing scripts; these can be included by specifying a file in the <SCRIPT> tag. This feature works only in Netscape Navigator 3.0 or later and Internet Explorer 4.0 or later.

Browsers and JavaScript

Like HTML, JavaScript requires a Web browser to be displayed, and different browsers may display it differently. Unlike HTML, the results of browser incompatibility with JavaScript are more drastic: Rather than simply displaying your text incorrectly, the script may not execute at all, may display an error message, or may even crash the browser.

We'll take a quick look at the way different browsers (and different versions of the same browser) treat JavaScript in the following sections.

Netscape and Internet Explorer

Today's Web is dominated by two popular Web browsers: Netscape Navigator and Microsoft Internet Explorer. Netscape has traditionally been the more popular of the two, but Internet Explorer has quickly caught up, particularly with its inclusion in Microsoft Windows 98.

Both of these browsers include some support for JavaScript. However, since the JavaScript language was developed by Netscape, the newest features of the language are supported only under Netscape Navigator. Internet Explorer does support the basic JavaScript commands, and newer versions may implement all of the new features.

 Since this book is about JavaScript 1.3, the latest and greatest version, you should definitely have a copy of the latest version of Netscape (version 4.5 or later) to try the examples. However, most of the scripts in this book will work with Netscape 4.0 and with Internet Explorer 4.0 or later.

Versions of JavaScript

The JavaScript language has evolved since its original release in Netscape 2.0. There have been four versions of JavaScript:

- JavaScript 1.0, the original version, is supported by Netscape 2.0 and Internet Explorer 3.0.
- JavaScript 1.1 is supported by Netscape 3.0 and mostly supported by Internet Explorer 4.0.
- JavaScript 1.2 is supported by Netscape 4.0, and partially supported by Internet Explorer 4.0.
- JavaScript 1.3 is supported by Netscape 4.5.

Each of these versions is an improvement over the previous version and includes a number of new features. Browsers that support the new version also support scripts written for earlier versions.

As mentioned earlier in this hour, the <SCRIPT> tag can specify a JavaScript version. One use for this feature is to prevent older browsers from accessing the script. If you specifically refer to JavaScript 1.3, Netscape 4.0 and earlier and IE4 and earlier will ignore the script.

The JavaScript language has been submitted to the ECMA, a European standards committee. This committee has finalized the ECMA-262 specification, a standard for the language. The standardized version of the language is sometimes referred to as ECMAScript. JavaScript 1.3 follows the ECMA-262 standard.

Another language you may hear of is JScript. This is how Microsoft refers to its implementation of JavaScript, which is partially compatible with the Netscape version.

Alternatives to JavaScript

JavaScript is not the only language used on the Web, and in some cases, it may not be the right tool for the job. Java, described earlier in this hour, can do some things better than JavaScript. In the following sections, we'll look at a few other commonly used Web languages and their advantages.

VBScript

VBScript, sometimes known as Visual Basic Scripting Edition, is Microsoft's answer to JavaScript. Just as JavaScript's syntax is loosely based on Java, VBScript's syntax is loosely based on Microsoft Visual Basic, a popular programming language for Windows machines.

Like JavaScript, VBScript is a simple scripting language, and you can include VBScript statements within an HTML document. To begin a VBScript script, you use the <SCRIPT LANGUAGE="VBScript"> tag.

VBScript can do many of the same things as JavaScript, and it even looks similar in some cases. It has two main advantages:

- For those who already know Visual Basic, it may be easier to learn than JavaScript.
- It is closely integrated with ActiveX, Microsoft's standard for Web-embedded applications.

VBScript's main disadvantage is that it is supported only by Microsoft Internet Explorer. JavaScript, on the other hand, is supported by both Netscape and Internet Explorer to some degree. JavaScript is also a much more popular language, and you can see it in use all over the Web.

CGI

CGI (Common Gateway Interface) is not really a language, but a specification that allows programs to run on Web servers. CGI programs can be written in a number of languages, including Perl, C, and Visual Basic.

CGI programs are heavily used on the Web. If you've ever typed information into a form and pressed a button to send it to a Web site, chances are the data was sent to a CGI application.

The main difference between CGI and JavaScript is that CGI executes on the server, while JavaScript applications execute on the client (the Web browser). The main disadvantage of CGI is that, since the data must be sent to the Web server and back, response time may be slow.

On the other hand, CGI can do things JavaScript can't do. It can read and write files on the server. While a client-side JavaScript program can read information from a form and manipulate it, it can't store the data in any permanent form. However, a server-side version of JavaScript is available and does not have this limitation.

ActiveX

ActiveX is a specification developed by Microsoft that allows ordinary Windows programs to be run within a Web page. ActiveX programs can be written in languages such as Visual C++ and Visual Basic, and they are compiled before being placed on the Web server.

ActiveX applications, called *controls*, are downloaded and executed by the Web browser, like Java applets. Unlike Java applets, controls can be installed permanently when they are downloaded, eliminating the need to download them again.

ActiveX's main advantage is that it can do just about anything. This can also be a disadvantage: Several enterprising programmers have already used ActiveX to bring exciting new capabilities to Web pages, such as "the Web page that turns off your computer" and "the Web page that formats your disk drive."

Fortunately, ActiveX includes a signature feature that identifies the source of the control and prevents controls from being modified. While this won't prevent a control from damaging your system, you can specify which sources of controls you trust.

ActiveX has two main disadvantages. First, it isn't as easy to program as a scripting language or Java. Second, ActiveX is proprietary: It works only in Microsoft Internet Explorer, and only under Windows platforms.

Along with VBScript, JavaScript applications can be used to work with ActiveX controls in Internet Explorer. This allows you to customize a downloaded control without having to compile your own version.

Summary

During this hour, you've learned what Web scripting is and what JavaScript is. You've also learned how to insert a script into an HTML document, and how JavaScript differs from other Web languages.

If you're waiting for some real JavaScript code, look no further. The next hour, "Creating a Simple Script," guides you through the process of creating a working JavaScript application.

Q&A

Q If I plan to learn Java anyway, will I have any use for JavaScript?

A Certainly. JavaScript is the ideal tool for many applications, such as form valida- tion. JavaScript is also faster than Java for simple tasks because there is usually a delay of 10 seconds or longer to start a Java applet.

Q Can a Web page include more than one set of <SCRIPT> tags?

A Yes. In fact, the larger scripts in this book will often include two or more script sections.

Q Can I make scripts that work on both Netscape and Internet Explorer?

A Yes, but it isn't always easy. Some JavaScript commands are supported by both browsers, and if you carefully test a simple script on both browsers, you can make it work. For more complex scripts, you may need to use different sections of code for each browser. JavaScript can detect the browser and then run the code for the appropriate browser.

Q What about supporting different versions of Netscape?

A If you don't specify a version number in the <SCRIPT> tag, you can write simple scripts that will run in Netscape 2.0 and later versions. In that case you will need to stick to the features of JavaScript 1.0.

Q What happens if a user's browser doesn't support JavaScript at all?

A You can use HTML comments to prevent older browsers from displaying JavaScript code. This is explained in Hour 4.

Workshop

Quiz

1. Why do JavaScript and Java have similar names?

    a. JavaScript is a stripped-down version of Java

    b. JavaScript's syntax is loosely based on Java's

    c. They both originated on the island of Java

2. When a user views a page containing a JavaScript program, which machine actually executes the script?

    a. The user's machine running a Web browser

    b. The Web server

    c. A central machine deep within Netscape's corporate offices

3. Which of the following languages is supported by both Microsoft Internet Explorer and Netscape Navigator?

    a. VBScript

    b. ActiveX

    c. JavaScript

Answers

1. b. Although they are different languages, JavaScript's syntax is based on Java.

2. a. JavaScript programs execute on the Web browser. (There is actually a server-side version of JavaScript, but that's another story.)

3. c. JavaScript is supported by both Netscape and MSIE, although the implementations are not identical.

Exercises

If you want to learn a bit about JavaScript or check out the latest developments before you proceed with the next hour, perform this activity:

- Visit Netscape's Developer Web site at `http://developer.netscape.com/` to view articles and news about JavaScript.

Hour 2

Creating a Simple Script

As you learned in Hour 1, "Understanding JavaScript," JavaScript is a scripting language for Web documents. You can include JavaScript commands directly in the HTML document, and the script is executed when the page is viewed in a browser.

During this hour, you will create a simple script, edit it, and test it using a Web browser. Along the way you'll learn the basic tasks involved in creating and using scripts. We will cover the following topics:

- The software tools you will need to create and test scripts
- Beginning and ending scripts
- Formatting JavaScript statements
- How a script can display a result
- Including a script within a Web document
- Testing a script using Netscape
- Modifying a script

Tools for Scripting

Unlike many programming languages, you won't need any special software to create JavaScript scripts. In fact, you probably already have everything you need.

The first thing you'll need to work with JavaScript is an *editor*. JavaScript scripts are stored in simple text files, usually as part of HTML documents. Any editor that can store ASCII text files will work.

You can choose from a wide range of editors, from simple text editors to word processors. If you don't have a favorite editor already, a simple editor is most likely included with your computer. For Windows computers, the Notepad accessory will work just fine.

If you use a word processor to create JavaScript programs, be sure you save the files as ASCII text rather than as word processing documents.

A variety of dedicated HTML editors are also available and will work with JavaScript. In fact, many include features specifically for JavaScript—for example, coloring the various JavaScript statements to indicate their purposes, or even creating simple scripts automatically.

For Windows computers, here are a few recommended editors:

- **Homesite**—An excellent HTML editor that includes JavaScript support.
- **Microsoft FrontPage 2000**—Microsoft's visual HTML editor. The Script Builder component allows you to easily create simple scripts.
- **NetObjects ScriptBuilder**—A script-oriented editor that simplifies the process of writing scripts.
- **EditPad**—A simple text editor that includes a number of features missing from Notepad.

For the Macintosh, BBEdit, BBEdit Lite, and Alpha are good HTML editors that you can use to create Web pages and scripts.

Appendix B, "Tools for JavaScript Developers," includes Web addresses to download these and other HTML and script editors.

You'll need two other things to work with JavaScript: a Web browser and a computer to run it on. Since this book deals with JavaScript 1.3, I recommend that you use the latest version of Netscape Navigator. Netscape is available for Windows, Macintosh, and UNIX platforms. See Netscape's Web page to download a copy:

`http://www.netscape.com/`

If you plan on making your script available over the Internet, you'll also need a Web server, or access to one. However, you can use all of the JavaScript examples in this book directly from your computer's hard disk.

2

Counting Down to the Year 2000

If you've watched the news recently, chances are you've heard something about the year 2000 and the problems it presents for computer systems: Since many system designers and programmers weren't thinking far enough ahead, they used only two digits to store dates.

The result of this is that on the first day of the year 2000, any software that is still using two-digit dates will wake up convinced that the current year is 1900. Depending on who you ask, this could cause problems ranging from minor billing errors to the decline of modern civilization.

How close is the year 2000? Whether you're expecting the end of the world or just expecting to work lots of overtime, you're probably curious as to how long we have until the big day.

As a simple example of scripting, you can create a JavaScript program that calculates the time remaining until the year 2000. Since computers are known for their precision, you'll start by calculating the time in seconds.

Beginning the Script

Your script, like most JavaScript programs, begins with the HTML <SCRIPT> tag. As you learned in Hour 1, you use the <SCRIPT> and </SCRIPT> tags to enclose a script within the HTML document.

Remember not to include anything but valid JavaScript statements between the starting and ending <SCRIPT> tags. If the browser finds any HTML tags that aren't explicitly part of the script within the <SCRIPT> tags, it will display a JavaScript error message.

To begin creating the script, open your favorite text editor and type the beginning and ending <SCRIPT> tags, as shown in Listing 2.1. (This listing and others in this book include line numbers for reference; be sure to type the script without the line numbers.)

LISTING 2.1   THE FRAMEWORK FOR A JAVASCRIPT SCRIPT.

```
1: <SCRIPT LANGUAGE="JavaScript1.1">
2: </SCRIPT>
```

Since the script is going to use some features that were not available in JavaScript 1.0, we specify JavaScript 1.1 in the <SCRIPT> tag. This script will work in Netscape 3.0 and later.

Adding JavaScript Statements

If you were asked to calculate on your own the number of seconds left until the year 2000, you'd probably start by determining the number of days and hours left, then do some math to convert your result to the number of seconds.

For your first JavaScript program, you will be working in the opposite direction. JavaScript stores dates in milliseconds (thousandths of a second), so you'll start with the number of milliseconds, then convert it to seconds.

Actually, JavaScript stores dates as the number of milliseconds since January 1, 1970. This means that if you travel back in time, you may not be able to use the script you're writing here. (This will probably be the least of your worries.)

Storing Data in Variables

To begin the script, you will use a *variable* to store the current date and another one to represent the beginning of the year 2000. You will learn more about variables in Hour 5, "Using and Storing Values." For now, think of them as containers that can hold some information (a number, or in this case, a date).

To start writing the script, add the following lines after the first <SCRIPT> tag. Be sure to use the same combination of capital and lowercase letters in your version, since JavaScript is case sensitive in some instances.

```
now = new Date();
y2k = new Date("Jan 01 2000 00:00:00");
```

Each of these statements assigns a value (a date) to a variable. The first statement creates a variable called now and stores the current date and time in it. The second statement creates a variable called y2k and stores the first moment of the year 2000 in it.

Both of these statements use JavaScript's built-in Date object, which allows you to conveniently handle dates. You'll learn more about working with dates in Hour 9, "Using Built-In Objects."

Notice the semicolons at the end of each of the above statements. These tell the browser that it has reached the end of a statement. You can actually omit the semicolons, but we'll use them throughout this book for clarity.

Calculating the Result

As I mentioned earlier, JavaScript stores dates in milliseconds; therefore, we now have two variables containing numbers of milliseconds. To calculate the time remaining until the year 2000, you can simply subtract today's date from the future date:

```
y2k - now
```

Of course, this would tell you the number of milliseconds until the year 2000. To work in more human terms, your script can convert the value to seconds. Insert a line in your editor before the final </SCRIPT> tag and add this statement:

```
seconds = (y2k - now) / 1000;
```

This statement tells the computer to create a third variable called seconds. To calculate this number, divide the number of milliseconds by 1000.

Notice the parentheses in the last statement. These ensure that the subtraction happens before the division. JavaScript has certain rules about which math operations are performed first, and in this case the division would be first without the parentheses. These rules are called *operator precedence*. Hour 5 takes a closer look at these rules.

Creating Output

You now have a variable, seconds, that contains the number of seconds until the year 2000. Of course, this variable doesn't do us much good unless we can read it. JavaScript includes a number of ways of displaying information, and one of the simplest is the document.write statement.

The document.write statement displays text, a number, or anything else you throw at it. Since your JavaScript program will be used within a Web page, the output will be displayed as part of the page. To display the result, add this statement before the final </SCRIPT> tag:

```
document.write("Seconds until the year 2000: " + seconds);
```

This statement tells the browser to add some text to the Web page containing your script. The output will include a bit of text explaining the result, followed by the contents of the seconds variable.

Notice the plus sign (+) between the text message and the seconds variable. In this case, it tells the browser to combine the two values into one string of text. If you use the plus sign between two numbers, they are added together.

Adding the Script to a Web Page

You should now have a complete script that calculates a result and displays it. Your listing should match Listing 2.2. In case you're still a little confused, Listing 2.3 is a line-by-line breakdown of the script with an explanation for each statement.

LISTING 2.2   THE COMPLETE YEAR 2000 SCRIPT.

```
1: <SCRIPT LANGUAGE="JavaScript1.1">
2:     now = new Date();
3:     y2k = new Date("Jan 01 2000 00:00:00");
4:     seconds = (y2k - now) / 1000;
5:     document.write("Seconds until the year 2000: " + seconds);
6: </SCRIPT>
```

LISTING 2.3   A DESCRIPTIVE BREAKDOWN OF THE YEAR 2000 SCRIPT.

```
1: The script begins here:
2:     Store the current date and time in the now variable
3:     Store January 1st, 2000 in the variable y2k
4:     Subtract now from y2k, divide by 1000, and store in seconds
5:     Display the value of seconds within the Web page
6: The script ends here.
```

In order to use your script, you'll need to add it to an HTML document. At its most basic, the HTML document should include the <HTML> tags and the <HEAD> and <BODY> tags.

If you add these tags to the document containing your script along with a descriptive heading, you should end up with something like Listing 2.4.

LISTING 2.4   THE YEAR 2000 SCRIPT INCLUDED IN AN HTML DOCUMENT.

```
1: <HTML>
2: <HEAD><TITLE>The Year 2000</TITLE></HEAD>
3: <BODY>
4: <H1>Countdown to the Year 2000</H1>
5: <HR>
6: <SCRIPT LANGUAGE="JavaScript1.1">
7: now = new Date();
8: y2k = new Date("Jan 01 2000 00:00:00");
9: seconds = (y2k - now) / 1000;
10: document.write("Seconds until the year 2000: " + seconds);
11: </SCRIPT>
12: </BODY>
13: </HTML>
```

Now that you have a complete HTML document, save it with the .htm or .html extension. (If you're using Windows 3.1, you'll need to use .htm; otherwise, either one will work.)

Notepad, and some other text editors, may try to be helpful and add the .txt extension to your script. Be sure your saved file has the correct extension.

Testing the Script

To test your script, you simply need to load the HTML document you created in a Web browser. Start Netscape and select Open Page from the File menu. Press the Choose File button, then browse to your HTML file. Once you've selected it, press the Open button to view the page.

If you typed the script correctly, your browser should display the result of the script, as shown in Figure 2.1. (Of course, your result won't be the same as mine, unless you really have been traveling back in time.)

FIGURE 2.1

Netscape displays the results of the Year 2000 script.

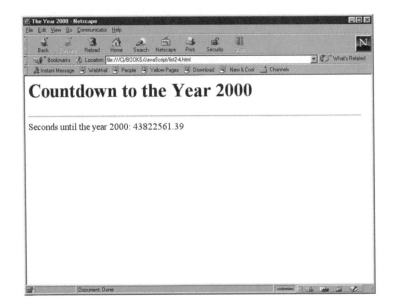

In case you're curious, the script you've just written is not vulnerable to the year 2000 problem, since JavaScript can handle dates well beyond the year 2000. Your script will work just fine during the year 2000, although it will display negative numbers and won't be terribly useful.

Modifying the Script

One thing you probably noticed when you ran the script is that there were two or more decimal places listed after the number of seconds. While this might be useful if you're interested in precision, it doesn't make for a very attractive display.

Luckily, JavaScript includes a feature that will round numbers for you. All you need to do is plug the number into the Math.round function, which rounds off the decimal places and leaves you with a nice integer.

To add this feature to your script, open the HTML file in your editor. Insert a line before the `document.write` statement and type this line:

```
seconds = Math.round(seconds);
```

This statement tells the browser to plug the value of the `seconds` variable into the `Math.round` function and store the resulting rounded number back into `seconds`.

Now that you have modified the script, save the HTML file and open the modified file using Netscape. If you left Netscape running, you can simply use the Reload button to load the new version of the script. Try it and verify that a rounded number is displayed. (If you repeatedly press the Reload button, you can watch the seconds count down before your eyes.)

Causing an Error

You have now created a slightly useful script using the JavaScript language and modified it to make it slightly more useful. Next, you will modify the script to cause an error.

You're probably wondering why you would want to deliberately cause an error. The reason is simple: You're going to run into an error sooner or later, and this will give you a demonstration of how Netscape behaves when it runs into a JavaScript error.

To cause an error, modify the statement you added in the previous section. We'll use a common error: omitting one of the parentheses. Change the `Math.round` statement to read:

```
seconds = Math.round(seconds;
```

Save your HTML document again and load the document into the browser. Depending on the browser version you're using, one of two things will happen:

- With Netscape 4.5 and earlier, an error message will be displayed.
- With Netscape 4.5 and later, no error message is displayed, but you will notice that your script stops executing (the number of seconds is not displayed).

A new feature of JavaScript 1.3 (Netscape 4.5 and later) is the JavaScript Console, which replaces the error messages in earlier versions. The console displays the last few JavaScript errors that have occurred (in some cases, your script may cause more than one error).

To display the console, type `javascript:` into the browser's Location field. The console is shown in Figure 2.2, displaying the same error message you probably see on your computer.

FIGURE 2.2

*The JavaScript
Console displays an
error message for the
script.*

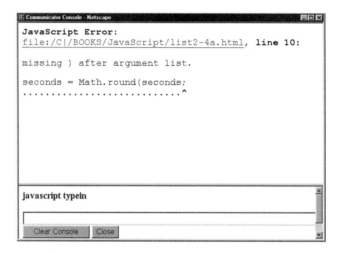

The error we get in this case is `missing ) after argument list`, which turns out to be exactly the problem. Be warned, however, that the error message may not always indicate the exact problem. However, it will at least let you know which line caused the error.

> Notice the field at the bottom of the JavaScript Console. This allows you to type a JavaScript statement, which will be executed immediately. This is a handy way to test JavaScript's features.

If you plan to do much work with JavaScript, you'll be using the JavaScript Console frequently. You can use the Preferences dialog in Navigator 4.5 to set the console to be displayed automatically when an error occurs.

Workshop: Adding Features to the Script

Your script now displays the number of seconds until the year 2000 as a nice round number. In case you'd rather comprehend a slightly smaller number, you can modify the script to display the number of minutes.

To modify the script, load the file into your editor again. Since you have already calculated the number of seconds, you can use the result, stored in the `seconds` variable to calculate the number of minutes. Add the following lines before the final `</SCRIPT>` tag:

```
minutes = seconds / 60;
minutes = Math.round(minutes);
document.write("<P>Minutes until the year 2000: " + minutes);
```

The first statement divides the `seconds` value by 60 and stores the result in a variable called `minutes`. Next, we use the `Math.round` function to round the number of minutes.

The final line uses the `document.write` statement to display the number of minutes left before the year 2000. Since the number of seconds has already been displayed, you can use the `<P>` (paragraph) HTML tag to ensure that your second result is displayed on a new line.

After adding the `minutes` feature, your script should resemble Listing 2.5. (Be sure you fix the error you created in the previous section!) Save the HTML document again and reload it into the browser. Figure 2.3 shows Netscape's display of the new and improved script.

LISTING 2.5 THE YEAR 2000 SCRIPT WITH THE MINUTES CALCULATION ADDED.

```
 1: <HTML>
 2: <HEAD><TITLE>The Year 2000</TITLE></HEAD>
 3: <BODY>
 4: <H1>Countdown to the Year 2000</H1>
 5: <HR>
 6: <SCRIPT LANGUAGE="JavaScript1.1">
 7: now = new Date();
 8: y2k = new Date("Jan 01 2000 00:00:00");
 9: seconds = (y2k - now) / 1000;
10: seconds = Math.round(seconds);
11: document.write("Seconds until the year 2000: " + seconds);
12: minutes = seconds / 60;
13: minutes = Math.round(minutes);
14: document.write("<P>Minutes until the year 2000: " + minutes);
15: </SCRIPT>
16: </BODY>
17: </HTML>
```

FIGURE 2.3

*Netscape's display of
the new and improved
script.*

Summary

During this hour, you wrote a simple JavaScript program and tested it using a browser.
You learned the tools you need to work with JavaScript—basically, an editor and a
browser. You also learned how to modify and test scripts and what happens when a
JavaScript program runs into an error.

In the process of writing this script, you have used some of JavaScript's basic features:
variables, the document.write statement, and functions for working with dates and
rounding. You'll learn more about all of these features in the remaining hours of this
book.

Q&A

**Q If this is a book about JavaScript 1.3, why didn't we specify the JavaScript
version number in the beginning <SCRIPT> tag?**

A Since this script doesn't use any features specific to JavaScript 1.3, it's best
to include the lowest possible version number. If we used the tag <SCRIPT
LANGUAGE="JavaScript 1.3">, the script would only run on Netscape 4.5 or later.
Since this script requires only JavaScript 1.1's features, we used the tag <SCRIPT
LANGUAGE="JavaScript1.1">. With this tag, the script will run on Netscape 3.0,
MSIE, and other JavaScript-compatible browsers.

Q When I try to run my script, Netscape displays the actual script in the browser window instead of executing it. What did I do wrong?

A This is most likely caused by one of three errors. First, you may be missing the beginning or ending `<SCRIPT>` tag. Check them, and verify that the first reads `<SCRIPT LANGUAGE="JavaScript">`. Second, your file may have been saved with a `.txt` extension, causing Netscape to treat it as a text file. Rename it to `.htm` or `.html` to fix the problem. Third, make sure your browser supports JavaScript and that it is not disabled in the Preferences dialog.

Q Why is the `<P>` tag allowed in the statement to print the number of minutes? I thought HTML tags weren't allowed within the `<SCRIPT>` tags.

A Since this particular tag is inside quotation marks, it's considered a valid part of the script. The script's output, including any HTML tags, is interpreted and displayed by the browser. You can use other HTML tags within quotation marks to add formatting, such as boldface or italics, to your script's output.

Q I can imagine a large script making a mess of my beautifully formatted HTML documents. Can I move the script to a separate file?

A Yes. Create a file with a `.js` extension and place the script statements (not including the `<SCRIPT>` tags) in this file. Leave the `<SCRIPT>` tags in the HTML file and modify the first tag to refer to the file, such as `<SCRIPT LANGUAGE="JavaScript" SRC="filename.js">`. This feature works only for JavaScript 1.1 and later (Netscape 3.0 and later).

Workshop

Quiz

1. What software do you use to create and edit JavaScript programs?

   a. A browser

   b. A text editor

   c. A pencil and a piece of paper

2. What are variables used for in JavaScript programs?

   a. Storing numbers, dates, or other values

   b. Varying randomly

   c. Causing high school algebra flashbacks

3. What should appear at the very end of your JavaScript script?

    a. The `<SCRIPT LANGUAGE="JavaScript">` tag

    b. The `</SCRIPT>` tag

    c. The `END` statement

Answers

1. b. Any text editor can be used to create scripts. You can also use a word processor, if you're careful to save the document as text.

2. a. Variables are used to store numbers, dates, or other values.

3. b. Your script should end with the `</SCRIPT>` tag.

Exercises

If you would like to gain a bit more practice working on the JavaScript features you learned in this hour, try these activities:

- Modify the Year 2000 script to display the number of hours left until the year 2000.
- Modify the script to display the number of days left until the year 2000.
- Instead of the year 2000, modify the script to count the minutes and seconds left until a date you choose, such as your birthday.

Hour 3

Exploring JavaScript's Capabilities

In Hour 2, "Creating a Simple Script," you created a working JavaScript program. While this should have given you a feeling of accomplishment, you probably didn't rush right in and add the "Countdown to the Year 2000" feature to all of your Web pages—and you're probably waiting to discover what truly useful things you can do with JavaScript.

Before you learn more about the details of the JavaScript language, you might find it useful to have a general idea of what JavaScript can do and what is being done with it on the Web. During this hour, you'll take a quick look at some of the most useful applications for JavaScript. (You'll take a longer look at most of these in later hours.) The following topics are covered in this hour:

- Improving a site's user interface with JavaScript
- Creating those pesky scrolling messages
- What JavaScript can do with images and animation
- Using JavaScript to automate and validate forms

- Detecting Web browsers with JavaScript
- How JavaScript works with browser plug-ins
- Creating complex applications with JavaScript
- How to copy a script to your own Web page

Improving a Site's User Interface

Have you ever been bored by a Web site? (If you haven't, you need to get out more.) One of the most popular uses for JavaScript is to add a bit of excitement to a Web page. This includes eye candy features like scrolling messages and animation, as well as useful navigational aids and new ways of presenting information.

Using the Status Line

The status line is the gray strip at the bottom of the browser window that is found in all of today's fashionable browsers. It usually serves two main purposes:

- Displaying descriptions of menu and toolbar items
- Displaying the URL of links as the mouse pointer moves over them

Using JavaScript, you can take control of the status line yourself. You've probably noticed scrolling messages in the status line of some pages. While this can be annoying in some cases (or am I the only one who thinks so?), it's one of the most popular uses of JavaScript.

> You'll learn how to create a script for scrolling status line messages in Hour 6, "Using Strings and Arrays." If you just can't wait three more hours, see the Workshop section at the end of this hour.

Along with scrolling messages, you can take advantage of the status line in other ways. One common example uses JavaScript to replace the URL display in the status line with a description of the link the mouse pointer is over.

Navigational Aids

You can also use JavaScript to make your site easier to navigate. You've probably seen drop-down lists on Web pages for navigation between a number of pages. You can select a page's title from the list, then press a button to load that page. In some cases, the page is loaded as soon as you select it.

This feature is usually accomplished with JavaScript, and you'll find out how to create your own version in Hour 14, "Getting Data with Forms." You can also use JavaScript for more complicated variations of this technique. For example, Netscape's Netcenter site, shown in Figure 3.1, uses a drop-down list for a search function.

FIGURE 3.1

Netscape's Netcenter site uses JavaScript to select a search engine.

The search box at the top of the Netcenter site allows you to enter a search string and then select a search engine from the drop-down list. When you use the Search button, a script reads your data from the form and sends the search string to the appropriate search engine.

Pop-up Windows and Other Features

JavaScript has a number of other features that allow you to communicate with the user in more exciting ways than HTML. For example, you can easily create pop-up alert, confirmation, or prompt messages with JavaScript. A simple example of an alert message is shown in Figure 3.2. These can alert the user to an error, present a warning or disclaimer, or prompt for information.

FIGURE 3.2

A pop-up alert message created with JavaScript.

For a more versatile display than an alert message, you can use JavaScript to create an entirely new browser window. You can choose how the window will be displayed—for example, its size and whether it has a toolbar and location bar.

Once you've created a new browser window, you can load a URL into it, or even create its content directly using JavaScript. You can also clear the contents of the normal browser window and display a new document in it. JavaScript can also work with frames, which allow you to divide a browser window into sections.

 Hour 10, "Working with Browser Objects," explains how to use pop-up alerts. In Hour 13, "Using Windows and Frames," you will use JavaScript to create custom browser windows and to work with frames.

The newest versions of Netscape and Internet Explorer support a feature called Dynamic HTML. One of the uses of Dynamic HTML is to create layers (also known as position-able elements) within a page. These are similar to frames, but they can overlap (similar to the windows on your computer's desktop) and can be moved around within the main browser window. JavaScript can work with layers to create some truly amazing effects.

 You'll learn about layers and Dynamic HTML in Hour 18, "Creating Dynamic Pages with Layers."

Graphics and Animation

One thing that separates an exciting, well-designed Web page from a boring one is the use of graphics. While you won't learn how to create graphics in this book, you will learn how JavaScript can work with graphics.

When a browser loads a normal HTML page, it displays the graphics along with the text, and the graphics don't change until you move on to a different HTML page. Using JavaScript, you can change the rules. JavaScript 1.1 and later include a feature called *dynamic images*, which allows you to replace one image on a page with another image without reloading the page.

One of the most common uses of this JavaScript feature is to create images that change when the mouse moves over them. This is usually used to highlight an image used as a link as the user moves the mouse pointer across it.

Graphics that change when the mouse pointer passes over them are variously known as rollovers, mouseovers, or simply "those cool graphics that change when the mouse pointer passes over them." Whatever they are, you'll learn to create them in Hour 15, "Using Graphics and Animation."

JavaScript can also be used to replace images in a sequence, creating a full-scale animation. While there are limitations to this approach (you can't use it to create a video game that competes with Quake, for example), it can be an attention-grabbing feature.

For automations, there are more powerful tools than JavaScript. The Java language can be used to create faster animations (although not nearly as easily). You can also create simple animations as animated GIFs using a graphics program. For more complex animations and video clips, you can use plug-ins such as ShockWave and QuickTime.

3

Validating Forms

One of the most powerful features of the Web is the use of interactive forms. These forms allow the user to enter information and interact with the site, instead of simply looking at the page. This makes everything from order forms to questionnaires to entirely customizable pages possible.

Traditionally, forms are handled by a CGI (Common Gateway Interface) script. This script runs on the Web server. When the user enters information on a form and presses the Submit button, it is sent to the CGI script for processing. The script then sends back a result in the form of another Web page.

CGI is not a language, but a standard that allows programs in any language to work within a Web server. CGI programs are often written in Perl, a powerful scripting language, or in more traditional languages such as C and Visual Basic.

While CGI is a powerful system, it has disadvantages for some uses of forms. The main disadvantage is that submitting the data requires communication with the Web server and may take anywhere from a few seconds to a few minutes.

Often, the CGI script is responsible for *validating* the form, or making sure the appropriate data has been entered. For example, if the user enters only four digits in a phone number field or leaves a required field blank, the script could alert him and prompt for the missing information.

While this method of form validation works, the slow speed can make it inconvenient— the user may be frustrated when, after waiting ten minutes for a reply from the server, he receives a response indicating that he needs to supply missing information and start over.

As you've probably guessed by now, JavaScript provides a convenient solution to this problem. A JavaScript program can read the data in the form instantly (without any communication with the server) and display an error message in an alert box. Your script can even move the cursor to the field that contains the error.

> You will learn how to write a JavaScript program to validate a form in Hour 14.

In some cases, JavaScript can be used to handle the form submission entirely, sending the results via email. The script can also pass the data on to a CGI script after validating it.

You can also use JavaScript to automate forms in ways CGI can't. For example, Figure 3.3 shows an order form that uses JavaScript to fill in the subtotals and keep a running total as the user enters product quantities.

FIGURE 3.3

An order form that uses JavaScript to keep running totals.

If JavaScript can work with forms faster than CGI and without communicating with the server, then you may be wondering, why use CGI? The answer is that CGI can do things a client-side scripting language can't do, such as writing data to a file on the server or working with a database. (A server-side version of JavaScript is available and can also perform these functions.)

Detecting Browser Versions

The HTML standard was designed to be cross-platform. In other words, if you follow the HTML standards, your page should look about the same in any browser on any computer platform.

If you've done much work designing HTML Web pages, you've probably noticed that this isn't always the case. While the newest browsers from Microsoft and Netscape have moved closer to a common standard, there are still differences in the way they treat HTML code. On top of that, each browser has a number of different versions with different features.

While it's possible to carefully construct a simple HTML document so that it will display properly in both browsers, new features such as Dynamic HTML aren't supported in the same way. One solution is to have browser-specific pages for each browser, or perhaps a specific page for one browser and a generic one for others.

Some sites have done just that and ask you to click on the link for the appropriate browser version. With JavaScript, you can automate this process: Your page can detect the user's browser type and version and either send him to the appropriate customized page or use JavaScript to customize the output from a single page.

Because of the differences in the ways browsers handle HTML, you should test the page in different browsers. If you plan to use JavaScript to detect browsers, you will want to keep a few different browsers (or at least the latest Microsoft and Netscape offerings) for testing.

One major difference between Microsoft's and Netscape's browsers—and even between different versions of each—is the way they handle JavaScript. It is possible to detect the browser version using a simple, universal script, and then to use separate JavaScript commands for different browsers. You'll learn more about these issues in Hour 16, "Creating Browser-Specific Scripts."

While detecting browser versions is usually something you would do to allow more users to comfortably access your site, it's also possible to make it difficult--or in some cases impossible--to access the site without using a particular browser. While I certainly don't recommend this, you'll probably run into a site or two using this technique.

Working with Plug-Ins

Plug-ins are browser add-ons that allow different types of content to be used within a Web page. Plug-ins are available for everything from audio to video to virtual reality, and much more. Here are some of the most common plug-ins:

- RealAudio, for streaming audio support
- QuickTime, for embedded video clips
- Adobe Acrobat, for precisely formatted documents
- ShockWave, for animations and interactive applications

While you can use plug-in content to add just about anything to your Web page, there is one major problem: Aside from a few default plug-ins that are included with browsers, you can't really count on the entire audience for your page to have the plug-in installed.

This makes plug-ins an issue similar to browser versions: Either you have to choose one particular plug-in to support and expect the users to install it, or you must create alternative pages (typically one using plug-ins and one without them).

Once again, JavaScript can make the situation a bit more controllable. You can use JavaScript to detect whether the browser has a particular plug-in installed and modify the HTML page appropriately. If the plug-in is not available, your script can send the user to a different page, or even send him to the download page for the plug-in.

Along with detecting installed plug-ins, you can use JavaScript to work with plug-in content. Netscape calls this feature LiveConnect. Using this system, you can control a plug-in with JavaScript.

Incidentally, the LiveConnect specification also allows JavaScript programs to communicate with Java applets, and it allows Java applets to access JavaScript variables and commands.

For example, you can include an embedded sound on a page and use JavaScript to play the sound at appropriate moments. Depending on the plug-in type, you can control a variety of aspects of the plug-in object with your script.

 You will learn how to use JavaScript to detect installed plug-ins and to control plug-in objects in Hour 20, "Working with Multimedia and Plug-Ins."

Complex Scripts

Throughout this hour, you've learned about some of the most common uses for JavaScript. You can implement any of these features using a simple script, or even a single command in some cases.

However, don't let this give you the impression that JavaScript can only do simple things. You can create full-scale JavaScript programs to do just about anything, although there are limitations.

In Hour 23, "Creating a Shopping Cart Script," you'll use JavaScript to create an ordering system that could be used for any Web site with products for sale, and in Hour 24, "Creating a JavaScript Game," you'll create a JavaScript program to play a game.

Workshop: Copying a Script

You should now have an idea of the many things you can do with JavaScript. In the remaining hours of this book, you'll learn the specifics of these and other uses for JavaScript.

Of course, you might want to make some improvements to your site right away. While you'll eventually learn to create useful and complicated scripts from scratch, sometimes it's nice to be able to use a feature without entirely understanding it.

For example, suppose you want to use a scrolling status-line message on your page. Rather than create a program to do this from scratch, you can copy a working script from someone else's page.

 Be warned: Scripts belong to the people who create them, just like anything else on a Web page, and you may be violating a copyright if you copy one. If you want to use a script from someone else's page, be sure to ask permission. A number of sites offer scripts free for the taking; some of these are listed in Appendix A, "Other JavaScript Resources."

For this example, you'll copy the scrolling message from an existing page (it's my page, so you have permission to copy it) and modify it to suit your own needs. To view the page containing the original script, use this URL:

`http://www.jsworkshop.com/scroll.html`

Figure 3.4 shows Netscape's display of this page, including the scrolling message.

FIGURE 3.4

The scrolling message example page as seen by Netscape.

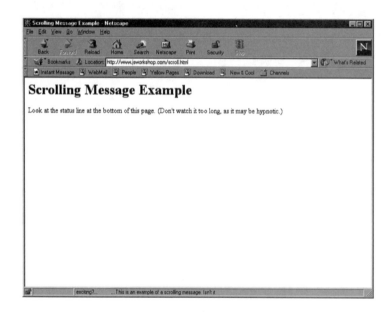

To copy the script from this page, use the Page Source option under Netscape's View menu. You should see the HTML source code of the page, including the script. Listing 3.1 shows the source code of the page.

LISTING 3.1   THE SOURCE CODE OF THE SCROLLING MESSAGE PAGE.

```
1: <HTML>
2: <HEAD><TITLE>Scrolling Message Example</TITLE>
3: <SCRIPT LANGUAGE="JavaScript">
4: var msg = "This is an example of a scrolling message. Isn't it
      exciting?";
5: var spacer = "...            ...";
6: var pos = 0;
7: function ScrollMessage() {
8:    window.status = msg.substring(pos, msg.length) + spacer +
        msg.substring(0, pos);
9:    pos++;
```

```
10:    if (pos > msg.length) pos = 0;
11:    window.setTimeout("ScrollMessage()",200);
12:  }
13:  ScrollMessage();
14:  </SCRIPT>
15:  </HEAD>
16:  <BODY>
17:  <H1>Scrolling Message Example</H1>
18:  Look at the status line at the bottom of this page. (Don't watch it
19:  too long, as it may be hypnotic.)
20:  </BODY></HTML>
```

You'll learn how to create this script from scratch in Hour 6. For now, you just need to know how to copy it to your own page. Start by highlighting the <SCRIPT> tag, the </SCRIPT> tag, and everything in between.

Copy the script to the Clipboard by using the Ctrl+C (Windows) or Cmd+C (Macintosh) key combination. (The View Source window doesn't have an Edit menu.) You can then use the Paste command in your favorite HTML or text editor to insert it into your own page.

As in the example page, the script should be within the <HEAD> tags. Be sure you copy the entire script, and be sure the ending </SCRIPT> tag appears before the </HEAD> tag.

Once it's copied, you can personalize the scrolling message. To do this, simply place your own message between the quotation marks on the line that begins with var msg=. This is the first line after the <SCRIPT> tag.

After you've inserted the script into your own HTML document and changed the message, save it and load it into the browser. You should see the message scrolling away. (If you don't, you probably changed part of the script by mistake. See Hour 6 for details about what each command in this script does.)

Summary

In this hour, you've taken a tour of the capabilities and uses of JavaScript. You learned how JavaScript can be used with windows and pop-up messages, graphics, and forms, and how it can be used to detect browsers and plug-ins.

You also learned how to copy a script from an existing page to your own page. In Hour 4, "How JavaScript Programs Work," you'll begin learning the details of the JavaScript language.

Q&A

Q I've seen scrolling messages that were in the upper part of a page, not the status line, and they included extra features, such as clicking on part of the message to jump to a page. Can JavaScript create this type of scrolling message?

A Most of these messages are created with Java, which is a bit more powerful. You can scroll messages in the body of the page with JavaScript, though, either using a text field in a form or using the layers feature of Dynamic HTML.

Q I know JavaScript can create graphics that change when the mouse moves over them. What about graphics that change when you click on them?

A Yes, JavaScript can also detect when a graphic is clicked on. You'll learn how to do this in Hour 15.

Q JavaScript can detect different versions of browsers. Can I use it to detect whether the browser supports JavaScript?

A You can't do this, strictly speaking, because a browser that doesn't support JavaScript won't run your script at all. However, for browsers that do support scripting, you can detect the version of JavaScript supported. You can also use HTML comments and the <NOSCRIPT> tag to handle browsers that don't handle JavaScript. You'll learn how to do this in the next hour.

Q I copied a different script to one of my pages, but it doesn't work. Have I made a mistake?

A There are many reasons why the script might not work, and you may have better luck after you've learned more about JavaScript. If you don't have luck getting the script to work, try asking the creator of the script to help.

Workshop

Quiz

1. What are rollovers?

    a. A trick performed by dogs

    b. Graphics that change when the mouse passes over them

    c. A type of cream-filled pastry

2. Which of the following *can't* be done with client-side JavaScript?

   a. Validating a form

   b. Sending a form's contents by email

   c. Storing the form's contents to a database file on the server

3. What is CGI (Common Gateway Interface)?

   a. A scripting language for Web servers

   b. A specification that lets programs run on Web servers

   c. A company that makes Web servers

Answers

1. b. Rollovers are graphics that change when the mouse pointer moves over them.

2. c. JavaScript can't access a database file on the server.

3. b. CGI is a specification (not a language) that lets programs run on Web servers.

Exercises

If you want to learn more about JavaScript's capabilities before you move on, try these activities:

- Browse the Web and see if you can find examples of each of the uses of JavaScript mentioned during this hour.

- Type about:plugins in the Location field in Netscape. This will display a list of the plug-ins you have installed and the types of files they handle.

HOUR **4**

How JavaScript Programs Work

Welcome to the end of Part I of this book. In the first three hours, you've learned what JavaScript is, created a simple script, and learned the variety of things JavaScript can do.

In this, the final hour of Part I, you'll learn a few basic concepts and script components that you'll use in just about every script you write. This will prepare you for the remaining hours of the book, in which you'll explore specific JavaScript functions and features.

Hour 4 covers the following topics:

- Organizing scripts using functions
- What objects are and how JavaScript uses them
- How JavaScript can respond to events
- Hiding JavaScript code from older browsers
- Adding alternatives to JavaScript for older browsers

Using Functions

The scripts you've seen so far, such as the Year 2000 script in Hour 2, "Creating a Simple Script," are simple lists of instructions. The browser begins with the first statement after the <SCRIPT> tag and follows each instruction in order until it reaches the closing </SCRIPT> tag (or encounters an error).

While this is a straightforward approach for short scripts, it can be confusing to read a huge script written in this fashion. To make it easier for you to organize your scripts, JavaScript supports *functions*.

Defining a Function

Functions are groups of JavaScript statements that can be treated as a single unit. In order to use a function, you must first define it. Listing 4.1 shows a simple example of a function definition.

LISTING **4.1**   A SIMPLE FUNCTION DEFINITION.

```
1: function Greet() {
2:     alert("Greetings.");
3: }
```

Listing 4.1 defines a function that displays an alert message to the user. This begins with the function keyword. The function's name is Greet. Notice the parentheses after the function's name. As you'll learn next, the space between them is not always empty.

The first and last lines of the function definition include braces ({ and }). You use these to enclose all of the statements in the function. The browser uses the braces to determine where the function begins and ends.

Between the braces, this particular function contains a single line. This uses the built-in alert function, which displays an alert message. The message will contain the text "Greetings."

Now, about those parentheses. The current Greet function always does the same thing: Each time you use it, it displays the same message. While this avoids a bit of typing, it doesn't really provide much of an advantage.

To make your function more flexible, you can add *parameters*, also known as *arguments*. These are variables that are received by the function each time it is called. For example, you can add a parameter called who that tells the function the name of the person to greet. Listing 4.2 shows the modified function.

LISTING **4.2** A FUNCTION THAT ACCEPTS A PARAMETER.

```
1: function Greet(who) {
2:     alert("Greetings," + who);
3: }
```

Of course, to use this function you should include it in an HTML document. Traditionally, the best place for a function definition is within the <HEAD> section of the document. Since the statements in the <HEAD> section are executed first, this ensures that the function is defined before it is used.

Listing 4.3 shows the Greet function embedded in the header section of an HTML document.

LISTING **4.3** THE Greet FUNCTION EMBEDDED IN THE HEADER SECTION OF AN HTML DOCUMENT.

```
 1: <HTML>
 2: <HEAD>
 3: <TITLE>Functions</TITLE>
 4: <SCRIPT LANGUAGE="JavaScript">
 5: function Greet(who) {
 6:     alert("Greetings," + who);
 7: }
 8: </SCRIPT>
 9: </HEAD>
10: <BODY>
11: This is the body of the page.
12: </BODY>
13: </HTML>
```

Calling the Function

You have now defined a function and placed it in an HTML document. However, if you load Listing 4.3 into a browser, you'll notice that it does absolutely nothing. This is because the function is defined—ready to be used—but we haven't used it yet.

Making use of a function is referred to as *calling* the function. To call a function, use the function's name as a statement in a script. You will need to include the parentheses and the values for the function's parameters. For example, here's a statement that calls the Greet function:

```
Greet("Fred");
```

This tells the JavaScript interpreter to transfer control to the first statement in the Greet function. It also passes the parameter "Fred" to the function. This value will be assigned to the who variable inside the function.

Functions can have more than one parameter. To define a function with multiple parameters, list a variable name for each parameter, separated by commas. To call the function, specify values for each parameter, separated by commas.

Listing 4.4 shows a complete HTML document that includes the function definition and a second script in the body of the page that actually calls the function. To demonstrate the usefulness of functions, we'll call it twice to greet two different people.

LISTING 4.4 THE COMPLETE FUNCTION EXAMPLE.

```
 1: <HTML>
 2: <HEAD>
 3: <TITLE>Functions</TITLE>
 4: <SCRIPT LANGUAGE="JavaScript">
 5: function Greet(who) {
 6:     alert("Greetings," + who);
 7: }
 8: </SCRIPT>
 9: </HEAD>
10: <BODY>
11: <H1>Function Example</H1>
12: <P>Prepare to be greeted twice.</P>
13: <SCRIPT LANGUAGE="JavaScript">
14: Greet("Fred");
15: Greet("Ethel");
16: </SCRIPT>
17: </BODY>
18: </HTML>
```

This listing includes a second set of <SCRIPT> tags in the body of the page. The second script includes two function calls to the Greet function, each with a different name. Now that you have a script that actually does something, try loading it into a browser. You should see something like Figure 4.1.

Notice that the second alert message isn't displayed until you press the OK button on the first alert. This is because JavaScript processing is halted while alerts are displayed.

FIGURE 4.1

The output of the Greeting example.

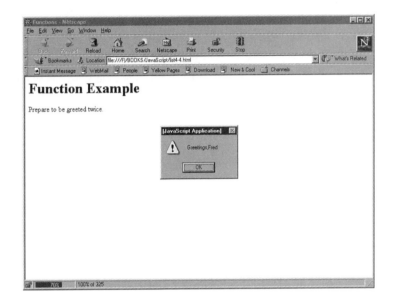

Returning a Value

4

While the function you just created displays a message to the user, functions can also return a value to the script that called them. This allows you to use functions to calculate values. As an example, you can create a function that averages four numbers.

Your function should begin with the function keyword, the function's name, and the parameters it accepts. We will use the variable names a, b, c, and d for the four numbers to average. Here is the first line of the function:

```
function Average(a,b,c,d) {
```

I've also included the first brace ({) on the first line of the function. This is a common style, but you can also place the brace on the next line, or on a line by itself.

Next, the function needs to calculate the average of the four numbers. You can calculate this by adding the numbers, then dividing by the number of numbers (in this case, 4). Thus, here is the next line of the function:

```
result = (a + b + c + d) / 4;
```

This statement creates a variable called result and calculates the result by adding the four numbers, then dividing by 4. (The parentheses are necessary to tell JavaScript to perform the addition before the division.)

To send this result back to the script that called the function, you use the return keyword. Here is the last part of the function:

```
return result;
}
```

Listing 4.5 shows the complete Average function.

LISTING 4.5   A FUNCTION TO AVERAGE FOUR NUMBERS.

```
1: <SCRIPT LANGUAGE="JavaScript">
2: function Average(a,b,c,d) {
3: result = (a + b + c + d) / 4;
4: return result;
5: }
6: </SCRIPT>
```

To use this function in a script, you can use a variable with the function call. For example, this statement averages the numbers 3, 4, 5, and 6 and stores the result in a variable called score:

```
score = Average(3,4,5,6);
```

You can also use the function call directly in an expression. For example, you can use the alert statement to display the result of the function:
alert(Average(1,2,3,4)).

Understanding Objects

In Chapter 2, you learned that variables are containers that can store a number, a string of text, or another value. JavaScript also supports *objects*. Like variables, objects can store data—but they can store two or more pieces of data at once.

The items of data stored in an object are called the *properties* of the object. For example, you could use objects to store information about people, as in an address book. The properties of each person object might include a name, an address, and other information.

JavaScript uses periods to separate object names and property names. For example, for a person object called Bob, the properties might include Bob.address and Bob.phone.

Objects can also include *methods*. These are functions that work with the object's data. For example, our person object for the address book might include a `display()` method to display the person's information. In JavaScript terminology, the statement `Bob.display()` would display Bob's details.

Don't worry if this sounds confusing—you'll be exploring objects in much more detail later in this book. For now, you just need to know the basics. JavaScript supports three kinds of objects:

- *Built-in objects* are objects built into the JavaScript language. You've already encountered two of these, `Date` and `Math`, in Hour 2. Some other built-in objects include `Array` and `String`, which you'll explore in Hour 6, "Using Strings and Arrays."

- *Browser objects* are objects that represent various components of the browser and the current HTML document. For example, the `alert()` function you used earlier in this chapter is actually a method of the `window` object. You'll explore these in more detail in Hour 10, "Working with Browser Objects."

- *Custom objects* are objects you create yourself. For example, you could create a person object, as in the examples in this section. You'll learn to use these in Hour 11, "Creating Custom Objects."

Handling Events

As mentioned in Chapter 1, not all scripts are located within `<SCRIPT>` tags. You can also use scripts as *event handlers*. While this might sound like a complex programming term, it actually means exactly what it says: Event handlers are scripts that handle events.

In real life, an event is something that happens to you. For example, the things you write on your calendar are events: "Dentist appointment" or "Fred's Birthday." You also encounter unscheduled events in your life, such as a traffic ticket, an IRS audit, or an unexpected visit from relatives.

Whether events are scheduled or unscheduled, you probably have normal ways of handling them. Your event handlers might include things like *When Fred's birthday arrives, send him a present* or *When relatives visit unexpectedly, turn out the lights and pretend nobody's home.*

Event handlers in JavaScript are similar: They tell the browser what to do when a certain event occurs. The events JavaScript deals with aren't as exciting as the ones you deal with—they include such events as *When the mouse button clicks* and *When this page is finished loading*. Nevertheless, they're a very useful part of JavaScript.

Many JavaScript events (such as mouse clicks) are caused by the user. Rather than doing things in a set order, your script can respond to the user's actions. Needless to say, this is essential for just about every practical use of JavaScript.

Event handlers are associated with particular browser objects, and you specify the event handler in the tag that defines the object. For example, images and text links have an event, onMouseOver, that happens when the mouse pointer moves over the object. Here is a typical HTML image tag with an event handler:

```
<IMG SRC="button.gif" onMouseOver="highlight()">
```

You specify the event handler as an attribute to the HTML tag and include the JavaScript statement to handle the event within the quotation marks. This is an ideal use for functions, since function names are short and to the point and can refer to a whole series of statements.

> You'll learn more about event handlers in Hour 12, "Responding to Events."

Hiding Scripts from Older Browsers

Many users are still using browsers that don't support JavaScript. More importantly, many people have JavaScript support turned off in their browsers, either due to security concerns or to avoid scrolling messages.

> Most of the security concerns people have about JavaScript are unfounded; there is really no way to do damage to a user's files with JavaScript, and scripts do not have access to the contents of hard drives by default. Some small security holes have been found in earlier versions of JavaScript, but none that allow serious damage.
>
> To add to JavaScript's capabilities, Netscape included features to access files on hard drives, change browser settings, and other functions in version 1.3; however, these functions require signed scripts, which must be authorized by the user before they can perform these functions.

Since older browsers don't understand the <SCRIPT> tag, they will not behave very well when they encounter a script in a Web page. In most cases, they will display the script in the middle of the page—probably not the effect you were looking for.

e the script within HTML comment tags. This tells older
completely. Newer browsers are smart enough to know that
ment.

the tag <!-- and end with the --> tag. Listing 4.6 shows a
ith comments.

OLDER BROWSERS.

aScript">

ur browser supports JavaScript.");

nning and ending HTML comment tags. The // in the last
; this prevents the HTML comment from being detected as a

hiding scripts is not perfect. Certain characters within your
arly the greater-than sign, >) may end the comment prema-

4

Supporting Non-JavaScript Browsers

You can now hide your script from older browsers so that they won't display the script
itself. But you may need to support these browsers (for example, displaying a notice that
the page requires JavaScript). The <NOSCRIPT> tag, supported in JavaScript 1.1 and later,
provides a convenient solution. This tag tells JavaScript-compatible browsers to ignore
everything between the beginning and ending <NOSCRIPT> tags; you can then include
HTML content for the non-JavaScript browser within the tags.

Old browsers that don't support JavaScript don't support the <NOSCRIPT> tag
either. However, this technique still works because, according to the HTML
standard, browsers should ignore unknown tags. Modern browsers support
the <NOSCRIPT> tag when JavaScript support is turned off.

For example, Listing 4.7 shows a section of HTML that displays a message for non-JavaScript browsers:

LISTING 4.7   SUPPORTING NON-JAVASCRIPT BROWSERS.

```
1: <NOSCRIPT>
2: Your browser does not support JavaScript. Please use the
3: <A href="nojs.html">Non-JavaScript Version</A> of this document.
4: </NOSCRIPT>
```

This allows you to conveniently support both types of browsers. The one exception is Netscape 2.0, which supports JavaScript but does not support the <NOSCRIPT> tag; this version will display the <NOSCRIPT> message, but will still support JavaScript 1.0.

Workshop: Using Comments

You have now used HTML comments to hide your script from browsers. JavaScript also includes its own type of comments. While these won't hide JavaScript from browsers, they are useful for their intended purpose: including comments in your script.

Comments allow you to include documentation within your script. This will be useful if someone else tries to understand the script, or even if you try to understand it after a long break. To include comments in a JavaScript program, begin a line with two slashes, as in this example:

```
//this is a comment.
```

You can also begin a comment in the middle of a line, which is useful for documenting a script. For example:

```
a = a + 1; // add one to the value of a
```

JavaScript also supports C-style comments, which begin with /* and end with */. These comments can extend across more than one line, as the following example demonstrates.

```
/*This script includes a variety
of features, including this comment. */
```

Since these comments are part of JavaScript syntax, they are only valid inside <SCRIPT> tags.

Summary

During this hour, you've learned some of the basics of JavaScript programming: how to define and use functions, the basics of objects and event handlers, and how to hide scripts from browsers that don't support JavaScript. You also learned how to use JavaScript comments to make your script easier to read.

You have now reached the end of Part I of this book and should have a good grasp of the fundamentals of JavaScript. In the next few hours, you will learn the specifics of JavaScript programming using various features.

Q&A

Q Netscape displays the error message "missing semicolon before statement" when I try the function example.

A This is probably because you mistyped something. JavaScript is case sensitive, so be sure you get the capitalization right. This specific error message will appear if you use the keyword `Function` instead of `function`.

Q I've heard the term object-oriented applied to languages such as C and Java. If JavaScript supports objects, is it an object-oriented language?

A Yes, although it might not fit some people's strict definitions. JavaScript objects do not support all of the features that languages such as C and Java support.

Q This hour explained how to hide JavaScript from older browsers. However, in Hour 2 I learned how easy it is to copy a script. How can I hide my source code from the prying eyes of users?

A Since JavaScript is part of the HTML document, there is really no way to do this. The solution employed by some Web pages is to make the script as confusing as possible, removing spaces and carriage returns. While this might annoy users, it doesn't really prevent a determined user from copying the script. The `<SCRIPT SRC>` tag (only supported in newer browsers) keeps the script out of the HTML document, but it is still accessible from the Web server.

4

Workshop

Quiz

1. A script that executes when the user clicks the mouse button is an example of what?

   a. An object

   b. An event handler

   c. An impossibility

2. Which of the following are capabilities of functions in JavaScript?

   a. Accept parameters

   b. Return a value

   c. Both of the above

3. What is the purpose of enclosing a script within HTML comments?

   a. To make it look more complicated

   b. To hide it from users

   c. To hide it from non-JavaScript browsers

Answers

1. b. A script that executes when the user clicks the mouse button is an event handler.

2. c. Functions can both accept parameters and return values.

3. c. HTML comments can be used to hide the script from non-JavaScript browsers.

Exercises

To further explore the JavaScript features you learned about in this hour, you can perform the following exercises:

1. Modify the Greet function to accept two parameters, who1 and who2, and to include both names in a single greeting dialog. Modify Listing 4.4 to use a single function call to the new function.

2. Add the Average function to the header of a simple HTML document. Add a function call that uses the alert statement to display the average and verify that the result is correct.

3. Add JavaScript comments to the Average function to explain what each line does.

PART II

Learning JavaScript Basics

Hour

Hour 5

Using and Storing Values

Welcome to Part II of this book! In the next four hours, you will learn some specific scripting features and techniques that you will use frequently in JavaScript programs.

During this hour, you will focus on variables and expressions. Hour 5 covers the following topics:

- Naming and declaring variables
- Choosing whether to use local or global variables
- Assigning values to variables
- How JavaScript stores various types of data
- How to convert between different data types
- Using variables and literals in expressions
- Using variables to store data entered by the user

Using Variables

Unless you skipped the first four hours of this book, you've already used a few variables. You probably can also figure out how to use a few more without any help. Nevertheless, there are some aspects of variables you haven't learned yet.

Choosing Variable Names

Variables are named containers that can store data (for example, a number, a text string, or an object). As you learned earlier in this book, each variable has a name. There are specific rules you must follow when choosing a variable name:

- Variable names can include letters of the alphabet, both upper- and lowercase. They can also include the digits 0–9 and the underscore (_) character.
- Variable names cannot include spaces or any other punctuation characters.
- The first character of the variable name must be either a letter or an underscore.
- Variable names are case sensitive—totalnum, Totalnum, and TotalNum are separate variable names.
- There is no official limit on the length of variable names, but they must fit within one line. (And you must be able to type the same name twice to make use of the variable.)

Using these rules, the following are examples of valid variable names:

```
total_number_of_fish
LastInvoiceNumber
temp1
a
_var39
```

> You can choose to use either friendly, easy-to-read names or completely cryptic ones. Do yourself a favor: use longer, friendly names whenever possible. While you might remember the difference between a, b, x, and x1 right now, you might not after a good night's sleep.

Using Local and Global Variables

Some computer languages require you to declare a variable before you use it. JavaScript includes the var keyword, which can be used to declare a variable. You can omit var in many cases; the variable is still declared the first time you assign a value to it.

To understand where to declare a variable, you will need to understand the concept of *scope*. A variable's scope is the area of the script in which that variable can be used. There are two types of variables:

- *Global variables* have the entire script (and other scripts in the same HTML document) as their scope. They can be used anywhere, even within functions.
- *Local variables* have a single function as their scope. They can be used only within the function they are created in.

To create a global variable, you declare it in the main script, outside any functions. You can use the var keyword to declare the variable, as in this example:

```
var students = 25;
```

This statement declares a variable called students and assigns it a value of 25. If this statement is used outside functions, it creates a global variable. The var keyword is optional in this case, so this statement is equivalent to the previous one:

```
students = 25;
```

Before you get in the habit of omitting the var keyword, be sure you understand exactly when it's required. It's actually a good idea to always use the var keyword—you'll avoid errors and make your script easier to read, and it won't ever cause any trouble.

For the most part, the variables you've used in earlier hours of this book have been global.

A local variable belongs to a particular function. Any variable you declare (or use for the first time) in a function is a local variable. For example, the variables in the function's parameter list are local variables.

To be sure you are creating a local variable within a function, you can use the var keyword. This forces JavaScript to create a local variable, even if there is a global variable with the same name.

To understand the types of variables and declarations better, look at Listing 5.1. This is a modified version of the Greet() example from Hour 4, "How JavaScript Programs Work."

5

LISTING 5.1   A SCRIPT USING BOTH LOCAL AND GLOBAL VARIABLES.

```
 1: <HTML>
 2: <HEAD>
 3: <TITLE>Functions</TITLE>
 4: <SCRIPT LANGUAGE="JavaScript">
 5: var name1 = "Fred";
 6: var name2 = "Ethel";
 7: function Greet(who) {
 8: alert("Greetings," + who);
 9:     var name2 = "Barney";
10: }
11: </SCRIPT>
12: </HEAD>
13: <BODY>
14: <H1>Function Example: the Sequel</H1>
15: <P>Prepare to be greeted twice.</P>
16: <SCRIPT LANGUAGE="JavaScript">
17: Greet(name1);
18: Greet(name2);
19: </SCRIPT>
20: </BODY>
21: </HTML>
```

The script in Listing 5.1 uses the following variables:

- name1 and name2 are global variables defined in the header.

- who is a local variable created in the Greet() function's parameter list.

- Here's the tricky bit: The Greet() function creates a local variable called name2. Since the var keyword is used, this does not affect the global variable name2. (If it did, the name in the second greeting would change.)

 If you think having two variables with the same name is confusing, you're right. To avoid this, it's best to use unique names for all variables.

Notice that the global variables are declared within the header of the HTML document. You can actually declare variables in any script in the document, but the header is a good place for global variables because it is executed first. If you attempt to use a variable before it is declared (or assigned a value), it will contain the null value.

You should now understand the difference between local and global variables. If you're still a bit confused, don't worry—if you use the var keyword every time, you'll almost always end up with the right type of variable.

Assigning Values to Variables

As you learned in Hour 2, "Creating a Simple Script," you can use the equal sign to assign a value to a variable. For example, this statement assigns the value 40 to the variable `lines`:

```
lines = 40;
```

You can use any expression to the right of the equal sign, including other variables. You have used this syntax earlier to add one to a variable:

```
lines = lines + 1;
```

Since incrementing or decrementing variables is quite common, JavaScript includes two types of shorthand for this syntax. The first uses the += operator:

```
lines += 1;
```

Similarly, you can subtract a number from a variable using the -= operator:

```
lines -= 1;
```

If you still think that's too much to type, JavaScript also includes the increment and decrement operators, ++ and --. This statement adds one to the value of `lines`:

```
lines++;
```

Similarly, this statement subtracts one from the value of `lines`:

```
lines--;
```

You can also use the ++ or -- operator before a variable name, as in ++lines. However, these are not identical. The difference is when the increment or decrement happens:

- If the operator is after the variable name, the increment or decrement happens *after* the current expression is evaluated.
- If the operator is before the variable name, the increment or decrement happens *before* the current expression is evaluated.

This difference is only an issue when you use the variable in an expression and increment or decrement it in the same statement. As an example, suppose you have assigned the `lines` variable the value 40. The following two statements have different effects:

```
alert(lines++);
```

```
alert(++lines);
```

The first statement displays an alert with the value 40, and then it increments `lines` to 41. The second statement first increments `lines` to 41, then displays an alert with the value 41.

5

These operators are strictly for your convenience. If it makes more sense to you to stick to lines = lines + 1, do it—your script won't suffer.

Data Types in JavaScript

In some computer languages, you have to specify the type of data a variable will store: for example, a number or a string. In JavaScript, you don't need to specify a data type except in rare cases. However, you should know the types of data JavaScript can deal with.

These are the basic JavaScript data types:

- *Numbers*, such as 3, 25, or 1.4142138. JavaScript supports both integers and floating-point numbers.

- *Boolean*, or logical values. These can have one of two values: true or false. These are useful for indicating whether a certain condition is true.

You'll learn more about Boolean values and about using conditions in JavaScript in Hour 7, "Testing and Comparing Values."

- *Strings*, such as "I am a jelly doughnut". These consist of one or more characters of text. (Strictly speaking, these are string objects, which you'll learn about in Hour 6.)

- *The null value*, represented by the keyword null. This is the value of an undefined variable. For example, the statement document.write(fig) will result in this value if the variable fig has not been previously used or defined.

Although JavaScript keeps track of the data type currently stored in each variable, it doesn't restrict you from changing types midstream. For example, suppose you declared a variable by assigning it a value:

```
total = 31;
```

This statement declares a variable called total and assigns it the value of 31. This is a numeric variable. Now suppose you changed the value of total:

```
total = "albatross";
```

This assigns a string value to total. JavaScript will not display an error when this statement executes; it's perfectly valid, although it's probably not a very useful total.

While this feature of JavaScript is convenient and powerful, it can also make it easy to make a mistake. For example, if the `total` variable was later used in a mathematical calculation, the result would be invalid—but JavaScript does not warn you that you've made this mistake.

Converting Between Data Types

JavaScript handles conversions between data types for you whenever it can. For example, you've already used statements like this:

```
document.write("The total is " + total);
```

This statement prints out a message such as "The total is 40." Since the `document.write` function works with strings, the JavaScript interpreter automatically converts any non-strings in the expression (in this case, the value of `total`) to strings before performing the function.

This works equally well with floating-point and Boolean values. However, there are some situations where it won't work. For example, the following statement will work fine if the value of `total` is 40:

```
average = total / 3;
```

However, the `total` variable could also contain a string; in this case, the statement above would result in an error.

In some situations, you may end up with a string containing a number and need to convert it to a regular numeric variable. JavaScript includes two functions for this purpose:

- `parseInt()` converts a string to an integer number.
- `parseFloat()` converts a string to a floating-point number.

Both of these functions will read a number from the beginning of the string and return a numeric version. For example, this statement converts the string "30 angry polar bears" to a number:

```
stringvar = "30 angry polar bears"
numvar = parseInt(stringvar);
```

After these statements execute, the `numvar` variable contains the number 30. The non-numeric portion of the string is ignored.

5

These functions look for a number of the appropriate type at the beginning of the string. If a valid number is not found, the function returns the string "NaN", meaning *not a number*.

Workshop: Storing User Data in Variables

One common use of variables is to store information that comes from the user. As an example, you will now create a script that prompts the user for information and creates an HTML document containing that information.

In this script, we'll create a customized home page for the user. (It won't be a good one, but it will be customized.) You will use the prompt function to prompt for each piece of information. This function is similar to alert, but prompts the user for an entry.

To begin the script, you will prompt for a first name, a last name, and a title for the page. These statements prompt for three variables:

```
first = prompt("Enter your first name.");
last = prompt("Enter your last name.");
title = prompt("Enter a page title.");
```

You can now use the contents of the variables to customize the HTML document. Begin with the title the user entered:

```
document.write("<H1>" + title + "</H1>");
```

This statement adds the title to the page, enclosed in <H1> (heading 1) tags. Next, we'll make use of the first and last names to give the user credit:

```
document.write("<H2>By " + first + " " + last + "</H2>");
```

This begins with an <H2> tag, followed by the word "By", the first name, a space, the last name, and the closing </H2> tag.

To complete this script, add the usual <SCRIPT> tags and an HTML framework. Listing 5.2 shows the final HTML document.

LISTING 5.2 A SCRIPT TO CREATE A CUSTOMIZED HTML DOCUMENT.

```
1: <HTML>
2: <HEAD>
3: <TITLE>Customized home page</TITLE>
4: </HEAD>
5: <BODY>
6: <SCRIPT LANGUAGE="JavaScript">
```

```
 7: first = prompt("Enter your first name.");
 8: last = prompt("Enter your last name.");
 9: title = prompt("Enter a page title.");
10: document.write("<H1>" + title + "</H1>");
11: document.write("<H2>By " + first + " " + last + "</H2>");
12: </SCRIPT>
13: <P>This page is under construction.</P>
14: </BODY>
15: </HTML>
```

To test this script, load the HTML document into a browser. You will be prompted for the three items, one at a time. After you have entered all three, the complete page is displayed. The final page should resemble Figure 5.1.

FIGURE 5.1

The customized HTML page script as seen by Netscape.

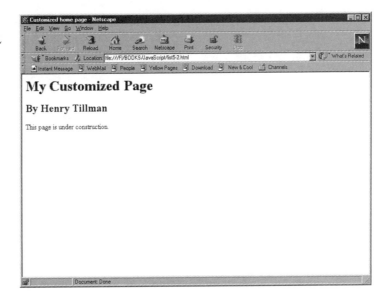

Summary

During this hour, you've focused on variables and how JavaScript handles them. You've learned how to name variables, how to declare them, and the differences between local and global variables.

You also explored the data types supported by JavaScript and how to convert between them and created expressions using variables in literals. In the next hour, you'll move on to two more complicated types of variables: strings and arrays.

Q&A

Q What is the importance of the var keyword? Should I always use it to declare variables?

A You only need to use var to define a local variable in a function, and then only if you want to ensure that a global variable of the same name is not used. However, if you're unsure at all, it's always safe to use var. Using it consistently will help you keep your scripts organized and error free.

Q Is there any reason I would want to use the var keyword to create a local variable with the same name as a global one?

A Not on purpose. The main reason to use var is to avoid conflicts with global variables you may not know about. For example, you may add a global variable in the future, or you may add another script to the page that uses a similar variable name. This is more of an issue with large, complex scripts.

Q What good are Boolean variables?

A Often in scripts you'll need a variable to indicate whether something has happened—for example, whether a phone number the user entered is in the right format. Boolean variables are ideal for this; they're also useful in working with conditions, as you'll see in Hour 7.

Workshop

Quiz

1. Which of the following is *not* a valid JavaScript variable name?

   a. 2names

   b. _first_and_last_names

   c. FirstAndLast

2. If the statement var fig=2 appears in a function, which type of variable does it declare?

   a. A global variable

   b. A local variable

   c. A constant variable

3. What will be the result of the JavaScript expression `31 + " angry polar bears"`?

    a. An error message

    b. 32

    c. "31 angry polar bears"

Answers

1. a. `2names` is an invalid JavaScript variable name since it begins with a number. The others are valid, although choice (b) is extremely silly.

2. b. Since the variable is declared in a function, it is a local variable. The `var` keyword ensures that a new local variable is created.

3. c. JavaScript converts the whole expression to the string "31 angry polar bears". (No offense to polar bears, who are seldom angry and rarely seen in groups this large.)

Exercises

If you would like to further explore the concepts you learned in this chapter, perform the following activities:

- Modify Listing 5.1 by removing the `var` keyword before `name2` in the `Greet()` function. Are the greetings different than the original version? If they are, try to understand why.

- Add some additional customizable features to Listing 5.2. For example, you could prompt the user for a URL and include a link on the page.

5

HOUR **6**

Using Strings and Arrays

In Hour 5, "Using and Storing Values," you used variables to store and work with numbers. Although you can do quite a bit with numbers, some of the most useful applications of JavaScript involve the use of strings (text) and arrays (groups of numbers, strings, or objects).

In Hour 6, you will learn to use strings and arrays in JavaScript. You will cover the following topics:

- How strings are stored in String objects
- Creating and using String objects
- Calculating the length of a string
- Working with parts of strings
- Finding a string within a larger string
- How arrays are stored in Array objects
- Creating and using arrays
- Working with string arrays
- Using strings to create scrolling messages

Using String Objects

You've already used several strings during the first few hours of this book. Strings store groups of text characters and are named similarly to other variables. As a simple example, this statement assigns the string `This is a test` to a string variable called `test`:

```
test = "This is a test";
```

Creating a String Object

JavaScript stores strings as *String objects*. You usually don't need to worry about this, but it will explain some of the techniques for working with strings, which use methods (built-in functions) of the `String` object.

There are two ways to create a new `String` object. The first is the one you've already used, while the second uses official object syntax. The following two statements create the same string:

```
test = "This is a test";
test = new String("This is a test");
```

The second statement uses the `new` keyword, which you use to create objects. This tells the browser to create a new `String` object containing the text `This is a test` and assigns it to the variable `test`.

> While you can create a string using object-oriented syntax, the standard JavaScript syntax is simpler, and there is no difference in the strings created by these two methods.

Assigning a Value

You can assign a value to a string in the same way as any other variable. Both of the examples in the previous section assigned an initial value to the string. You can also assign a value after the string has already been created. For example, the following statement replaces the contents of the `test` variable with a new string:

```
test = "This is only a test.";
```

You can also use the concatenation operator (+) to combine the values of two strings. Listing 6.1 shows a simple example of assigning and combining the values of strings.

LISTING 6.1 ASSIGNING VALUES TO STRINGS AND COMBINING THEM.

```
 1: <HTML>
 2: <HEAD>
 3: <TITLE>String Test</TITLE>
 4: </HEAD>
 5: <BODY>
 6: <H1>String Test</H1>
 7: <SCRIPT LANGUAGE="JavaScript">;
 8: test1 = "This is a test.";
 9: test2 = "This is only a test.";
10: both = test1 + test2;
11: alert(both);
12: </SCRIPT>
13: </BODY>
14: </HTML>
```

This script assigns values to two string variables, test1 and test2, and then displays an alert with their combined value. If you run this script in Netscape, your output should resemble Figure 6.1.

FIGURE 6.1

The output of the string example script.

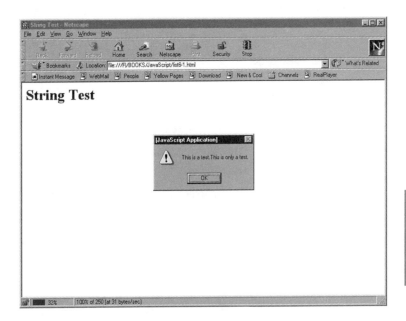

6

In addition to using the + operator to concatenate two strings, you can use the += operator to add to a string. For example, this statement adds a period to the current contents of the string sentence:

sentence += ".";

The plus sign (+) is also used to add numbers in JavaScript. The browser knows whether to use addition or concatenation based on the types of data you use with the plus sign. If you use it between a number and a string, the number is converted to a string and concatenated.

Calculating the String's Length

From time to time, you may find it useful to know how many characters a string variable contains. You can do this with the `length` property of `String` objects, which you can use with any string. To use this property, type the string's name followed by `.length`.

For example, `test.length` refers to the length of the `test` string. Here is an example of this property:

```
test = "This is a test.";
document.write(test.length);
```

The first statement assigns the string `This is a test` to the `test` variable. The second statement displays the length of the string—in this case, 15 characters.

Remember that although `test` refers to a string variable, the value of `test.length` is a number and can be used in any numeric expression.

Converting the String's Case

Two methods of the `String` object allow you to convert the contents of a string to all uppercase or all lowercase:

- `toUpperCase()` converts all characters in the string to uppercase.
- `toLowerCase()` converts all characters in the string to lowercase.

For example, the following statement displays the value of the `test` string variable in lowercase:

```
document.write(test.toLowerCase());
```

Assuming that this variable contained the text `This Is A Test`, the result would be the following string:

```
this is a test
```

Note that the statement doesn't change the value of the text variable. These methods return the upper- or lowercase version of the string, but they don't change the string itself. If you want to change the string's value, you can use a statement like this:

```
test = test.toLowerCase();
```

> Note that the syntax for these methods is similar to the length property introduced earlier. The difference is that methods always use parentheses, while properties don't. The toUpperCase and toLowerCase methods do not take any parameters, but you still need to use the parentheses.

Working with Substrings

So far, you've worked with entire strings. JavaScript also allows you to work with *substrings*, or portions of a string. You can use the substring method to retrieve a portion of a string, or the charAt method to get a single character. These are explained in the sections below.

Using Part of a String

The substring() method returns a string consisting of a portion of the original string between two index values, which you must specify in parentheses. For example, the following statement displays the fourth through sixth characters of the text string:

```
document.write(text.substring(3,6));
```

At this point, you're probably wondering where the 3 and the 6 come from. There are three things you need to understand about the index parameters:

- Indexing starts with 0 for the first character of the string, so the fourth character is actually index 3.
- The second index is noninclusive. A second index of 6 includes up to index 5 (the sixth character).
- You can specify the two indexes in either order. The smaller one will be assumed to be the first index. In the previous example, (6,3) would have produced the same result. Of course, there is rarely a reason to use the reverse order.

As another example, suppose you defined a string called alpha to hold the alphabet:

```
alpha = "ABCDEFGHIJKLMNOPQRSTUVWXYZ";
```

6

The following are examples of the `substring()` method using this string:

- `alpha.substring(0,4)` returns ABCD.
- `alpha.substring(10,12)` returns KL.
- `alpha.substring(12,10)` also returns KL. Because it's smaller, 10 is used as the first index.
- `alpha.substring(6,7)` returns G.
- `alpha.substring(24,26)` returns YZ.
- `alpha.substring(0,26)` returns the entire alphabet.
- `alpha.substring(6,6)` returns the null value, an empty string. This is true whenever the two index values are the same.

Getting a Single Character

The `charAt` method is a simple way to grab a single character from a string. You specify the character's index, or position, in parentheses. The indices begin at 0 for the first character. Here are a few examples using the `alpha` string:

- `alpha.charAt(0)` returns A.
- `alpha.charAt(12)` returns M.
- `alpha.charAt(25)` returns Z.
- `alpha.charAt(27)` returns an empty string because there is no character at that position.

Finding a Substring

Another use for substrings is to find a string within another string. One way to do this is with the `indexOf` method. To use this method, add `indexOf` to the string you want to search, and specify the string to search for in the parentheses. This example searches for text in the `test` string:

```
location = test.indexOf("text");
```

 As with most JavaScript methods and property names, `indexOf` is case sensitive. Make sure you type it exactly as shown here when you use it in scripts.

The value returned in the `location` variable is an index into the string, similar to the first index in the `substring` method. The first character of the string is index 0.

You can specify an optional second parameter to indicate the index value at which to begin the search. For example, this statement searches for the word `fish` in the `temp` string, starting with the 20th character:

```
location = temp.indexOf("fish",19);
```

> One use for the second parameter is to search for multiple occurrences of a string. After finding the first occurrence, you search starting with that location for the second one, and so on.

A second method, `lastIndexOf()`, works the same way, but finds the *last* occurrence of the string. It searches the string backwards, starting with the last character. For example, this statement finds the last occurrence of `Fred` in the `names` string:

```
location = names.lastIndexOf("Fred");
```

As with `indexOf()`, you can specify a location to search from as the second parameter. In this case, the string will be searched backward starting at that location.

Using Numeric Arrays

An array is a numbered group of data items that you can treat as a single unit. For example, you might use an array called `scores` to store several scores for a game. Arrays can contain strings, numbers, objects, or other types of data.

Creating a Numeric Array

Unlike most other types of JavaScript variables, you must declare an array before you use it. The following example creates an array with 30 elements:

```
scores = new Array(30);
```

To assign values to the array, use brackets and an index. Indices begin with `0`, so the elements of the array in this example would be numbered `0` to `29`. These statements assign values to the first four elements of the array:

```
scores[0] = 39;
scores[1] = 40;
scores[2] = 100;
scores[3] = 49;
```

6

Like strings, arrays have a `length` property. This tells you the number of elements in the array, usually the same number you used when creating the array. For example, this statement would print the number 30:

```
document.write(scores.length);
```

Accessing Array Elements

You can read the contents of an array using the same notation you used when assigning values. For example, the following statements would display the values of the first four elements of the `scores` array:

```
scoredisp = "Scores: " + scores[0] + "," + scores[1] + "," + scores[2] +
"," + scores[3];
document.write(scoredisp);
```

Looking at this example, you might imagine it would be inconvenient to display all 30 elements of the `scores` array—and working with a larger array would be even more difficult. This is an ideal job for loops, which allow you to perform the same statements several times with different values. You'll learn all about loops in Hour 8, "Repeating Yourself: Using Loops."

Using String Arrays

So far, you've used arrays of numbers. JavaScript also allows you to use *string arrays*, or arrays of strings. This is a powerful feature that allows you to work with a large number of strings at the same time.

Creating a String Array

You define a string array in the same way as a numeric array (in fact, JavaScript does not make a distinction between them):

```
names = new Array(30);
```

You can then assign string values to the array elements:

```
names[0] = "Henry J. Tillman";
names[1] = "Sherlock Holmes";
```

You can use these array elements anywhere you would use a string. You can even use the string methods introduced earlier. For example, the following statement prints the first five characters of the first element of the `names` array, resulting in `Henry`:

```
document.write(names[0].substring(0,5));
```

Splitting a String

JavaScript includes a string method called split, which splits a string into its component parts. To use this method, specify the string to split and a character to divide the parts:

```
test = "John Q. Public";
parts = test.split(" ");
```

In this example, the test string contains the name John Q. Public. The split method in the second statement splits the name string at each space, resulting in three strings. These are stored in a string array called parts. After the example statements execute, the elements of parts contain the following:

- parts[0] = "John"
- parts[1] = "Q."
- parts[2] = "Public"

JavaScript also includes an array method, join, that performs the opposite function. This statement reassembles the parts array into a string:

```
fullname = parts.join(" ");
```

The value in the parentheses specifies a character to separate the parts of the array. In this case, a space is used, resulting in the final string John Q. Public. If you do not specify a character, commas are used.

Sorting an Array

JavaScript also includes a sort method for arrays, which returns a sorted version of the array (alphabetically or numerically). For example, the following statements initialize an array of four names and sort it:

```
names[0] = "Public, John Q.";
names[1] = "Tillman, Henry J.";
names[2] = "Clinton, Bill";
names[3] = "Mouse, Mickey";
sortednames = names.sort();
```

The last statement assigns the sortednames array to the sorted version of names using the join method.

Workshop: Displaying Scrolling Messages

In Hour 3, "Exploring JavaScript's Capabilities," you learned that JavaScript can be used to create a scrolling message in the status line of a Web page, and you copied an existing script. With your knowledge of strings, you can now create the scrolling message program from scratch.

6

To begin, you'll need to define the message to be scrolled. You will use a variable called msg to store the message. To begin the script, initialize the variable (feel free to choose your own text for the message):

```
msg = "This is an example of a scrolling message. Isn't it exciting?";
```

Next, define a second string called spacer. This string will be displayed between the copies of the message to make it clear where one ends and the other begins. Here is the definition for spacer:

```
spacer = "...           ...";
```

You'll need one more variable: a numeric variable to store the current position of the string. Call it pos and initialize it with 0:

```
pos = 0;
```

The actual scrolling will be done by a function called ScrollMessage. Listing 6.2 shows this function.

LISTING 6.2   THE ScrollMessage FUNCTION.

```
1: function ScrollMessage() {
2:    window.status = msg.substring(pos, msg.length) + spacer +
      msg.substring(0, pos);
3:    pos++;
4:    if (pos > msg.length) pos = 0;
5:    window.setTimeout("ScrollMessage()",200);
6: }
```

Here is a line-by-line breakdown of the ScrollMessage function:

- Line 1—The function keyword is used to begin the function.
- Line 2—This statement displays a string in the status line. The string is composed of the portion of msg from pos to the end, followed by the space, followed by the portion of msg from the beginning to pos.
- Line 3—The pos variable is incremented.
- Line 4—This statement checks whether pos is larger than the length of msg. If it is, it resets it to 0. (You'll learn more about the if statement in the next hour.)
- Line 5—This statement uses the window.setTimeout method, which allows you to set a statement to be executed after a time delay. In this case, it executes the ScrollMessage function after .2 seconds.
- Line 6—The closing bracket ends the function.

To complete the example, add the <SCRIPT> tags and the HTML tags that make up a Web document. Listing 6.3 shows the complete scrolling message example.

LISTING 6.3 THE COMPLETE SCROLLING MESSAGE EXAMPLE.

```
 1: <HTML>
 2: <HEAD><TITLE>Scrolling Message Example</TITLE>
 3: <SCRIPT LANGUAGE="JavaScript">
 4: msg = "This is an example of a scrolling message. Isn't it exciting?";
 5: spacer = "...          ...";
 6: pos = 0;
 7: function ScrollMessage() {
 8:    window.status = msg.substring(pos, msg.length) + spacer +
        msg.substring(0, pos);
 9:    pos++;
10:    if (pos > msg.length) pos = 0;
11:    window.setTimeout("ScrollMessage()",200);
12: }
13: ScrollMessage();
14: </SCRIPT>
15: </HEAD>
16: <BODY>
17: <H1>Scrolling Message Example</H1>
18: Look at the status line at the bottom of this page. (Don't watch it
      too long, as it may be hypnotic.)
19: </BODY></HTML>
```

Figure 6.2 shows the output of the scrolling message program.

FIGURE 6.2

*The scrolling message
example in action.*

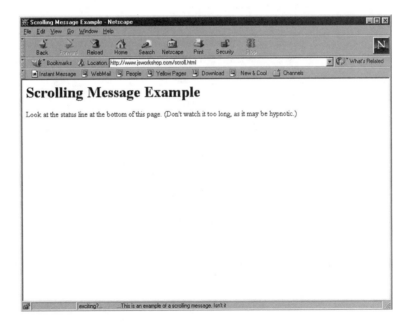

6

Summary

In this hour, you learned how to store strings in JavaScript and how to work with portions of strings. You also learned how to use arrays and how to store numbers or strings in them.

You applied your knowledge of strings to create a scrolling message. In the next hour, you'll learn how to use the `if` statement and other JavaScript features to test the values of variables, including strings and arrays.

Q&A

Q Can I store other types of data in an array? For example, can I have an array of dates?

A Absolutely. JavaScript allows you to store any data type in an array.

Q What about two-dimensional arrays?

A These are arrays with two indices (such as columns and rows). JavaScript does not directly support this type of array, but you can use objects to achieve the same effect. You will learn more about objects in Hour 11, "Creating Custom Objects."

Q If I assign values to array elements manually anyway, what is the advantage of using arrays?

A First of all, you can use a loop to work with the array elements and use methods such as `join` and `sort` to work with the array. Arrays can also be used to store several lines of data from a form, as you'll see in Hour 14, "Getting Data with Forms."

Workshop

Quiz

1. If the string `test` contains the value `The eagle has landed.`, what would be the value of `test.length`?

   a. 4

   b. 21

   c. The

2. Using the same example string, which of these statements would return the word `eagle`?

    a. `test.substring(4,9)`

    b. `test.substring(5,9)`

    c. `test.substring("eagle")`

3. What does the `join` method of an array do?

    a. Allows a new member to join the array.

    b. Combines the array with another array.

    c. Combines the array's elements into a string.

Answers

1. b. The length of the string is 21 characters.

2. a. The correct statement is `test.substring(4,9)`. Remember that the indices start with `0`, and that the second index is non-inclusive.

3. c. The `join` method combines the array's elements into a string.

Exercises

You can further your knowledge of strings and arrays by performing these activities:

- Use the JavaScript Console to create several strings and experiment with them. The console was introduced in Hour 2, "Creating a Simple Script." To use it, type `javascript:` in Netscape's Location field.

- Modify the scrolling message example to scroll the message in the opposite direction.

6

HOUR 7

Testing and Comparing Values

Having survived Hours 5 and 6 of this book, you should now be familiar with creating and using variables of all sorts. In this hour, you'll learn how to make better use of variables by comparing, testing, and evaluating their values with the tools provided by JavaScript.

In Hour 7, you'll learn to use conditional statements in JavaScript. You will cover the following topics:

- Testing variables with the `if` statement
- Using various operators to compare values
- Using logical operators to combine conditions
- Using alternate conditions with `else`
- Creating expressions with conditional operators
- Testing for multiple conditions
- Evaluating data received from the user

The `if` Statement

One of the most important features of a computer language is the capability to test and compare values. This allows your scripts to behave differently based on the values of variables or based on input from the user.

The `if` statement is the main conditional statement in JavaScript. This statement means much the same in JavaScript as it does in English—for example, here is a typical conditional statement in English:

If the phone rings, answer it.

This statement consists of two parts: a condition (*If the phone rings*) and an action (*answer it*). The `if` statement in JavaScript works much the same way. Here is an example of a basic `if` statement:

```
if (a == 1) window.alert("Found a 1!");
```

This statement includes a condition (if a equals 1) and an action (display a message). This statement checks the variable a and, if it has a value of 1, prints a message. Otherwise, it does nothing.

If you use an `if` statement like the preceding example, you can use a single statement as the action. You can also use multiple statements for the action by enclosing them in braces (`{}`), as shown in Listing 7.1.

LISTING 7.1 AN `if` STATEMENT WITH MULTIPLE ACTION STATEMENTS.

```
1: if (a == 1) {
2:    window.alert("Found a 1!");
3:    a = 0;
4: }
```

This block of statements checks the variable a once again. If it finds a value of 1, it displays a message and sets a back to 0.

Conditional Operators

While the action part of an `if` statement can include any of the JavaScript statements you've already learned (and any others, for that matter), the condition part of the statement uses its own syntax. This is called a *conditional expression*.

A conditional expression includes two values to be compared (in the preceding example, the values were a and 1). These values can be variables, constants, or even expressions in themselves.

Either side of the conditional expression can be a variable, a constant, or an expression. You can compare a variable and a value or compare two variables. (You can compare two constants, but there's usually no reason to.)

Between the two values to be compared is a *conditional operator*. This operator tells JavaScript how to compare the two values. For instance, the == operator is used to test whether the two values are equal. A variety of conditional operators are available:

- == (is equal to)
- != (is not equal to)
- < (is less than)
- > (is greater than)
- <= (is less than or equal to)
- >= (is greater than or equal to)

Be sure not to confuse the equality operator (==) with the assignment operator (=), even though they both might be read as "equals." Remember to use = when *assigning* a variable and == when *comparing* values. Confusing these two is one of the most common mistakes in JavaScript programming.

Combining Conditions with Logical Operators

Often, you'll want to check a variable for more than one possible value or check more than one variable at once. JavaScript includes logical operators, also known as Boolean operators, for this purpose. For example, the following two statements check different conditions and use the same action:

```
if (phone == " ") window.alert("error!");
if (email == " ") window.alert("error!");
```

Using a logical operator, you can combine them into a single statement:

```
if (phone == " " || email == " ") window.alert("error!");
```

This statement uses the logical Or operator (||) to combine the conditions. Translated to English, this would be "If the phone number or the email address is blank, display an error message."

An additional logical operator is the And operator, &&. Consider this statement:

```
if (phone == " " && email == " ") window.alert("error!");
```

7

This statement uses && (And) instead of ¦¦ (Or), so the error message will only be displayed if *both* the email address and phone number variables are blank. (In this particular case, Or is a better choice.)

> If the JavaScript interpreter discovers the answer to a conditional expression before reaching the end, it does not evaluate the rest of the condition. For example, if the first of two conditions separated by the && operator is false, the second is not evaluated. You can take advantage of this to improve the speed of your scripts.

The third logical operator is the exclamation mark (!), which means Not. It can be used to invert an expression—in other words, a true expression would become false, and a false one would become true. For example, here's a statement that uses the Not operator:

```
if (phone != " ") alert("phone is OK");
```

In this case, the Not operator is used as part of the not-equal operator, !=. This operator inverts the condition, so the action of the if statement is executed only if the phone number variable is *not* blank.

> The logical operators are powerful, but it's easy to accidentally create an impossible condition with them. For example, the condition (a < 10 && a > 20) might look correct at first glance. However, if you read it out loud, you get "If a is less than 10 and a is greater than 20"—an impossibility in our universe. In this case, Or (¦¦) should have been used.

The else Keyword

An additional feature of the if statement is the else keyword. Much like its English equivalent, else tells the JavaScript interpreter what to do if the condition isn't true. Listing 7.2 shows a simple example of the else keyword in action.

LISTING 7.2 AN EXAMPLE USING THE if AND else KEYWORDS.

```
1: if (a == 1) {
2:     alert("Found a 1!");
3:     a = 0;
4: }
5: else {
6:     alert("Incorrect value: " + a);
7: }
```

This is a modified version of Listing 7.1. This displays a message and resets the variable a if the condition is met. If the condition is not met (if a is not 1), a different message is displayed.

Like the `if` statement, `else` can be followed either by a single action statement or by a number of statements enclosed in braces.

Using Conditional Expressions

In addition to the `if` statement, JavaScript provides a shorthand type of conditional expression that you can use to make quick decisions. This uses a peculiar syntax, which is also found in other languages, such as C. A conditional expression looks like this:

```
variable = (condition) ? if true : if false;
```

This assigns one of two values to the variable: one if the condition is true, and another if it is false. Here is an example of a conditional expression:

```
value = (a == 1) ? 1 : 0;
```

This statement may look confusing, but it is equivalent to the following `if` statement:

```
if (a == 1)
   value = 1;
else
   value = 0;
```

In other words, the value after the question mark (?) will be used if the condition is true, and the value after the colon (:) will be used if the condition is false. The colon represents the `else` portion of this statement and, like the `else` portion of the `if` statement, is optional.

These shorthand expressions can be used anywhere JavaScript expects a value. They provide an easy way to make simple decisions about values. As an example, here's an easy way to display a grammatically correct message about the `counter` variable:

```
document.write("Found " + counter + ((counter == 1) ? " word." : "
words."));
```

This will print the message Found 1 word if counter has a value of 1, and Found 2 words if it's a value of 2 or greater. This is one of the most common uses for a conditional expression.

7

Using Multiple Conditions with switch

Often, you'll use several if statements in a row to test for different conditions. Listing 7.3 shows one example of this technique.

LISTING 7.3 USING MULTIPLE if STATEMENTS.

```
1: if (button=="next") window.location="next.html";
2: if (button=="previous") window.location="prev.html";
3: if (button=="home") window.location="home.html";
4: if (button=="back") window.location="menu.html";
```

Although this is a pretty compact way of doing things, this method can get messy if each if statement has its own block of code with several statements. As an alternative, JavaScript includes the switch statement, which allows you to combine several tests of the same variable or expression into a single block of statements. Listing 7.4 shows the same example converted to use switch.

The switch statement is included in JavaScript 1.2 (Netscape 4.0) and later. Be sure your browser supports this version before you try the examples. To ensure that scripts won't cause errors, specify the LANGUAGE="JavaScript1.2" parameter in the <SCRIPT> tag.

LISTING 7.4 TESTING MULTIPLE CONDITIONS WITH switch.

```
 1: switch(button) {
 2:     case "next" :
 3:         window.location="next.html";
 4:         break;
 5:     case "previous":
 6:         window.location="prev.html";
 7:         break;
 8:     case "home":
 9:         window.location="home.html";
10:         break;
11:     case "back":
12:         window.location="menu.html";
13:         break;
14:     default :
15:         window.alert("Wrong button.");
16: }
```

The `switch` statement has several components:

- The initial `switch` statement. This statement includes the value to test (in this case, `button`) in parentheses.

- Braces ({ and }) enclose the `switch` statement, similar to a function or an `if` statement.

- One or more `case` statements. Each of these statements specifies a value to compare with the value specified in the `switch` statement. If the values match, the statements after the `case` statement are executed. Otherwise, the next case is tried.

- The `break` statement is used to end each case.

- Optionally, the `default` statement can be included and followed by a default case—one or more statements that are executed if none of the `case` statements were matched.

> You can use multiple statements after each `case` statement within the `switch` structure. You don't need to enclose them in braces. If the `case` matches, the JavaScript interpreter executes statements until it encounters a `break` or the next case.

Workshop: Evaluating a User Response

As a practical example of the `switch` statement, you will now create a Web page that asks the user a question and then evaluates the user's response to determine what to do next. Specifically, you'll ask the user for a keyword that represents a Web page.

If the keyword matches one of those in your script, the user will be sent to the appropriate page. If the response doesn't match one of the predetermined keywords, the user will be sent to a default page.

Your script starts by prompting the user with the `window.prompt` function. To use this function, you include a statement that prompts the user as a parameter and assigns the returned value to a variable. Here's the prompt statement:

```
where = window.prompt("Where do you want to go today?");
```

Next, use a `switch` statement and several `case` statements to evaluate the response:

```
switch (where) {
    case "Netscape" :
    window.location="http://www.netscape.com";
    break;
```

7

```
case "Microsoft" :
    window.location="http://www.microsoft.com";
    break;
case "Yahoo" :
    window.location="http://www.yahoo.com";
    break;
```

Next, use the `default` statement to send the user to a default page (in this case, Macmillan Computer Publishing's page):

```
default :
    window.location="http://www.mcp.com";
}
```

Because this is the last statement in the `switch` structure, you don't need to use the `break` statement here. The final brace ends the `switch` statement.

Listing 7.5 shows the complete script embedded in a Web document. To test it, load the page. You should see a prompt, as shown in Figure 7.1. Next, enter one of the keywords. You should be sent to the appropriate page. If you specify an unknown keyword, you will be sent to the default page.

LISTING 7.5 THE COMPLETE USER RESPONSE EXAMPLE.

```
 1: <HTML>
 2: <HEAD><TITLE>User Response Example</TITLE>
 3: </HEAD>
 4: <BODY>
 5: <H1> User Response Example</H1>
 6: Enter your destination.<BR>
 7: <SCRIPT LANGUAGE="JavaScript1.2">
 8: where = window.prompt("Where do you want to go today?");
 9: switch (where) {
10:     case "Netscape" :
11:         window.location="http://www.netscape.com";
12:         break;
13:     case "Microsoft" :
14:         window.location="http://www.microsoft.com";
15:         break;
16:     case "Yahoo" :
17:         window.location="http://www.yahoo.com";
18:         break;
19:     default :
20:         window.location="http://www.mcp.com";
21: }
22: </SCRIPT>
23: </BODY>
24: </HTML>
```

FIGURE 7.1

Prompting for a user response.

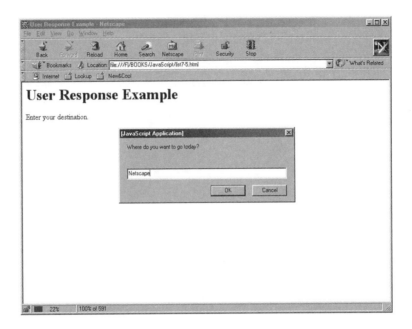

Summary

In this hour, you've learned to use JavaScript statements such as `if` and `else` to test and compare values. You've also learned a quick way to test values with the `?` operator and used the `switch` statement to test for a number of different values. Finally, you've applied this knowledge by asking the user a question and testing the answer.

In the next hour, you'll learn another fundamental JavaScript programming tool, loops, which you can use to make JavaScript perform repetitive tasks without repetitive typing.

Q&A

Q What happens if I compare two items of different data types (for example, a number and a string) in a conditional expression?

A The JavaScript interpreter does its best to make the values a common format and compare them. In this case, it would convert them both to strings before comparing. In JavaScript 1.3, you can use the special equality operator `===` to compare two values and their types—using this operator, the expression will be true only if the expressions have the same value *and* the same data type.

Q Why don't I get a friendly error message if I accidentally use = instead of ==?

A In some cases, this will result in an error. However, the incorrect version often appears to be a correct statement. For example, in the statement `if (a=1)`, the

7

variable a will be assigned the value 1. The if statement is considered true, and the value of a is lost.

Q Why does the script in Listing 7.5 specify JavaScript 1.2?

A The `switch` statement was added in JavaScript 1.2. Specifying that version prevents older browsers from attempting to execute the script and becoming confused.

Workshop

Quiz

1. What does the statement if (fig==1) do?

    a. Assigns the variable `fig` the value 1.

    b. Displays an error message because the names of fruits cannot be used as variable names.

    c. Checks `fig` for a value of 1 and performs an action if it matches.

2. Which of the following operators means "Is not equal to" in JavaScript?

    a. !

    b. !=

    c. <>

3. What does the `switch` statement do?

    a. Tests a variable for a number of different values.

    b. Turns a variable on or off.

    c. Makes ordinary `if` statements longer and more confusing.

Answers

1. c. This statement checks the `fig` variable and performs an action if its value is 1.

2. b. The != operator means *is not equal to*.

3. a. The `switch` statement can test the same variable or expression for a number of different values.

Exercises

If you want to explore the `if` statement and conditional expressions further, perform the following exercise:

- You might have noticed that the example in Listing 7.5 is case sensitive. If you enter `netscape`, you won't be sent to the correct page. Modify the script to ignore case. (You can use the `toLowerCase` string method, described in Hour 6, "Using Strings and Arrays," and then compare the value with all-lowercase keywords.)

HOUR 8

Repeating Yourself: Using Loops

Welcome to the final hour of Part II. To end your journey through the basics of JavaScript programming, you will now learn how to use JavaScript's looping features to make the computer perform repetitive tasks for you.

Hour 8 covers the following topics:

- Performing repeated statements with the for loop
- Using while for a different type of loop
- Using do and while for loops
- Creating infinite loops (and why you shouldn't)
- Escaping from a loop
- Continuing a loop
- Using for…in to loop through an array

Using for Loops

The `for` keyword is the first tool to consider for creating loops. A `for` loop typically uses a variable (called a *counter* or *index*) to keep track of how many times the loop has executed, and it stops when the counter reaches a certain number. A basic `for` statement looks like this:

```
for (var = 1; var < 10; var++) {
```

There are three parameters to the `for` loop, separated by semicolons:

- The first parameter (`var = 1` in the example) specifies a variable and assigns an initial value to it. This is called the *initial expression* because it sets up the initial state for the loop.
- The second parameter (`var < 10` in the example) is a condition that must remain true to keep the loop running. This is called the *condition* of the loop.
- The third parameter (`var++` in the example) is a statement that executes with each iteration of the loop. This is called the *increment expression* because it is usually used to increment the counter.

After the three parameters are specified, a left brace (`{`) is used to signal the beginning of a block. A right brace (`}`) is used at the end of the block. All the statements between the braces will be executed with each iteration of the loop.

As with `if` statements, if you use only a single statement within the loop, you can include it rather than a block of statements. In this case, the braces are not required.

This may sound a bit confusing, but once you're used to it, you'll use `for` loops frequently. A simple example of this type of loop is shown in Listing 8.1.

LISTING 8.1   A LOOP USING THE `for` KEYWORD.

```
1: for (i=1; i<10; i++) {
2:    document.write("This is line ",i,"\n");
3: }
```

This example displays a message with the loop's counter during each iteration. The output of Listing 8.1 would look like this:

```
This is line 1
This is line 2
This is line 3
This is line 4
This is line 5
```

```
This is line 6
This is line 7
This is line 8
This is line 9
```

Notice that the loop was executed only nine times. This is because the conditional is i<10. When the counter (i) is incremented to 10, the expression is no longer true. If you need the loop to count to 10, you could change the conditional; either i<=10 or i<11 will work fine.

> You might notice that the variable name i is often used as the counter in loops. This is a programming tradition that began with an ancient language called Forth. There's no need for you to follow this tradition, but it is a good idea to use one consistent variable for counters. (To learn more about Forth, see the Forth Interest Group's Web site at www.forth.org.)

The structure of the for loop in JavaScript is based on Java, which in turn is based on C. Although it is traditionally used to count from one number to another, you can use just about any statement for the initialization, condition, and increment. However, there's usually a better way to do other types of loops with the while keyword, described in the next section.

Using while Loops

Another keyword for loops in JavaScript is while. Unlike for loops, while loops don't necessarily use a variable to count. Instead, they execute as long as *(while)* a condition is true. In fact, if the condition starts out as false, the statements might not execute at all.

The while statement includes the condition in parentheses, and it is followed by a block of statements within braces, just like a for loop. Listing 8.2 shows a simple while loop.

LISTING 8.2   A SIMPLE LOOP USING while.

```
1: while (total < 10) {
2: n++;
3: total += values[n];
4: }
```

This loop uses a counter, n, to iterate through the values array. Rather than stopping at a certain count, however, it stops when the total of the values reaches 10.

You might have noticed that you could have done the same thing with a `for` loop:

```
for (n=0;total < 10; n++) {
total += values[n];
}
```

As a matter of fact, the `for` loop is nothing more than a special kind of `while` loop that handles an initialization and an increment for you. You can generally use `while` for any loop. However, it's best to choose whichever type of loop makes the most sense for the job or takes the least amount of typing.

Using do...while Loops

JavaScript 1.2 introduced a third type of loop: the `do…while` loop. This type of loop is similar to an ordinary `while` loop, with one difference: The condition is tested at the *end* of the loop rather than the beginning. Listing 8.3 shows a typical `do…while` loop.

LISTING 8.3 AN EXAMPLE OF A `do…while` LOOP.

```
1: do {
2:   n++;
3:   total += values[n];
4: }
5: while (total < 10);
```

As you've probably noticed, this is basically an upside-down version of the `while` example in Listing 8.2. There is one difference: With the `do` loop, the condition is tested at the end of the loop. This means that the statements in the loop will always be executed at least once, even if the condition is never true.

> As with the `for` and `while` loops, the `do` loop can include a single statement without braces, or a number of statements enclosed in braces.

Working with Loops

Although you can use simple `for` and `while` loops for straightforward tasks, there are some considerations you should make when using more complicated loops. In the next sections, we'll look at infinite loops and the `break` and `continue` statements, which give you more control over your loops.

Creating an Infinite Loop

The `for` and `while` loops give you quite a bit of control over the loop. In some cases, this can cause problems if you're not careful. For example, look at the loop in Listing 8.4.

LISTING 8.4 AN EXAMPLE OF AN INFINITE LOOP.

```
1: while (j < 10) {
2: n++;
3: values[n] = 0;
4: }
```

There's a mistake in this example. The condition of the `while` loop refers to the `j` variable, but that variable doesn't actually change during the loop. This creates an *infinite loop*. The loop will continue executing until it is stopped by the user, or until it generates an error of some kind.

Infinite loops can't always be stopped by the user, except by quitting the browser—and some loops can even prevent the browser from quitting or cause a crash.

Obviously, infinite loops are something to avoid. They can also be difficult to spot, because JavaScript won't give you an error that actually tells you there is an infinite loop. Thus, each time you create a loop in a script, you should be careful to make sure there's a way out.

> Depending on the browser version in use, an infinite loop may even make the browser stop responding to the user. Be sure you provide an escape route from infinite loops, and save your script before you test it just in case.

Occasionally, you may want to create an infinite loop deliberately. This might include situations when you want your program to execute until the user stops it, or if you are providing an escape route with the `break` statement, which is introduced in the next section. Here's an easy way to create an infinite loop:

```
while (true) {
```

Because the value `true` is the conditional, this loop will always find its condition to be true.

Escaping from a Loop

There is one way out of an infinite loop. You can use the break statement during a loop to exit it immediately and continue with the first statement after the loop. Listing 8.5 shows one example of the use of break.

LISTING 8.5 ESCAPING FROM AN INFINITE LOOP WITH break.

```
1: while (true) {
2: n++;
3: if (values[n] == 1) break;
4: }
```

Although the while statement is set up as an infinite loop, the if statement checks the corresponding value of an array. If it finds a 1, it exits the loop.

When the JavaScript interpreter encounters a break statement, it skips the rest of the loop and continues the script with the first statement after the right brace at the loop's end. You can use the break statement in any type of loop, whether infinite or not. This provides an easy way to exit if an error occurs, or if you've found what you were looking for.

Continuing a Loop

One more statement is available to help you control the execution of statements in a loop. The continue statement skips the rest of the loop, but unlike break, it continues with the next iteration of the loop. Listing 8.6 shows a simple example.

LISTING 8.6 USING continue TO SKIP PART OF A LOOP.

```
1: for (i=1; i<21; i++) {
2: if (score[i]==0) continue;
3: document.write("Student number ",i, " Score: ", score[i], "\n");
4: }
```

This script uses a for loop to print out scores for 20 students, stored in the score array. The if statement is used to check for scores with a value of 0. The script assumes that a score of 0 means that the student didn't take the test, so it continues the loop without printing that score.

Using for...in Loops

A third type of loop is available in JavaScript. The for...in loop is not as flexible as an ordinary for or while loop. Instead, it is specifically designed to perform an operation on each property of an object.

For example, the navigator object contains properties that describe the user's browser, as you'll learn in Hour 16, "Creating Browser-Specific Scripts." You can use for...in to display this object's properties:

```
for (i in navigator) {
document.write("property: " + i);
document.write(" value: " + navigator[i]);
}
```

Like an ordinary for loop, this type of loop uses an index variable (i in the example). For each iteration of the loop, the variable is set to the next property of the object. This makes it easy when you need to check or modify each of an object's properties.

> This type of loop is useful for arrays, but it also works with any JavaScript object. For example, the preceding loop would still work if counters was an object with properties such as hits and misses. The index variable would be set to each of the property names. You'll learn how to create your own objects and properties in Hour 11, "Creating Custom Objects."

Workshop: Working with Arrays and Loops

To apply your knowledge of loops, you will now create a script that deals with arrays using loops. (As you progress through this script, try to imagine how difficult it would be without loops.)

This simple script will prompt the user for a series of names. After all of the names have been entered, it will display the list of names in a numbered list. To begin the script, initialize some variables:

```
names = new Array();
i = 0;
```

The names array will store the names the user enters. You don't know how many names will be entered, so you did not specify a dimension for the array. The i variable will be used as a counter in the loops.

Next, use the `window.prompt` statement to prompt the user for a series of names. Use a loop to repeat the prompt for each name. You want the user to enter at least one name, so a do loop is ideal:

```
do {
    next = window.prompt("Enter the Next Name");
    if (next > " ") names[i] = next;
    i = i + 1;
    }
    while (next > " ");
```

> If you're interested in making your scripts as short as possible, remember that you could use the increment (++) operator to combine the i = i + 1 statement with the previous statement.

This loop prompts for a string called `next`. If a name was entered (and if it's greater than a space), it's stored as the next entry in the `names` array. The `i` counter is then incremented. The loop repeats until the user doesn't enter a name or clicks Cancel in the Prompt dialog.

Next, just to show off, your script can display the number of names that were entered:

```
document.write("<H2>" + (names.length) + " names entered.</H2>");
```

This statement displays the `length` property of the `names` array, surrounded by header 2 tags for emphasis.

Next, the script should display all of the names in the order they were entered. Because the names are in an array, the for...in loop is a good choice:

```
document.write("<OL>");
for (i in names) {
    document.write("<LI>" + names[i] + "<BR>");
}
document.write("</OL>");
```

Here you have a for...in loop that loops through the `names` array, assigning the counter `i` to each index in turn. The script then prints the name with an `<LI>` tag as an item in an ordered list. Before and after the loop, the script prints beginning and ending `<OL>` tags.

You now have everything you need for a working script. Listing 8.7 shows a complete version of the script, including the usual HTML and <SCRIPT> tags.

LISTING 8.7   A SCRIPT TO PROMPT FOR NAMES AND DISPLAY THEM.

```
 1: <HTML>
 2: <HEAD>
 3: <TITLE>Loops Example</TITLE>
 4: </HEAD>
 5: <BODY>
 6: <H1>Loop Example</H1>
 7: <P>Enter a series of names. I will then
 8: display them in a nifty numbered list.</P>
 9: <SCRIPT LANGUAGE="JavaScript1.2">
10: names = new Array();
11: i = 0;
12: do {
13:     next = window.prompt("Enter the Next Name");
14:     if (next > " " && next != "undefined") names[i] = next;
15:     i = i + 1;
16:     }
17:     while (next > " " && next != "undefined");
18: document.write("<H2>" + (names.length) + " names entered.</H2>");
19: document.write("<OL>");
20: for (i in names) {
21:     document.write("<LI>" + names[i] + "<BR>");
22: }
23: document.write("</OL>");
24: </SCRIPT>
25: </BODY>
26: </HTML>
```

When you load this document into a browser, you'll be prompted for a name. Enter several names, and then click Cancel to indicate that you're finished. Figure 8.1 shows what the final results should look like, as displayed by Netscape.

FIGURE 8.1

The output of the names example.

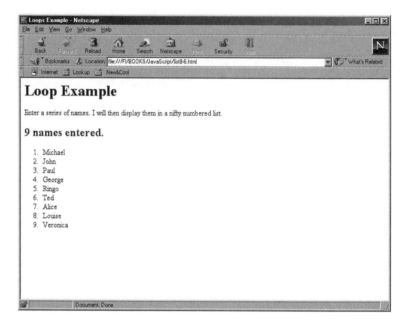

Summary

In Hour 8, you learned to use the `for`, `while`, and do statements to make various kinds of loops. You also learned about the `for…in` loop for arrays and objects and created a simple application using loops and arrays.

You've reached the end of Part II, which covered some basic building blocks of JavaScript programs. In Part III, "Moving On to Advanced JavaScript Features," you'll learn some of JavaScript's more advanced features, including objects and event handlers.

Q&A

Q It seems like I could use a `for` loop to replace any of the other loop methods (`while`, `do`, and so on). Why so many choices?

A You're right. In most cases a simple `for` loop would work, and you can do all of your loops that way if you want. The other methods provide simpler and easier-to-understand methods of looping for some applications.

Q I want to support JavaScript 1.1. Is there an alternative to the `do…while` loop?

A Yes. Use a `while` statement to create an infinite loop, as shown in this hour, and then use an `if` statement at the end of the loop to check the condition. If the condition is met, use the `break` statement to end the loop.

Q **Entering names in repeated prompt dialogs is annoying. Is there an easier way to ask the user for many pieces of information?**

A The ideal way to do this is to use a form. You'll learn all about forms in Hour 14, "Getting Data with Forms."

Workshop

Quiz

1. Which type of JavaScript loop checks the condition at the *end* of the loop?

    a. `for`

    b. `while`

    c. `do…while`

2. Within a loop, what does the `break` statement do?

    a. Breaks the user's computer.

    b. Starts the loop over.

    c. Escapes the loop entirely.

3. The statement `while (3==3)` is an example of:

    a. A typographical error.

    b. An infinite loop.

    c. An illegal JavaScript statement.

Answers

1. c. The `do…while` loop uses a condition at the end of the loop.

2. c. The `break` statement escapes the loop.

3. b. This statement creates an infinite loop.

Exercises

To further your knowledge of JavaScript programming basics, perform the following exercises:

- Modify Listing 8.7 to sort the names in alphabetical order before displaying them. You can use the `sort` method of arrays, described in Hour 6, "Using Strings and Arrays."

- Modify Listing 8.7 to prompt for exactly ten names. What happens if you click the Cancel button instead of entering a name?

PART III

Moving On to Advanced JavaScript Features

Hour

HOUR 9

Using Built-In Objects

You've arrived at Part III of this book. (If you've been reading nonstop, it's been eight hours, so you might want to get some sleep before you continue.) In this part, you'll learn all about two advanced features of JavaScript: objects and event handlers.

In Hour 9, you'll learn the basics of objects in JavaScript and the details of using the Math and Date objects. This hour covers the following topics:

- What JavaScript objects are and how to use them
- How to access an object's properties
- Using an object's methods
- Using with to work with objects
- Using the Math object's methods
- Using the Date object to work with dates
- Creating an application using JavaScript math functions

What Is an Object?

As you should know from earlier hours of this book, *objects* allow you to combine several kinds of data (properties) and functions to act on the data (methods) into a single, convenient package. In this hour, you'll learn more about the built-in `Math` and `Date` objects—but first, here's a quick overview of the way objects work in JavaScript.

Creating Objects

Each object has a special function, called a *constructor*, that's used to create objects. For example, JavaScript includes a built-in function called `String` to create `String` objects. That's why you can create a string variable like this:

```
myname=new String("Figby");
```

The `new` keyword tells JavaScript to create a new object—or in technical terms, a new *instance* of the `String` object. This particular instance will have the value `Figby` and will be stored in the variable `myname`.

You can use the same basic syntax to create `String` objects, `Date` objects, `Array` objects, and even your own custom objects. (The `Math` object is an exception, which you'll learn about later in this hour.)

> If you're dying to crete some custom objects right away, you should probably get some sleep. If you're serious, you can skip to Hour 11, "Creating Custom Objects."

Object Properties and Values

Each object can have one or more *properties*, or attributes. Each property is basically a variable in itself, and is contained within the object. Each property can be assigned a value. You can use properties to store any type of data a variable can store.

You've already used a few object properties, such as the `length` property of strings and arrays. To refer to a property, you use the object's name, a period, and the property's name. For example, the length of the `names` array is referred to with this property:

```
names.length
```

Object properties can even contain objects themselves. For example, each of an array's elements is a special type of property, named with an index value. If the names array contains strings, it is an array of String objects. Here is the syntax for the length of the first element of names:

```
names[0].length
```

Understanding Methods

9

As you learned in Hour 4, "How JavaScript Programs Work," functions are combinations of statements that can be executed as a single unit. Methods are functions that are stored as properties of an object.

You've already used methods. For example, the toUpperCase method of String objects converts a string to uppercase. Here is an example using a string called value:

```
value.toUpperCase();
```

Like ordinary functions, methods can optionally return a value. For example, this statement rounds a number using the round method of the Math object and stores the result in the variable final:

```
final = Math.round(num);
```

Using the with Keyword

The with keyword is one you haven't seen before. You can use it to make JavaScript programming easier—or at least easier to type.

The with keyword specifies an object, and it is followed by a block of statements enclosed in braces. For each statement in the block, any properties you mention without specifying an object are assumed to be for that object.

As an example, suppose you have a string called lastname. You can use with to perform string operations on it without specifying the name of the string every time:

```
with (lastname) {
   window.alert("length of last name: " + length);
   toUpperCase();
}
```

In this example, the length property and the toUpperCase method refer to the lastname string, although it is only specified once with the with keyword.

Obviously, the `with` keyword only saves a bit of typing in situations like this. However, you will find it very useful when you're dealing with an object throughout a large procedure, or when you are using a built-in object, such as the `Math` object.

The `Math` Object

The `Math` object is a built-in JavaScript object that includes math constants and functions. You don't need to create a `Math` object, because it exists automatically in any JavaScript program. The `Math` object's properties represent mathematical constants, and its methods are mathematical functions.

> Because you may use the `Math` object's properties and methods throughout an entire group of statements, you might find it useful to use the `with` keyword, introduced earlier in this hour, to specify the `Math` object for those statements.

Rounding and Truncating

Three of the most useful methods of the `Math` object allow you to round decimal values up and down:

- `Math.ceil()` rounds a number up to the next integer.
- `Math.floor()` rounds a number down to the next integer.
- `Math.round()` rounds a number to the nearest integer.

All of these take the number to be rounded as their single parameter. You might notice one thing missing: the capability to round to a decimal place, such as for dollar amounts. You can easily simulate this, though. Listing 9.1 shows a function that rounds numbers to two decimal places.

LISTING 9.1   A FUNCTION THAT ROUNDS NUMBERS TO TWO DECIMAL PLACES.

```
1: function round(num) {
2:    return Math.round(num * 100) / 100;
3: }
```

This function multiplies the value by 100 to move the decimal, and then rounds the number to the nearest integer. Finally, the value is divided by 100 to restore the decimal.

Generating Random Numbers

One of the most commonly used methods of the Math object is the Math.random() method, which generates a random number. This method doesn't require any parameters. The number it returns is a random decimal number between 0 and 1.

You'll usually want a random number between 1 and a value. You can do this with a general-purpose random number function. Listing 9.2 shows a function that generates random numbers between 1 and the parameter you send it.

LISTING 9.2   A GENERAL-PURPOSE RANDOM NUMBER FUNCTION.

```
1: function rand(num) {
2:     return Math.floor(Math.random() * num) + 1;
3: }
```

This function multiplies a random number by the value you send it and then converts it to an integer between 1 and the number by using the Math.floor() method.

Working with Dates

The Date object is a built-in JavaScript object that enables you to work conveniently with dates and times. You can create a Date object any time you need to store a date and use the Date object's methods to work with the date.

You encountered one example of a Date object in Hour 2, "Creating a Simple Script," with the Year 2000 script. The Date object has no properties. To set or obtain values from a Date object, you must use the methods described in the next section.

JavaScript dates are stored as the number of milliseconds since midnight, January 1, 1970. This date is called the *epoch*. Dates before 1970 aren't allowed. This means I can't store my birthday in a Date object, and there's a good chance you can't either. Fortunately, your scripts will usually be more concerned with the present than the past.

Creating a Date Object

You can create a Date object using the new keyword. You can also optionally specify the date to store in the object when you create it. You can use any of the following formats:

```
birthday = new Date();
birthday = new Date("June 20, 1999 08:00:00");
```

```
birthday = new Date(6, 20, 1999);
birthday = new Date(6, 20, 1999, 8, 0, 0);
```

You can choose any of these formats, depending on which values you want to set. If you use no parameters, as in the first example, the current date is stored in the object. You can then set the values using the set methods, described in the next section.

Setting Date Values

A variety of set methods enable you to set components of a Date object to values:

- setDate() sets the day of the month.
- setMonth() sets the month. JavaScript numbers the months from 0 to 11, starting with January (0).
- setFullYear() sets the year.
- setTime() sets the time (and the date) by specifying the number of milliseconds since January 1, 1970.
- setHours(), setMinutes(), and setSeconds() set the time.

As an example, the following statement sets the year of a Date object called holiday to 99:

```
holiday.setYear(99);
```

Getting Date Values

You can use the get methods to get values from a Date object. This is the only way to obtain these values, because they are not available as properties. Here are the available get methods for dates:

- getDate() gets the day of the month.
- getMonth() gets the month.
- getFullYear() gets the year.
- getTime() gets the time (and the date) as the number of milliseconds since January 1, 1970.
- getHours(), getMinutes(), and getSeconds() get the time.

Along with setFullYear and getFullYear, which require 4-digit years, JavaScript includes setYear and getYear methods, which use two-digit dates. You should always use the four-digit version to avoid Year 2000 issues.

Working with Time Zones

Finally, a few functions are available to help your `Date` objects work with local time values and time zones:

- `getTimeZoneOffset()` gives you the local time zone's offset from GMT (Greenwich Mean Time, also known as UTC). In this case, *local* refers to the location of the browser (Of course, this only works if the user has set his system clock accurately.)
- `toGMTString()` converts the `date` object's time value to text, using GMT.
- `toLocalString()` converts the `date` object's time value to text, using local time.

Converting Between Date Formats

Two special methods of the `Date` object allow you to convert between date formats. Instead of using these methods with a `Date` object you created, you use them with the built-in object `Date` itself. These include the following:

- `Date.parse()` converts a date string, such as `June 20, 1996`, to a `Date` object (number of milliseconds since 1/1/1970).
- `Date.UTC()` does the opposite. It converts a `Date` object value (number of milliseconds) to a UTC (GMT) time.

Workshop: Working with the `Math` Object

The `Math.random` method, discussed earlier in this hour, generates a random number between `0` and `1`. However, it's very difficult for a computer to generate a truly random number. (It's also hard for a human being to do so—that's why dice were invented.)

Today's computers do reasonably well at generating random numbers, but just how good is JavaScript's `Math.random` function? One way to test it is to generate many random numbers and calculate the average of all of them.

In theory, the average should be somewhere near `.5`, halfway between `0` and `1`. The more random values you generate, the closer the average should get to this middle ground.

As an example of the use of the `Math` object, you can create a script that tests JavaScript's random number function. To do this, you'll generate 5,000 random numbers and calculate their average.

In case you skipped Hour 8, "Repeating Yourself: Using Loops," and are getting out your calculator, don't worry—you'll use a loop to generate the random numbers. (You'll be surprised how fast JavaScript can do this.)

To begin your script, you will initialize a variable called `total`. This variable will store a running total of all of the random values, so it's important that it starts at 0:

```
total = 0;
```

Next, begin a loop that will execute 5,000 times. Use a `for` loop because you want it to execute a fixed number of times:

```
for (i=0; i<5000; i++) {
```

Within the loop, you will need to create a random number and add its value to `total`. Here are the statements that do this and continue with the next iteration of the loop:

```
    num = Math.random();
    total += num;
}
```

Depending on the speed of your computer, it might take a few minutes to generate those 5,000 random numbers. Just to be sure something's happening, update the status line to tell the user how many numbers are left and the current total:

```
window.status = "Generated " + i + " numbers. Current total: " + total;
```

The final part of your script will calculate the average by dividing `total` by 5,000. You'll also round the average to three decimal places, using the trick you learned earlier in this hour:

```
average = total / 5000;
average = Math.round(average * 1000) / 1000;
document.write("<H2>Average of 5000 numbers: " + average + "</H2>");
```

If you're using a particularly slow computer (say, less than 60 MHz), you may want to consider changing the three instances of the number 5000 to a lower number. Or you can go out to lunch while the script executes.

To test this script and see just how random those numbers are, combine the complete script with an HTML document and <SCRIPT> statements. Listing 9.3 shows the complete random number testing script.

LISTING 9.3   A SCRIPT TO TEST JAVASCRIPT'S RANDOM NUMBER FUNCTION.

```
1: <HTML>
2: <HEAD>
3: <TITLE>Math Example</TITLE>
4: </HEAD>
```

```
 5: <BODY>
 6: <H1>Math Example</H1>
 7: <P>How random are JavaScript's random numbers?
 8: Let's generate 5000 of them and find out.</P>
 9: <SCRIPT LANGUAGE="JavaScript">
10: total = 0;
11: for (i=0; i<5000; i++) {
12:     num = Math.random();
13:     total += num;
14:     window.status = "Generated " + i + " numbers.";
15: }
16: average = total / 5000;
17: average = Math.round(average * 1000) / 1000;
18: document.write("<H2>Average of 5000 numbers: " + average + "</H2>");
19: </SCRIPT>
20: </BODY>
21: </HTML>
```

9

To test the script, load the HTML document into a browser. The status line will immediately begin counting up to 5,000. After a short delay, you should see a result. If it's close to .5, the numbers are reasonably random. My result was .502, as shown in Figure 9.1.

FIGURE 9.1

The random number testing script in action.

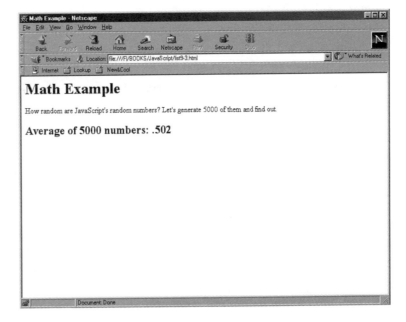

The average you've used here is called an *arithmetic mean*. This type of average isn't a perfect way to test randomness. Actually, all it tests is the distribution of the numbers above and below .5. For example, if the numbers turned out to be 2,500 .4's and 2,500 .6's, the average would be a perfect .5—but they wouldn't be very random numbers. (Thankfully, JavaScript's random numbers don't have this problem.)

Summary

In this hour, you learned the fundamentals of JavaScript objects, which you'll use throughout Part III as you learn more about objects. You also learned some specifics about the Math and Date objects and learned more than you ever wanted to know about random numbers.

In Hour 10, "Working with Browser Objects," you'll learn about the most useful objects in JavaScript: the browser objects, which refer to various parts of the browser window and HTML document.

Q&A

Q Can one of an object's properties be another object?

A Absolutely. In this case, the second object is called a *child object*. You'll encounter quite a few parent and child objects, such as window.location, in Hour 10.

Q You mentioned that the properties of the Math object are constants. What are they?

A They include a wide variety of mathematical constants, such as Math.PI and Math.E. A wide variety of more esoteric constants are included. There are also some methods of the Math object that weren't discussed here, such as the trigonometric functions. For details, see Netscape's *JavaScript Guide*; you'll find its URL in Appendix A, "Other JavaScript Resources."

Q I tried the random number example in Listing 9.3, and I'm surprised it takes more than a few seconds to add a few numbers together—aren't computers supposed to be really good at that sort of thing?

A Actually, the slowest part of the loop in the example script is the command that updates the status line. If you remove this command, the script will execute much faster, but you won't be able to watch its progress.

Workshop

Quiz

1. Which of the following objects *cannot* be used with the `new` keyword?

   a. `Date`

   b. `Math`

   c. `String`

2. How does JavaScript store dates in a `Date` object?

   a. The number of milliseconds since January 1, 1970.

   b. The number of days since January 1, 1900.

   c. The number of seconds since Netscape's public stock offering.

3. What is the range of random numbers generated by the `Math.random` function?

   a. Between 1 and 100.

   b. Between 1 and the number of milliseconds since January 1, 1970.

   c. Between 0 and 1.

Answers

1. b. The `Math` object is static; you can't create a `Math` object.

2. a. Dates are stored as the number of milliseconds since January 1, 1970.

3. c. JavaScript's random numbers are between 0 and 1.

Exercises

If you want to spend more time working with the `Math` and `Date` objects in JavaScript, perform the following activities:

- Modify the random number script in Listing 9.3 to prompt the user for the number of random numbers to generate.

- Modify the random number script to run three times, calculating a total of 15,000 random numbers, and display separate totals for each set of 5,000. (You'll need to use a `for` loop that encloses most of the script.)

- Look at the Year 2000 script in Hour 2, Listing 2.5. Now that you understand the `Date` object better, see if you can tell exactly what each line of the script does.

Hour **10**

Working with Browser Objects

In Hour 9, "Using Built-In Objects," you learned about JavaScript's support for objects, which allow you to store data in all sorts of interesting ways. However, the way you'll use objects the most is in accessing the browser objects, which let your scripts manipulate Web pages, windows, and documents.

In this hour, you will explore the hierarchy of browser objects. Hour 10 covers the following topics:

- How to access the various browser objects
- Working with windows using the `window` object
- Working with Web documents with the `document` object
- Using objects for links and anchors
- Using the `location` object to work with URLs
- Getting information about the browser with the `navigator` object
- Creating JavaScript-based Back and Forward buttons

Understanding Browser Objects

One advantage that JavaScript has—even over more sophisticated languages like Java—is that scripts can manipulate the Web browser. Your script can load a new page into the browser, work with parts of the browser window and document, and even open new windows.

In order to work with the browser and documents, JavaScript uses a variety of *browser objects*. Each object represents part of a Web page—for example, a window, a document, or an image. Browser objects have *properties*, which describe the Web page or document, and *methods*, which allow you to work with parts of the Web page.

The browser objects are arranged into a hierarchy of parent and child objects. When you refer to an object, you use the parent object name followed by the child object name or names, separated by periods. For example, JavaScript stores objects to represent images in a document as children of the `document` object. The following refers to the `image9` object, a child of the `document` object, which is a child of the `window` object:

```
window.document.image9
```

The `window` object is at the top of the browser object hierarchy. Figure 10.1 shows the object hierarchy and a variety of its objects.

FIGURE 10.1

The JavaScript browser object hierarchy.

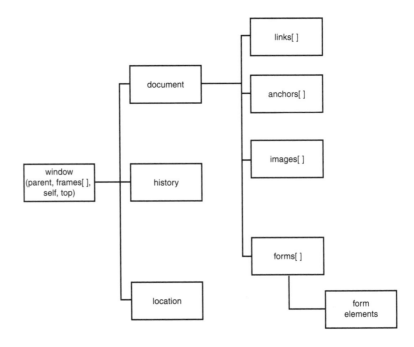

This diagram includes only the basic browser objects that will be covered in this hour. A variety of other objects also fit into the hierarchy, and they will be discussed in later hours of this book.

Using `window` Objects

At the top of the browser object hierarchy is the `window` object, which represents a browser window. You've already used a few methods and properties of the `window` object:

- You used the `window.status` property to change the contents of the browser's status line.
- The `window.alert`, `window.confirm`, and `window.prompt` methods display message dialogs to the user.

There can be several `window` objects at a time, each representing an open browser window. Frames are also represented by `window` objects. You'll learn more about windows and frames in Hour 13, "Using Windows and Frames."

Layers, which allow you to change the content of a Web document dynamically, are also similar to `window` objects. These are explained in Hour 18, "Creating Dynamic Pages with Layers."

Working with Web Documents

The `document` object represents a Web document, or page. Web documents are displayed within browser windows, so it shouldn't surprise you to learn that the `document` object is a child of the `window` object.

Because the `window` object always represents the current window (the one containing the script), you can use `window.document` to refer to the current document. You can also simply refer to `document`, which automatically refers to the current window.

You've already used the `document.write` method to display text within a Web document. The examples in earlier hours used only a single window and document, so it was unnecessary to use `window.document.write`—but this longer syntax would have worked equally well.

If multiple windows or frames are in use, there might be several window objects, each with its own document object. To use one of these document objects, you use the name of the window and the name of the document.

In the following sections, you will look at some of the properties and methods of the document object that will be useful in your scripting.

Getting Information About the Document

Several properties of the document object include information about the current document in general:

- The URL property specifies the document's URL. This is a simple text field. You can't change this property. If you need to send the user to a different location, use the window.location object, described later in this hour.

- The title property lists the title of the current page, defined by the HTML <TITLE> tag.

- The referrer property is the URL of the page the user was viewing prior to the current page—usually, the page with a link to the current page.

- The lastModified property is the date the document was last modified. This date is sent from the server along with the page.

As an example, Listing 10.1 shows a short HTML document that displays its last modified date.

LISTING 10.1   DISPLAYING THE LAST MODIFIED DATE.

```
1: <HTML><HEAD><TITLE>Test Document</TITLE></HEAD>
2: <BODY>
3: This page was last modified on:
4: <SCRIPT>
5: document.write(document.lastModified);
6: </SCRIPT>
7: <BR>
8: </HTML>
```

This can tell the user when the page was last changed. If you use JavaScript, you don't have to remember to update the date each time you modify the page. (You could also use the script to always print the current date, but that would be cheating.)

You might find that the document.lastModified property doesn't work on your Web pages. The date is received from the Web server, and some servers do not maintain modification dates correctly.

Writing Text in a Document

The simplest document object methods are also the ones you will use most often. In fact, you've used one of them already. The document.write method prints text as part of the HTML page in a document window. This statement is used whenever you need to include output in a Web page.

An alternative statement, document.writeln, also prints text, but it also includes a newline (\n) character at the end. This is handy when you want your text to be the last thing on the line.

10

Bear in mind that the newline character is ignored by HTML, except inside the <PRE> container. You will need to use the <BR> tag if you want an actual line break.

You can use these methods only within the body of the Web page, so they will be executed when the page loads. You can't add to a page that has already loaded without reloading it. You can write new content for a document, however, as the next section explains.

The document.write method can be used only within a <SCRIPT> tag in the body of an HTML document. You can also use it in a function, provided you include a call to the function within the body of the document.

Clearing and Rewriting Documents

The document object includes open and close methods. Unlike the window object methods of the same name, these methods don't actually open and close new documents or windows. Instead, the open method opens a *stream*, which clears the document and allows you to create a new one with the write or writeln method.

When you use the `document.open` method, the current document is cleared. Any data already displayed in the document is erased, and you can begin writing new content to the document.

The data you write after `document.open` isn't actually displayed until you close the stream with the `document.close` method. You can use this to ensure that blocks of `write` commands execute at the same time.

> If you use the `document.open` method on the current window, your script—part of the current document—will be cleared and will stop executing. For this reason, these methods are best used with separate windows and frames. You'll learn about this in Hour 13.

You can optionally specify a MIME document type in the `document.open` command. This enables you to create a document of any type, including images and documents used by plug-in applications. You'll learn about plug-ins in detail in Hour 20, "Working with Multimedia and Plug-Ins."

> MIME stands for *multipurpose Internet mail extensions*. It's an Internet standard for document types. Web servers send a MIME type to the browser with documents to tell the browser how to display them. Typical browser documents are HTML (MIME type `text/html`) and text (MIME type `text/plain`).

Using Links and Anchors

Another child of the `document` object is the `link` object. Actually, there can be multiple `link` objects in a document. Each one includes information about a link to another location or anchor.

> Anchors are named places in an HTML document that can be jumped to directly. You define them with a tag like this: `<A NAME="part2">`. You can then link to them: `<A HREF="#part2">`.

You can access link objects with the links array. Each member of the array is one of the link objects in the current page. A property of the array, document.links.length, indicates the number of links in the page.

Each link object (or member of the links array) has a list of properties defining the URL. These are the same properties as the location object, defined earlier in this chapter. You can refer to a property by indicating the link number and property name. For example, the following statement assigns the entire URL of the first link to the variable link1:

```
link1 = links[0].href;
```

The anchor objects are also children of the document object. Each anchor object represents an anchor in the current document—a particular location that can be jumped to directly.

Like links, you can access anchors with an array: anchors. Each element of this array is an anchor object. The document.anchors.length property gives you the number of elements in the anchors array.

Accessing Browser History

The history object is another child (property) of the window object. This object holds information about the URLs that have been visited before and after the current one, and it includes methods to go to previous or next locations.

The history object has three properties:

- history.length keeps track of the length of the history list—in other words, the number of different locations that the user has visited.

- history.current contains the value of the current history entry—the URL of the page that the user is currently staring at.

- history.next is the value of the next entry in the history list—the URL the user will be sent to if he presses the browser's Forward button. Because the Forward button only works when you've already used the Back button, there may not always be a value for the history.next property.

- history.previous is the previous history entry—the URL the user will be sent to if he uses the browser's Back button.

10

You can also treat the `history` object as an array. Each entry contains one of the URLs in the history list, with `history[0]` being the current entry. Last but not least, the `history` object has three methods:

- `history.go` opens a URL from the history list. To use this method, specify a positive or negative number in parentheses. For example, `history.go(-2)` is equivalent to pressing the Back button twice.

- `history.back` loads the previous URL in the history list—equivalent to pressing the Back button.

- `history.forward` loads the next URL in the history list, if available. This is equivalent to pressing the Forward button.

You'll use these methods in the Workshop at the end of this hour.

The `history.back` and `history.forward` methods don't work correctly in some versions of Netscape Navigator. For this reason, it's best to use `history.go(-1)` and `history.go(1)` instead.

Working with the `location` Object

A third child of the `window` object is the `location` object. This object stores information about the current URL stored in the window. For example, the following statement loads a URL into the current window:

```
window.location.href="http://www.starlingtech.com";
```

The `href` property used in this statement contains the entire URL of the window's current location. You can also access portions of the URL with various properties of the `location` object—for example, `location.protocol` is the protocol part of the URL (typically `http:`).

Although the `location.href` property usually contains the same URL as the `document.URL` property described earlier in this chapter, you can't change the `document.URL` property. Always use `location.href` to load a new page.

The location object has two methods:

- location.reload reloads the current document. This is the same as the Reload button on Netscape's toolbar.

- location.replace replaces the current location with a new one. This is similar to setting the location object's properties yourself. The difference is that the replace method does not affect the browser's history. In other words, the Back button can't be used to go to the previous location.

Reading Information About the Browser

The navigator object isn't part of the browser object hierarchy, but it is another useful object for scripting. This object contains information about the browser version. You can use this object to find out which browser and computer platform the user is running, and your script can change its behavior to match that browser.

The navigator object is named after Netscape Navigator, which was the only browser that supported JavaScript when the language first appeared in Navigator 2.0. Despite its Netscape-specific name, this object is now supported in Microsoft Internet Explorer.

Browser-specific scripting can be complicated, and you'll learn more about the navigator object in Hour 16, "Creating Browser-Specific Scripts."

Workshop: Creating Back and Forward Buttons

One common use for the back and forward methods of the history object is to add your own Back and Forward buttons to a Web document. This can improve the user interface of your pages.

As an example of the use of the history object, you will now create a script that displays Back and Forward buttons and uses these methods to navigate the browser.

10

You will use graphic images for the Back and Forward buttons. You can use the images included on this book's CD-ROM or make your own images to match the other graphics on your page.

Here's the part of the script that will handle the Back button:

```
<A HREF="javascript:history.go(-1);">
  <IMG BORDER = 0 SRC="left.gif">
</A>
```

This uses a javascript: URL to execute a command when the user clicks on a link. In this case, the link is the left-arrow image. The script for the Forward button is nearly identical:

```
<A HREF="javascript:history.go(1);">
  <IMG BORDER = 0 SRC="right.gif">
</A>
```

With these out of the way, you just need to build the rest of an HTML document. Listing 10.2 shows the complete HTML document, and Figure 10.2 shows Netscape's display of the document. After you load this document into a browser, visit other URLs and make sure the Back and Forward buttons work.

LISTING 10.2   A WEB PAGE THAT USES JAVASCRIPT TO INCLUDE BACK AND FORWARD BUTTONS.

```
 1: <HTML>
 2: <HEAD><TITLE>Graphic Back and Forward Buttons</TITLE>
 3: </HEAD>
 4: <BODY>
 5: <H1>Graphical Back and Forward Buttons</H1>
 6: <HR>
 7: This page allows you to go back or forward to pages in the history
 8: list. These should be equivalent to the back and forward arrow buttons
 9: in the browser's toolbar.
10: <HR>
11: <A HREF="javascript:history.go(-1);">
12:   <IMG BORDER = 0 SRC="left.gif">
13: </A>
14: <A HREF="javascript:history.go(1);">
15:   <IMG BORDER = 0 SRC="right.gif">
16: </A>
17: <HR>
18: </BODY>
19: </HTML>
```

FIGURE 10.2

The Back and Forward buttons in Netscape.

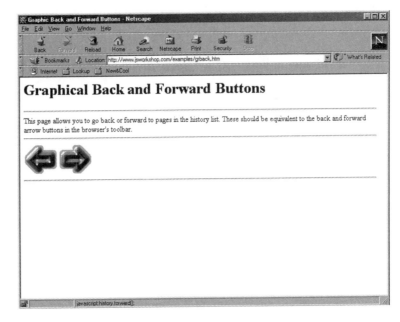

This script is an example of how much JavaScript can do with very little scripting. In fact, Listing 10.2 doesn't use any <SCRIPT> tags at all, and only two JavaScript commands.

Summary

In this hour, you've learned about JavaScript's hierarchy of browser objects. You've learned how you can use the document object to work with documents and used the history and location objects to control the current URL displayed in the browser.

You should now be comfortable working with a variety of objects in JavaScript. In the next hour, you'll learn how to create your own objects to store and work with data.

Q&A

Q I can use `history` and `document` instead of `window.history` and `window.document`. Can I leave out the `window` object in other cases?

A Yes. For example, you can use `alert` instead of `window.alert` to display a message. The `window` object contains the current script, so it's treated as a default object. However, be warned that you shouldn't omit the `window` object's name when you're using frames, layers, or multiple windows, or in an event handler.

Q I used the `document.lastModified` method to display a modification date for my page, but it displays a date in 1970, or a date that I know is incorrect. What's wrong?

A This function depends on the server sending the last modified date of the document to the browser. Some Web servers don't do this properly or require specific file attributes in order for this to work.

Q Can I change history entries or prevent the user from using the Back and Forward buttons?

A You can't change the history entries. You can't prevent the use of the Back and Forward buttons, but you can use the `location.replace()` method to load a series of pages that don't appear in the history. However, the Back button will still take the user to the page he visited before yours.

Workshop

Quiz

1. Which of the following objects can be used to load a new URL into the browser window?

    a. `document.url`

    b. `window.location`

    c. `window.url`

2. What information is stored by the `navigator` object?

    a. The current browser and version.

    b. The user's name, phone number, and hair color.

    c. The previous and next pages in the navigation history.

3. Which of the following object properties contains the URL of the current document?

    a. `window.location.href`

    b. `document.URL`

    c. `history.current`

Answers

1. b. The `window.location` object can be used to send the browser to a new URL.

2. a. The `navigator` object can tell you the current browser version.

3. b. The `document.URL` property contains the URL of the current document. Actually, this is a bit of a trick question: The `window.location.href` and `history.current` properties usually contain the current URL as well.

Exercises

To gain more experience working with browser objects in JavaScript, perform the following exercises:

- Modify the Back and Forward example in Listing 10.2 to include a Reload button along with the Back and Forward buttons. (This button would trigger the `location.reload()` method.)

- Modify the Back and Forward example to display the current number of history entries.

10

Hour 11

Creating Custom Objects

In the last two hours, you've learned to use JavaScript's built-in objects, such as Date. You've also learned about the browser objects, which allow you to manipulate Web documents. These are the most commonly used JavaScript objects, but you can also create custom objects.

In this hour, you'll learn how to create your own custom objects with JavaScript, and in the process learn a bit more about how JavaScript handles all kinds of objects. Hour 11 covers the following topics:

- How objects can simplify scripts
- Defining an object
- Adding methods to an object
- Creating instances of an object
- Using objects to store and manage data

Using Objects to Simplify Scripting

Although JavaScript's variables and arrays are versatile ways to store data, sometimes you need a more complicated structure. For example, suppose you are creating a script to work with a business card database that contains names, addresses, and phone numbers for a variety of people.

If you were using regular variables, you would need several separate variables for each person in the database: a name variable, an address variable, and so on. This would be very confusing.

Arrays would improve things slightly. You could have a names array, an addresses array, and a phone number array. Each person in the database would have an entry in each array. This would be more convenient, but still not perfect.

With objects, you can make the variables that store the database as logical as business cards. Each person is represented by a Card object, which has properties for name, address, and phone number. You can even add methods to the object to display or work with the information.

In the following sections, you'll use JavaScript to actually create the Card object and its properties and methods. Later in this hour, you'll use the Card object in a script to display information for several members of the database.

Defining an Object

The first step in creating an object is to name it and its properties. We've already decided to call the object a Card object. Each object will have the following properties:

- name
- address
- workphone
- homephone

The first step in using this object in a JavaScript program is to create a function to create new Card objects. This function is called the *constructor* for an object. Here is the constructor function for the Card object:

```
function Card(name,address,work,home) {
   this.name = name;
   this.address = address;
   this.workphone = work;
   this.homephone = home;
}
```

The constructor is a simple function that accepts parameters to initialize a new object and assigns them to the corresponding properties. This function accepts several parameters from the statement that calls the function and then assigns them as properties of an object. Because the function is called Card, the object is the Card object.

Notice the `this` keyword. You'll use it any time you create an object definition. Use `this` to refer to the current object—the one that is being created by the function.

Defining an Object Method

Next, you will create a method to work with the `Card` object. Because all `Card` objects will have the same properties, it might be handy to have a function that prints out the properties in a neat format. Let's call this function `PrintCard`.

Your `PrintCard` function will be used as a method for `Card` objects, so you don't need to ask for parameters. Instead, you can use the `this` keyword again to refer to the current object's properties. Here is a function definition for the `PrintCard()` function:

```
function PrintCard() {
   line1 = "Name: " + this.name + "<BR>\n";
   line2 = "Address: " + this.address + "<BR>\n";
   line3 = "Work Phone: " + this.workphone + "<BR>\n";
   line4 = "Home Phone: " + this.homephone + "<BR>\n";
   document.write(line1, line2, line3, line4);
}
```

This function simply reads the properties from the current object (`this`), prints each one with a caption, and skips to a new line.

You now have a function that prints a card, but it isn't officially a method of the `Card` object. The last thing you need to do is make `PrintCard` part of the function definition for `Card` objects. Here is the modified function definition:

```
function Card(name,address,work,home) {
   this.name = name;
   this.address = address;
   this.workphone = work;
   this.homephone = home;
   this.PrintCard = PrintCard;
}
```

The added statement looks just like another property definition, but it refers to the `PrintCard` function. This will work so long as the `PrintCard` function is defined with its own function definition.

Creating an Object Instance

Now let's use the object definition and method you created above. In order to use an object definition, you create a new object. This is done with the `new` keyword. This is the same keyword you've already used to create `Date` and `Array` objects.

11

The following statement creates a new `Card` object called `tom`:

```
tom = new Card("Tom Jones", "123 Elm Street", "555-1234", "555-9876");
```

As you can see, creating an object is easy. All you do is call the `Card()` function (the object definition) and give it the required attributes, in the same order as the definition.

Once this statement executes, a new object is created to hold Tom's information. This is called an *instance* of the `Card` object. Just as there can be several string variables in a program, there can be several instances of an object you define.

Rather than specify all of the information for a card with the `new` keyword, you can assign them after the fact. For example, Listing 11.1 creates an empty `Card` object called `holmes` and then assigns its properties.

LISTING 11.1 CREATING AN OBJECT AND ASSIGNING PROPERTIES.

```
1: holmes = new Card();
2: holmes.name = "Sherlock Holmes";
3: holmes.address = "221B Baker Street";
4: holmes.workphone = "555-2345";
5: holmes.homephone = "555-3456";
```

Once you've created an instance of the `Card` object using either of these methods, you can use the `PrintCard()` method to display its information. For example, this statement displays the properties of the `tom` card:

```
tom.PrintCard();
```

Customizing Built-In Objects

JavaScript includes a feature that allows you to extend the definitions of built-in objects. For example, if you think the `String` object doesn't quite fit your needs, you can extend it, adding a new property or method. This might be very useful if you were creating a large script that used many strings.

You can add both properties and methods to an existing object by using the `prototype` keyword. (A *prototype* is another name for an object's definition, or constructor function.) The `prototype` keyword allows you to change the definition of an object outside its constructor function.

As an example, let's add a method to the `String` object definition. You will create a method called `heading`, which converts a string into an HTML heading. The following statement defines a string called `title`:

```
title = "Fred's Home Page";
```

This statement would output the contents of the `title` string as an HTML level 1 header:

```
document.write(title.heading(1));
```

Listing 11.2 adds a `heading` method to the `String` object definition that will display the string as a heading and then display a simple example.

LISTING 11.2 ADDING A METHOD TO THE `String` OBJECT.

```
 1: <HTML>
 2: <HEAD><TITLE>Test of heading method</TITLE>
 3: </HEAD>
 4: <BODY>
 5: <SCRIPT LANGUAGE="JavaScript1.1">
 6: function addhead (level) {
 7:    html = "H" + level;
 8:    text = this.toString();
 9:    start = "<" + html + ">";
10:    stop = "</" + html + ">";
11:    return start + text + stop;
12: }
13: String.prototype.heading = addhead;
14: document.write ("This is a test".heading(1));
15: </SCRIPT>
16: </BODY>
17: </HTML>
```

First, you define the `addhead()` function, which will serve as the new string method. It accepts a number to specify the heading level. The `start` and `stop` variables are used to store the HTML "begin header" and "end header" tags, such as `<H1>` and `</H1>`.

After the function is defined, use the `prototype` keyword to add it as a method of the `String` object. You can then use this method on any `String` object, or in fact any JavaScript string. This is demonstrated by the last statement, which displays a quoted text string as a level 1 header.

Workshop: Storing Data in Objects

Now you've created a new object to store business cards and a method to print them out. As a final demonstration of objects, properties, functions, and methods, you will now use this object in a Web page to display data for several cards.

The HTML document will need to include the function definition for `PrintCard`, along with the function definition for the `Card` object. You will then create three cards and print

them out in the body of the document. Listing 11.3 shows the complete HTML
document.

LISTING 11.3 AN HTML DOCUMENT THAT USES THE Card OBJECT.

```
 1: <HTML>
 2: <HEAD>
 3: <TITLE>JavaScript Business Cards</TITLE>
 4: <SCRIPT LANGUAGE="JavaScript">
 5: function PrintCard() {
 6: line1 = "<B>Name: </B>" + this.name + "<BR>\n";
 7: line2 = "<B>Address: </B>" + this.address + "<BR>\n";
 8: line3 = "<B>Work Phone: </B>" + this.workphone + "<BR>\n";
 9: line4 = "<B>Home Phone: </B>" + this.homephone + "<BR>\n";
10: document.write(line1, line2, line3, line4);
11: }
12: function Card(name,address,work,home) {
13:     this.name = name;
14:     this.address = address;
15:     this.workphone = work;
16:     this.homephone = home;
17:     this.PrintCard = PrintCard;
18: }
19: </SCRIPT>
20: </HEAD>
21: <BODY>
22: <H1>JavaScript Business Card Test</H1>
23: Script begins here.<HR>
24: <SCRIPT LANGUAGE="JavaScript">
25: // Create the objects
26: sue = new Card("Sue Suthers", "123 Elm Street", "555-1234",
        "555-9876");
27: phred = new Card("Phred Madsen", "233 Oak Lane", "555-2222",
        "555-4444");
28: henry = new Card("Henry Tillman", "233 Walnut Circle", "555-1299",
        "555-1344");
29: // And print them
30: sue.PrintCard();
31: phred.PrintCard();
32: henry.PrintCard();
33: </SCRIPT>
34: End of script.
35: </BODY>
36: </HTML>
```

Notice that the `PrintCard()` function has been modified slightly to make things look good, with HTML line breaks and boldface. The Netscape output of this document is shown in Figure 11.1.

> This example isn't a very sophisticated database because you have to include the data for each person in the HTML document. However, the `Card` object just as easily could be used to store a database record retrieved from a database server with thousands of records.

FIGURE 11.1

Netscape displays the output of the business card example.

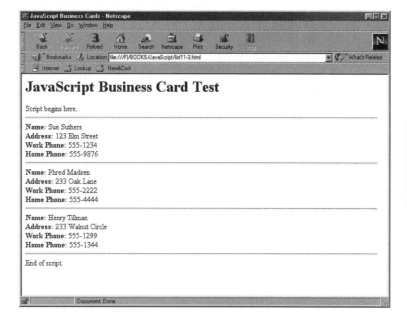

11

Summary

In this hour, you learned how to create your own objects in JavaScript. You created an object definition, added object properties and methods, created object instances, and learned to use all of them together in a complete script. You also learned how to modify JavaScript's built-in objects, such as the `String` object.

You're nearing the end of Part III. In the final hour of this part, you'll learn about event handlers, which allow your script to respond when the user clicks the mouse, presses a key, or otherwise gets its attention.

Q&A

Q The objects described in Hour 10 included parent and child objects. Can I include child objects in my custom object definitions?

A Yes. Just create a constructor function for the child object, and then add a property to the parent object that corresponds to it. For example, if you created a `Nicknames` object to store several nicknames for a person in the card file example, you could add it as a child object in the `Card` object's constructor: `this.nick = new Nicknames();`.

Q Can I create an array of custom objects?

A Yes. First, create the object definition as usual and define an array with the required number of elements. Then use a loop to assign a new object to each array element (for example, `cardarray[1] = new Card();`).

Q Which browsers support custom objects?

A The features described in this hour are included in JavaScript 1.1 and should be supported by Netscape 3.0 and later and Internet Explorer 4.0 and later.

Workshop

Quiz

1. What JavaScript keyword is used to create an instance of an object?

    a. `object`

    b. `new`

    c. `instance`

2. What is the meaning of the `this` keyword in JavaScript?

    a. The current object.

    b. The current script.

    c. It has no meaning.

3. What does the `prototype` keyword allow you to do in a script?

    a. Change the syntax of JavaScript commands.

    b. Modify the definitions of built-in objects.

    c. Modify the user's browser so only your scripts will work.

Answers

1. b. The new keyword creates an object instance.

2. a. The this keyword refers to the current object.

3. b. The prototype keyword allows you to modify the definitions of built-in objects.

Exercises

If you'd like to gain more experience in using custom objects, perform the following exercises:

- Modify the definition of the Card object to include a property called email for the person's email address. Modify the PrintCard function to include this property.

- Make a script that adds a first5 method, which returns the first five characters, to the String object. You'll need to use the substring method, described in Hour 6, "Using Strings and Arrays."

11

HOUR 12

Responding to Events

You've nearly reached the halfway point in your 24-hour study of JavaScript. So far, most of the scripts you've written have executed in a calm, orderly fashion, moving from the first statement to the last.

In this hour, you'll learn to use the wide variety of event handlers supported by JavaScript. Rather than executing in order, scripts using event handlers can interact directly with the user. You'll use event handlers in just about every script you write in the last 12 hours of this book.

Hour 12 covers the following topics:

- How event handlers work
- How event handlers relate to objects
- Creating an event handler
- Testing an event handler
- Detecting mouse actions
- Detecting keyboard actions
- Intercepting events with a special handler
- Adding friendly link descriptions to a Web page

Understanding Event Handlers

As you learned in Hour 4, "How JavaScript Programs Work," JavaScript programs don't have to execute in order. They can also detect *events* and react to them. Events are things that happen to the browser—the user clicking a button, the mouse pointer moving, or a Web page or image loading from the server. A wide variety of events allows your scripts to respond to the mouse, the keyboard, and other circumstances.

The script that you use to detect and respond to an event is called an *event handler*. Event handlers are among the most powerful features of JavaScript. Luckily, they're also among the easiest features to learn and use—often, a useful event handler requires only a single statement.

Objects and Events

As you learned in Hour 10, "Working with Browser Objects," JavaScript uses a set of objects to store information about the various parts of a Web page—buttons, links, images, windows, and so on. An event can often happen in more than one place (for example, the user could click any one of the links on the page), so each event is associated with an object.

Each event has a name. For example, the onMouseOver event occurs when the mouse pointer moves over an object on the page. When the pointer moves over a particular link, the onMouseOver event is sent to that link's event handler, if it has one.

To define an event handler, you add the word on to the beginning of the event's name. For example, the onMouseOver event handler is called when the mouse moves over a link. To define the event handler, you add it to that particular link's <A> HTML tag.

> Notice the strange capitalization on the onMouseOver keyword. This is the standard notation for event handlers. The on is always lowercase, and each word in the event name is capitalized.

Creating an Event Handler

You don't need the <SCRIPT> tag to define an event handler. Instead, you add an event handler attribute to an individual HTML tag. For example, here is a link that includes an onMouseOver event handler:

```
<A HREF="http://www.jsworkshop.com/"
   onMouseOver="window.alert('You moved over the link.');">
Click here</A>
```

Note that this is all one <A> tag, although it's split into multiple lines. This specifies a statement to be used as the onMouseOver event handler for the link. This statement displays an alert message when the mouse moves over the link.

The previous example uses single quotation marks to surround the text. This is necessary in an event handler because double quotation marks are used to surround the event handler itself. (You can also use single quotation marks to surround the event handler and double quotes within the script statements.)

You can use JavaScript statements like the previous one in an event handler, but if you need more than one statement, it's a good idea to use a function instead. Just define the function in the header of the document, and then call the function as the event handler like this:

```
<A HREF="#bottom" onMouseOver="DoIt();">Move the mouse over this link.</A>
```

This example calls a function called DoIt() when the user moves the mouse over the link. Using a function is convenient because you can use longer, more readable JavaScript routines as event handlers. You'll use a longer function to handle events in the "Workshop: Adding Link Descriptions to a Web Page" section of this hour.

For simple event handlers, you can use two statements if you separate them with a semicolon. However, in most cases it's easier to use a function to perform the statements.

12

Changing Event Handlers with JavaScript

Rather than specifying an event handler in an HTML document, you can use JavaScript to assign a function as an event handler. This allows you to set event handlers conditionally and turn them on and off, as well as change the function that handles an event dynamically.

To define an event handler in this way, first define a function and then assign it as an event handler. Event handlers are stored as properties of the document object or another object that can receive an event. For example, the following statements define a function called mousealert and then assign it as the onMouseDown event handler for the document:

```
function mousealert() {
alert ("You clicked the mouse!");
}
document.onmousedown = mousealert;
```

Using the event Object

The event object, available in JavaScript 1.2 and later, is a special object that is sent to an event handler with each event. Your event handler can receive this object as a parameter. The properties of the event object give you more information about the event that has occurred. The following properties are available:

- type is the type of event that has occurred, such as mouseover.
- target is the target object for the event (such as the document or a link).
- which is a numeric value that specifies the mouse button that was clicked for mouse events or the key that was pressed for keyboard events.
- modifiers is a list of modifier keys that were pressed during a keyboard or mouse event (such as Alt, Ctrl, and Shift).
- data is a list of dropped data for drag-and-drop events.
- pageX and pageY are the mouse's X and Y position when the event occurred, measured from the upper-left corner of the page.
- layerX and layerY are the mouse's X and Y position, measured from the upper-left corner of the current layer. (Layers are explained in Hour 18, "Creating Dynamic Pages with Layers.")
- screenX and screenY are the mouse's X and Y position, measured from the upper-left corner of the screen.

Using Mouse Events

JavaScript includes a number of event handlers for detecting mouse actions. Your script can detect the movement of the mouse pointer and when a button is clicked, released, or both.

Over and Out

You've already seen the first and most common event handler, onMouseOver. This handler is called when the mouse pointer moves over a link, image, or other object.

The onMouseOut handler is the opposite—it is called when the mouse pointer moves out of the object's border. Unless something strange happens, this always happens some time after the onMouseOver event is called.

This handler is particularly useful if your script made a change when the pointer moved over the object—for example, displaying a message in the status line or changing an image. You can use an onMouseOut handler to undo the action when the pointer moves away.

You'll use both onMouseOver and onMouseOut handlers in the "Workshop: Adding Link Descriptions to a Web Page" section later in this hour.

One of the most common uses for the onMouseOver and onMouseOut event handlers is to create *rollovers*—images that change when the mouse moves over them. You'll learn how to create these in Hour 15, "Using Graphics and Animation."

A third handler, onMouseMove, is called when any mouse movement at all occurs. Because this happens so often, this handler isn't available by default. To use it, you must use event capturing, which you'll learn about later in this hour.

Ups and Downs

You can also use events to detect when the mouse button is clicked. The basic event handler for this is onClick. This event handler is called when the mouse button is clicked while positioned over the appropriate object.

The object in this case can be a link. It can also be a form element. You'll learn more about forms in Hour 14, "Getting Data with Forms."

For example, you can use the following event handler to display an alert when a link is clicked:

```
<A HREF="http://www.jsworkshop.com/"
onClick="alert('You are about to leave this site.');">Click Here</A>
```

In this case, the onClick event handler runs before the linked page is loaded into the browser. This is useful for making links conditional or displaying a disclaimer before launching the linked page.

If your onClick event handler returns the false value, the link will not be followed. For example, the following is a link that displays a confirmation dialog. If you click Cancel, the link is not followed; if you click OK, the new page is loaded:

12

```
<A HREF="http://www.jsworkshop.com/"
onClick="return(window.confirm('Are you sure?'));">
Click Here</A>
```

This example uses the `return` statement to enclose the event handler. This ensures that the `false` value that is returned when the user clicks Cancel is returned from the event handler, which prevents the link from being followed.

The `onDblClick` event handler is similar, but is used only if the user double-clicks on an object. Because links usually require only a single click, you could use this to make a link do two different things, depending on the number of clicks. (Needless to say, this could be confusing.) You can also detect double-clicks on images and other objects.

To give you even more control of what happens when the mouse button is pressed, two more events are included:

- `onMouseDown` is used when the user presses the mouse button.
- `onMouseUp` is used when the user releases the mouse button.

These two events are the two halves of a mouse click. If you want to detect an entire click, use `onClick`. Use `onMouseUp` and `onMouseDown` to detect just one or the other.

To detect which mouse button is pressed, you can use the `which` property of the `event` object. This property is assigned the value 1 for the left button or 3 for the right button. This property is assigned for `onClick`, `onDblClick`, `onMouseUp`, and `onMouseDown` events.

For example, this script creates an `onMouseDown` event handler that displays an alert indicating which button was pressed.

```
function mousealert(e) {
whichone = (e.which == 1) ? "Left" : "Right";
message = "You clicked the " + whichone + " button.";
alert(message);
}
document.onmousedown = mousealert;
```

Using Keyboard Events

Prior to the release of Netscape 4.0, JavaScript programs couldn't detect keyboard actions—just mouse actions. This made it difficult to create some types of programs in JavaScript. For example, games were difficult to play using Go Left and Go Right buttons.

Thankfully, JavaScript 1.2 and 1.3 can detect keyboard actions. The main event handler for this purpose is `onKeyPress`, which occurs when a key is pressed and released, or held down. As with mouse buttons, you can detect the down and up parts of the keypress with the `onKeyDown` and `onKeyUp` event handlers.

Of course, you may find it useful to know which key the user pressed. You can find this out with the event object, which is sent to your event handler when the event occurs. The event.which property stores the ASCII character code for the key that was pressed.

> ASCII (American Standard Code for Information Interchange) is the standard numeric code used by most computers to represent characters. It assigns the numbers 0–128 to various characters—for example, the letters A through Z are ASCII values 65 to 90.

If you'd rather deal with actual characters, you can use the fromCharCode string method to convert it. This method converts a numeric ASCII code to its corresponding string character. For example, the following <BODY> tag includes an event handler that displays the character for the key that was pressed in an alert message:

```
<BODY onKeyPress="window.alert('You pressed:' +
String.fromCharCode(event.which));"
```

This statement uses the String.fromCharCode method to convert the event.which property to a string and then displays the string as part of an alert dialog.

Using the onLoad Event

Another event you'll use frequently is onLoad. This event occurs when the current page (including all of its images) finishes loading from the server.

The onLoad event is related to the document object, and to define it you use an event handler in the <BODY> tag. For example, the following is a <BODY> tag that uses a simple event handler to display an alert when the page finishes loading:

```
<BODY onLoad="alert('Loading complete.');">
```

> Since the onLoad event occurs after the HTML document has finished loading and displaying, you cannot use the document.write or document.open statement within an onLoad event handler. This would overwrite the current document.

JavaScript includes a variety of other events. Many of these are related to forms, which you'll learn more about in Hour 14. Another useful event is onError, which you can use to prevent error messages from displaying. This event is described in Hour 21, "Debugging JavaScript Applications."

Workshop: Adding Link Descriptions to a Web Page

One of the most common uses for an event handler is to display a message on the status line when the user moves the mouse over a link. For example, moving the mouse over the Order Form link might display a message like "Order a product or check an order's status" on the status line.

Status line descriptions like these are typically displayed with the onMouseOver event handler. You will now create a script that displays messages in this manner and clears the message using the onMouseOut event handler. You'll use functions to simplify the process.

> When you use this technique, your status line message will replace the URL that is usually displayed there. Make sure your description is at least as useful as the URL. All too often, Web designers use this technique to display a redundant message: For example, a link labeled "Order Form" displays the description "Goes to the Order Form."

To begin the script, you will define a function to display a message on the status line. Although you don't need to use a function, it makes your job a bit easier. For example, a link with an event handler that displays a message on the status line might look like this:

```
<A HREF="order.html"
    onMouseOver="window.status='Order a product'; return true;">
Order Form</A>
```

In this example, the return true statement is necessary to prevent the status message from being overwritten immediately by the URL display. As you can see, this makes the <A> tag complicated—and there isn't even a way to clear the message.

Using a function simplifies the link tags slightly. More importantly, it will make it easy to add other features (such as graphics) at a later time. You will call the function to display a describe message. Listing 12.1 shows its function definition.

LISTING 12.1 THE DEFINITION FOR THE describe FUNCTION.

```
1    <SCRIPT LANGUAGE="JavaScript">

3    function describe(text) {
2        window.status = text;
4        return true;
5    }
6    </SCRIPT>
```

This function accepts a parameter called text. The contents of this variable are placed on the status line. Because the function returns a true value, the status line will continue to display this message until it is cleared. To clear the message, you can create a small function to call using the onMouseOut handler, as shown in Listing 12.2.

LISTING 12.2 THE FUNCTION TO CLEAR THE STATUS LINE.

```
1    function clearstatus() {
2        window.status="";
3    }
```

Last but not least, your HTML document needs to include the actual links, with the appropriate event handlers to call these two functions. Listing 12.3 shows the complete HTML document with three typical links.

LISTING 12.3 THE COMPLETE DESCRIPTIVE LINKS EXAMPLE.

```
1    <HTML>
2    <HEAD>
3    <TITLE>Descriptive Links</TITLE>
4    <SCRIPT LANGUAGE="JavaScript">
5    function describe(text) {
6        window.status = text;
7        return true;
8    }
9    function clearstatus() {
10       window.status="";
11   }
12   </SCRIPT>
13   </HEAD>
14   <BODY>
15   <H1>Descriptive Links</H1>
16   <P>Move the mouse pointer over one of
17   these links to view a description:</P>
```

12

continues

LISTING 12.3   CONTINUED

```
18     <UL>
19     <LI><A HREF="order.html"
20        onMouseOver="describe('Order a product'); return true;"
21        onMouseOut="clearstatus();">
22     Order Form</A>
23     <LI><A HREF="email.html"
24        onMouseOver="describe('Send us a message'); return true;"
25        onMouseOut="clearstatus();">
26     Email</A>
27     <LI><A HREF="complain.html"
28        onMouseOver="describe('Insult us, our products, or our
              families'); return true;"
29        onMouseOut="clearstatus();">
30     Complaint Department</A>
31     </UL>
32     </BODY>
33     </HTML>
```

In this example, the functions are defined in the header portion of the document. Each link includes onMouseOver and onMouseOut event handlers to call the two status line functions.

To test the script, load it into a browser; this script should work on any JavaScript-capable browser. Netscape's display of the example is shown in Figure 12.1.

FIGURE 12.1

Netscape's display of the descriptive links example.

Summary

In this hour, you've learned to use events to detect mouse actions, keyboard actions, and other events, such as the loading of the page. You can use event handlers to perform a simple JavaScript statement when an event occurs, or to call a more complicated function.

Congratulations! You're halfway through your 24-hour tour of JavaScript. In the next few chapters, you'll move on to some more advanced methods of working with Web pages—for example, you'll learn how to use frames, forms, and graphics, and how to make scripts that detect the user's browser.

Q&A

Q I noticed that the `<IMG>` tag in HTML can't have `onMouseOver` or `onClick` event handlers. How can my scripts respond when the mouse moves over an image?

A The easiest way to do this is to make the image a link by surrounding it with an `<A>` tag. You can include the `BORDER=0` attribute to prevent the blue link border from being displayed around the image. You'll see an example of this in Hour 15.

Q What happens if I define both `onKeyDown` and `onKeyPress` event handlers? Will they both be called when a key is pressed?

A The `onKeyDown` event handler is called first. If it returns `true`, the `onKeyPress` event is called. Otherwise, no keypress event is generated.

Q Is there any way at all to detect keypresses in a script and support browsers older than Netscape 4.0?

A In general, no. However, you can detect keys pressed in certain circumstances, such as when text is entered into a text field of a form. This is explained in Hour 14.

Q When I use the `onLoad` event, my event handler sometimes executes before the page is done loading, or before some of the graphics. Is there a better way?

A This is a bug in some older versions of JavaScript. One solution is to add a slight delay to your script using the `setTimeout` method. You'll learn how to use this method in Hour 13, "Using Windows and Frames."

12

Workshop

Quiz

1. Which of the following is the correct event handler to detect a mouse click on a link?

   a. onMouseUp

   b. onLink

   c. onClick

2. When does the onLoad event handler execute?

   a. When an image is finished loading.

   b. When the entire page is finished loading.

   c. When the user attempts to load another page.

3. Where should you include the onLoad event handler in an HTML document?

   a. Within <SCRIPT> tags.

   b. Within the <BODY> tag.

   c. At the very end of the document.

Answers

1. c. The event handler for a mouse click is onClick.

2. b. The onLoad handler executes when the page and all of its images are finished loading.

3. b. The onLoad event handler should be placed within the <BODY> tag.

Exercises

To gain more experience using event handlers in JavaScript, try the following exercises:

- Add several additional links to the document in Listing 12.3. Include event handlers that display a unique description for each link.

- Modify Listing 12.3 to display a default welcome message in the status line whenever a description isn't being displayed. (Hint: you'll need to include a statement to display the welcome message when the page loads. You'll also need to change the clearstatus function to restore the welcome message.)

PART IV
Working with Web Pages

Hour

Hour 13

Using Windows and Frames

Welcome to Part IV! You should now have a good foundation of knowledge about JavaScript programming. In the next four hours, you'll learn some more specific techniques for making JavaScript work with various parts of Web pages and browsers.

In Hour 13, you'll begin by learning more about browser windows and frames and how JavaScript can work with them. This hour covers the following topics:

- The window object hierarchy
- Creating new windows with JavaScript
- Delaying your script's actions with timeouts
- Displaying alerts, confirmations, and prompts
- Using JavaScript to work with frames
- Creating a JavaScript-based navigation frame

Controlling Windows with Objects

In Hour 10, "Working with Browser Objects," you learned that you can use browser objects to represent various parts of the browser window and the current HTML document. You also learned that the window object is at the top of the object hierarchy. The history, document, and location objects are all children of the window object.

In this hour, you'll take a closer look at the window object itself. As you've probably guessed by now, this means you'll be dealing with browser windows. A version of the window object also allows you to work with frames, as you'll see later in this hour.

The window object always refers to the current window (the one containing the script). The self keyword is also a synonym for the current window. As you'll learn in the next section, you can have more than one window on the screen at the same time, and you can refer to them with different names.

Creating a New Window

One of the most convenient uses for the window object is to create a new window. You can do this to display a document—for example, the instructions for a game—without clearing the current window. You can also create windows for specific purposes, such as navigation windows.

You can create a new browser window with the window.open() method. A typical statement to open a new window looks like this:

```
WinObj=window.open("URL", "WindowName", "Feature List");
```

The following are the components of the window.open() statement:

- The WinObj variable is used to store the new window object. You can access methods and properties of the new object by using this name.
- The first parameter of the window.open() method is a URL, which will be loaded into the new window. If it's left blank, no Web page will be loaded.
- The second parameter specifies a window name (here, WindowName). This is assigned to the window object's name property and is used to refer to the window.
- The third parameter is a list of optional features, separated by commas. You can customize the new window by choosing whether to include the toolbar, status line, and other features. This enables you to create a variety of "floating" windows, which may look nothing like a typical browser window.

The features available in the third parameter of the window.open() method include width and height, to set the size of the window, and several features that can be set to either yes (1) or no (0): toolbar, location, directories, status, menubar, scrollbars, and resizable. You can list only the features you want to change from the default. This example creates a small window with no toolbar or status line:

```
SmallWin =
window.open("","small","width=100,height=120,toolbar=0,status=0");
```

 You can also manipulate the current window in a variety of ways from a signed script, which has the user's permission to gain greater control over the browser. See Appendix A, "Other JavaScript Resources," for a list of Web sites with information about signed scripts and other advanced features.

Opening and Closing Windows

Of course, you can close windows as well. The window.close() method closes a window. Netscape doesn't allow you to close the main browser window without the user's permission; its main purpose is for closing windows you have created. For example, this statement closes a window called updatewindow:

```
updatewindow.close();
```

As another example, Listing 13.1 shows an HTML document that enables you to open a new window by pressing a button. (I have specified a very small size for the second window so you can tell them apart.) You can then press another button to close the new window. The third button attempts to close the current window. Netscape allows this, but asks for confirmation first.

LISTING 13.1 AN HTML DOCUMENT THAT USES JAVASCRIPT TO ENABLE YOU TO CREATE AND CLOSE WINDOWS.

13

```
1    <HTML>
2    <HEAD><TITLE>Create a New Window</TITLE>
3    </HEAD>
4    <BODY>
5    <H1>Create a New Window</H1>
6    <HR>
7    Use the buttons below to test opening and closing windows in
       JavaScript.
```

continues

LISTING 13.1   CONTINUED

```
8    <HR>
9    <FORM NAME="winform">
10   <INPUT TYPE="button" VALUE="Open New Window"
11   onClick="NewWin=window.open('','NewWin',
12   'toolbar=no,status=no,width=200,height=100'); ">
13   <P><INPUT TYPE="button" VALUE="Close New Window"
14   onClick="NewWin.close();" >
15   <P><INPUT TYPE="button" VALUE="Close Main Window"
16   onClick="window.close();">
17   </FORM>
18   <BR>Have fun!
19   <HR>
20   </BODY>
21   </HTML>
```

This example uses event handlers to do its work, one for each of the buttons. Figure 13.1 shows Netscape's display of this page, with the small new window on top.

FIGURE 13.1

A new Netscape window opened with JavaScript.

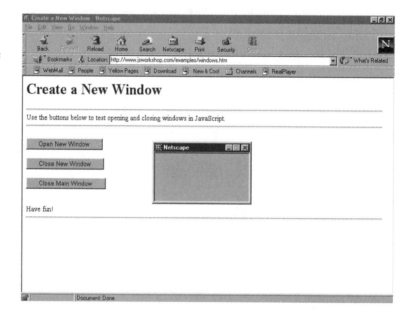

Using Timeouts

Sometimes the hardest thing to get a script to do is to do nothing at all—for a specific amount of time. Fortunately, JavaScript includes a built-in function to do this. The `window.setTimeout` method allows you to specify a time delay and a command that will execute after the delay passes.

> Timeouts don't actually make the browser stop what it's doing. Although the statement you specify in the `setTimeout` method won't be executed until the delay passes, the browser will continue to do other things while it waits (for example, acting on event handlers).

You begin a timeout with a call to the `setTimeout()` method, which has two parameters. The first is a JavaScript statement, or group of statements, enclosed in quotes. The second parameter is the time to wait in milliseconds (thousandths of a second). For example, the following statement displays an alert dialog after 10 seconds:

```
ident=window.setTimeout("alert('Time's up!')",10000);
```

> Like event handlers, timeouts use a JavaScript statement within quotation marks. Make sure that you use a single quote (apostrophe) on each side of each string within the statement, as shown in the preceding example.

A variable (`ident` in this example) stores an identifier for the timeout. This enables you to set multiple timeouts, each with its own identifier. Before a timeout has elapsed, you can stop it with the `clearTimeout()` method, specifying the identifier of the timeout to stop:

```
window.clearTimeout(ident);
```

Updating a Page with Timeouts

Normally, a timeout only happens once because the statement you specify in the `setTimeout` statement is only executed once. But often, you'll want your statement to execute over and over. For example, your script may be updating a clock or countdown and need to execute once per second.

You can make a timeout repeat by issuing the `setTimeout()` method call again in the function called by the timeout. Listing 13.2 shows an HTML document that demonstrates a repeating timeout.

13

LISTING 13.2   USING TIMEOUTS TO UPDATE A PAGE EVERY TWO SECONDS.

```
1    <HTML>
2    <HEAD><TITLE>Timeout Example</TITLE>
3    <SCRIPT>
4    var counter = 0;
5    // call Update function in 2 seconds after first load
6    ID=window.setTimeout("Update();",2000);
7    function Update() {
8       counter++;
9       window.status="The counter is now at " + counter;
10      document.form1.input1.value="The counter is now at " + counter;
11   // set another timeout for the next count
12      ID=window.setTimeout("Update();",2000);
13   }
14   </SCRIPT>
15   </HEAD>
16   <BODY>
17   <H1>Timeout Example</H1>
18   <HR>
19   The text value below and the status line are being updated every two
       seconds.
20   Press the RESET button to restart the count, or the STOP button to
       stop it.
21   <HR>
22   <FORM NAME="form1">
23   <INPUT TYPE="text" NAME="input1" SIZE="40"><BR>
24   <INPUT TYPE="button" VALUE="RESET" onClick="counter = 0;"><BR>
25   <INPUT TYPE="button" VALUE="STOP" onClick="window.clearTimeout(ID);">
26   <HR>
27   </BODY>
28   </HTML>
```

This program displays a message in the status line and in a text field every two seconds, including a counter that increments each time. You can use the Reset button to start the count over and the Stop button to stop the counting.

This script calls the setTimeout() method when the page first loads, and again at each update. The Update() function performs the update, adding one to the counter and setting the next timeout. The Reset button sets the counter to zero, and the Stop button demonstrates the clearTimeout() method. Figure 13.2 shows Netscape's display of the timeout example after the counter has been running for a while.

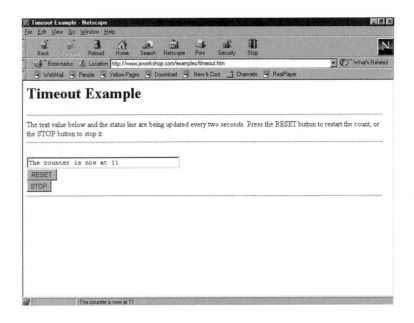

FIGURE 13.2

The output of the timeout example, as displayed by Netscape.

This example and the next one use buttons, which are a simple example of what you can do with HTML forms and JavaScript. You'll learn much more about forms in Hour 14, "Getting Data with Forms."

Displaying Dialog Boxes

The window object includes three methods that are useful for displaying messages and interacting with the user. You've already used these in some of your scripts. Here's a summary:

- The alert method displays an alert dialog box, shown in Figure 13.3. This dialog simply gives the user a message.

- The confirm method displays a confirmation dialog. This displays a message and includes OK and Cancel buttons. This method returns true if OK is pressed and false if Cancel is pressed. A confirmation is displayed in Figure 13.4.

- The prompt method displays a message and prompts the user for input. It returns the text entered by the user.

13

FIGURE 13.3

A JavaScript alert dialog displays a message.

FIGURE 13.4

A JavaScript confirm dialog asks for confirmation.

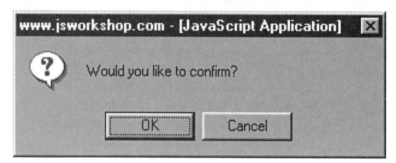

Creating a Script to Display Dialogs

As a further illustration of these types of dialogs, Listing 13.3 shows an HTML document that uses buttons and event handlers to enable you to test dialogs.

LISTING 13.3   AN HTML DOCUMENT THAT USES JAVASCRIPT TO DISPLAY ALERTS, CONFIRMATIONS, AND PROMPTS.

```
 1    <HTML>
 2    <HEAD><TITLE>Alerts, Confirmations, and Prompts</TITLE>
 3    </HEAD>
 4    <BODY>
 5    <H1>Alerts, Confirmations, and Prompts</H1>
 6    <HR>
 7    Use the buttons below to test dialogs in JavaScript.
 8    <HR>
 9    <FORM NAME="winform">
10     <INPUT TYPE="button" VALUE="Display an Alert"
11     onClick="window.alert('This is a test alert.');  ">
12     <P><INPUT TYPE="button" VALUE="Display a Confirmation"
13     onClick="temp = window.confirm('Would you like to confirm?');
14     window.status=(temp)?'confirm: true':'confirm: false'; ">
15     <P><INPUT TYPE="button" VALUE="Display a Prompt"
```

```
16    onClick="var temp = window.prompt('Enter some Text:','This is the
       default value');
17    window.status=temp;   ">
18    </FORM>
19    <BR>Have fun!
20    <HR>
21    </BODY>
22    </HTML>
```

This document displays three buttons, and each one uses an event handler to display one of the dialogs. Let's take a detailed look at each one:

- The alert dialog is displayed when you click on the button.
- The confirmation dialog is displayed when you press the button and displays a message in the status line indicating whether true or false was returned. The returned value is stored in the temp variable.
- The third button displays the prompt dialog. Notice that the prompt method accepts a second parameter, which is used to set a default value for the entry. The value you enter is stored in the temp variable and displayed on the status line. Notice that if you press the Cancel button in the prompt dialog, the null value is returned.

Figure 13.5 shows the script in Listing 13.3 in action. The prompt dialog is currently displayed and shows the default value, and the status line still displays the result of a previous confirmation dialog.

FIGURE 13.5

The dialog box example's output, including a prompt dialog.

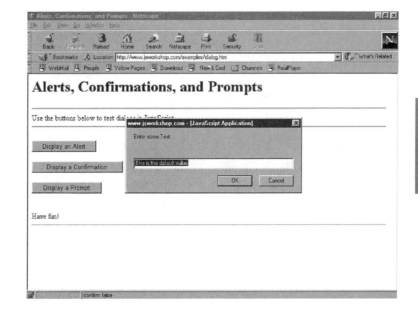

13

Working with Frames

Some browsers (including the latest Netscape and Microsoft browsers) support frames or framesets, which enable you to divide the browser window into multiple panes. Each frame can contain a separate URL or the output of a script.

Using JavaScript Objects for Frames

When a window contains multiple frames, each frame is represented in JavaScript by a frame object. This object is equivalent to a window object, but it is used for dealing with that frame. The frame object's name is the same as the NAME attribute you give it in the <FRAME> tag.

Remember the window and self keywords, which refer to the current window? When you are using frames, these keywords refer to the current frame instead. Another keyword, parent, enables you to refer to the main window.

Each frame object in a window is a child of the parent window object. Suppose you define a set of frames using the HTML in Listing 13.4.

LISTING 13.4 A FRAMED DOCUMENT THAT DIVIDES THE PAGE INTO QUARTERS.

```
1    <FRAMESET ROWS="*,*" COLS="*,*">
2    <FRAME NAME="topleft" SRC="topleft.htm">
3    <FRAME NAME="topright" SRC="topright.htm">
4    <FRAME NAME="bottomleft" SRC="botleft.htm">
5    <FRAME NAME="bottomright" SRC="botright.htm">
6    </FRAMESET>
```

This simply divides the window into quarters. If you have a JavaScript program in the topleft.htm file, it would refer to the other windows as parent.topright, parent. bottomleft, and so on. The keywords window and self would refer to the topleft frame.

> If you use nested framesets, things are a bit more complicated. window still represents the current frame, parent represents the frameset containing the current frame, and top represents the main frameset that contains all the others.

The `frames` Array

Rather than referring to frames in a document by name, you can use the `frames` array. This array stores information about each of the frames in the document. The frames are indexed starting with zero and beginning with the first `<FRAME>` tag in the frameset document.

For example, you could refer to the frames defined in Listing 13.4 using array references:

- `parent.frames[0]` is equivalent to the `topleft` frame.
- `parent.frames[1]` is equivalent to the `topright` frame.
- `parent.frames[2]` is equivalent to the `bottomleft` frame.
- `parent.frames[3]` is equivalent to the `bottomright` frame.

You can refer to a frame using either method interchangeably, and depending on your application, you should use the most convenient method. For example, a document with 10 frames would probably be easier to use by number, but a simple two-frame document is easier to use if the frames have meaningful names.

Workshop: Creating a Navigation Frame

A common use for frames is to display a navigation frame along the side or top of a page. Using `frame` objects, you can create a navigation frame that controls the document in another frame.

To begin, you'll need a document to define the frameset. This is the simple part. Listing 13.5 defines a frameset with frames on the left and right.

LISTING 13.5 AN HTML DOCUMENT TO DIVIDE THE WINDOW INTO TWO FRAMES.

```
1    <HTML>
2    <HEAD>
3    <TITLE>Frame Navigation Example</TITLE>
4    </HEAD>
5    <FRAMESET COLS="*,*">
6    <FRAME NAME="left" SRC="left.html">
7    <FRAME NAME="right" SRC="about:blank">
8    </FRAMESET>
9    </HTML>
```

13

Next, you will need the document for the left-hand frame, which will act as the navigation frame. Listing 13.6 shows the HTML document for this frame.

LISTING 13.6 THE HTML DOCUMENT FOR THE NAVIGATION FRAME.

```
1    <HTML>
2    <HEAD>
3    <TITLE>Navigation Frame</TITLE>
4    <BODY>
5    <P>
6    Follow one of these links
7    to load a page into the right-hand
8    frame:
9    </P>
10   <UL>
11   <LI><A HREF="#"
12   onClick="parent.right.location='order.html';
               window.location='ordernav.html';">
13   Order form</A>
14   <LI><A HREF="#"
15   onClick="parent.right.location='email.html';
               window.location='emailnav.html';">
16   Email</A>
17   <LI><A HREF="#"
18   onClick="parent.right.location='sales.html';
               window.location='salesnav.html';">
19   Sales Dept.</A>
20   <LI><A HREF="#"
21   onClick="parent.right.location='link.html';">
22   Other Links</A>
23   </UL>
24   </BODY>
25   </HTML>
```

This listing looks complicated, but it actually uses two simple JavaScript statements to do its job. These statements are repeated for each of the links, with a slight variation. Here's one example:

```
onClick="parent.right.location='email.html';
         window.location='emailnav.html';">
```

These statements are an event handler that loads a document into the right-hand frame and also loads a new document into the navigation frame. Because the current script is itself in a frame, you need to use the parent keyword before the name of the other frame's object.

> If you're only loading one document when the user clicks on a link, you can use the TARGET attribute of the <A> tag and avoid JavaScript. However, using JavaScript allows you to update two frames at once, as seen in this example.

To test this script, make sure that you've saved Listing 13.6 as `left.html`, and then load Listing 13.5 into the browser. Try one of the links. (You can download a complete set of HTML documents for this example from this book's Web site, `www.jsworkshop.com`.) Figure 13.6 shows Netscape's display of this example.

FIGURE 13.6

The frame example as displayed by Netscape.

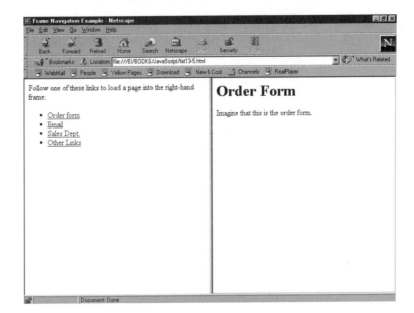

Summary

In this hour, you've learned how to use the `window` object to work with browser windows and used its properties and methods to set timeouts and display dialogs. You've also learned how JavaScript can work with framed documents.

In the next hour, you'll move on to another unexplored area of the JavaScript object hierarchy—the `form` object. You'll learn how to use forms to create some of the most useful applications of JavaScript.

13

Q&A

Q When a script is running in a window created by another script, how can it refer back to the original window?

A In Netscape 3.0 and later, JavaScript includes the `window.opener` property, which lets you refer to the window that opened the current window.

Q I've heard about layers, which are similar to frames, but more versatile, and are supported in Netscape 4.0. Can I use them with JavaScript?

A Yes. Like windows and frames, each layer has its own `window` object. You'll learn how to use layers in Hour 18, "Creating Dynamic Pages with Layers."

Q How can I update two frames at once when the user clicks on a single link?

A You can do this by using an event handler, as in Listing 13.6, and including two statements to load different frames. To simplify things, you can also create a function that loads both frames and then call the function from the event handler.

Quiz

1. Which of the following methods displays a dialog with OK and Cancel buttons and waits for a response?

    a. `window.alert`

    b. `window.confirm`

    c. `window.prompt`

2. What does the `window.setTimeout` method do?

    a. Executes a JavaScript statement after a delay.

    b. Locks up the browser for the specified amount of time.

    c. Sets the amount of time before the browser exits automatically.

3. You're working with a document that contains three frames with the names `first`, `second`, and `third`. If a script in the second frame needs to refer to the first frame, what is the correct syntax?

    a. `window.first`

    b. `parent.first`

    c. `frames.first`

Answers

1. b. The `window.confirm` method displays a dialog with OK and Cancel buttons.

2. a. The `window.setTimeout` method executes a JavaScript statement after a delay.

3. b. The script in the second frame would use `parent.first` to refer to the first frame.

Exercises

If you want to study the window object and its properties and methods further, perform these exercises:

- Return to the Year 2000 script you created in Hour 2, "Creating a Simple Script." This script only displays a new countdown value when you reload the page. Using timeouts, you can modify the script to reload automatically every second or two. (Use the window.location.reload method, described in Hour 10.)
- Modify the examples in Listings 13.5 and 13.6 to use three frames instead of two. For each link in the left frame, use the script to load new documents into both the middle and right frames.

13

HOUR 14

Getting Data with Forms

In this hour you'll explore one of the most powerful uses for JavaScript: working with HTML forms. You can use JavaScript to make a form more interactive, validate data the user enters, and enter data based on other data.

This hour covers the following topics:

- Understanding HTML forms
- Creating a form
- Using the `form` object to work with forms
- How form elements are represented by JavaScript
- Getting data from a form
- Sending form results by email
- How JavaScript can work with CGI forms
- Validating a form with JavaScript

The Basics of HTML Forms

Forms are among the most useful features of the HTML language. As you'll learn during this hour, adding JavaScript to forms can make them more interactive and provide a number of useful features. The first step in creating an interactive form is to create the HTML form itself.

Defining a Form

An HTML form begins with the <FORM> tag. This tag indicates that a form is beginning, and it enables form elements to be used. The <FORM> tag includes three parameters:

- NAME is simply a name for the form. You can use forms without giving them names, but you'll need to assign a name to a form in order to easily use it with JavaScript.

- METHOD is either GET or POST; these are the two ways the data can be sent to the server.

- ACTION is the CGI script that the form data will be sent to when submitted. You can also use the mailto: action to send the form's results to an email address, as described later in this hour.

For example, here is a <FORM> tag for a form named Order. This form uses the GET method and sends its data to a CGI script called order.cgi in the same directory as the Web page itself:

```
<FORM NAME="Order" METHOD="GET" ACTION="order.cgi">
```

For a form that will be processed entirely by JavaScript (such as a calculator or interactive game), the METHOD and ACTION attributes are not needed. You can use a simple <FORM> tag that names the form:

```
<FORM NAME="calcform">
```

The <FORM> tag is followed by one or more form elements. These are the data fields in the form, such as text fields, buttons, and check boxes. In the next section, you'll learn how JavaScript assigns objects to each of the form elements.

Using the form Object with JavaScript

Each form in your HTML page is represented in JavaScript by a form object, which has the same name as the NAME attribute in the <FORM> tag you used to define it.

Alternately, you can use the `forms` array to refer to forms. This array includes an item for each form element, indexed starting with 0. For example, if the first form in a document has the name `form1`, you can refer to it in one of two ways:

```
document.form1
document.forms[0]
```

The `form` Object's Properties

Along with the elements, each `form` object also has a list of properties, most of which are defined by the corresponding `<FORM>` tag. You can also set these from within JavaScript. They include the following:

- `action` is the form's `ACTION` attribute, or the program to which the form data will be submitted.

- `encoding` is the `MIME` type of the form, specified with the `ENCTYPE` attribute. In most cases, this is not needed.

- `length` is the number of elements in the form. You cannot change this property.

- `method` is the method used to submit the form, either `GET` or `POST`.

- `target` specifies the window in which the result of the form (from the CGI script) will be displayed. Normally, this is done in the main window, replacing the form itself.

Submitting and Resetting Forms

The `form` object has two methods, `submit` and `reset`. You can use these methods to submit the data or reset the form yourself, without requiring the user to press a button. One reason for this is to submit the form when the user clicks an image or performs another action that would not usually submit the form.

> If you use the `submit` method to send data to a server or by email, Netscape will prompt the user to verify that she wants to submit the information. There's no way to do this behind the user's back.

Detecting Form Events

The `form` object has two event handlers, `onSubmit` and `onReset`. You can specify a group of JavaScript statements or a function call for these events within the `<FORM>` tag that defines the form.

14

If you specify a statement or function for the onSubmit event, the statement is called before the data is submitted to the CGI script. You can prevent the submission from happening by returning a value of false from the onSubmit event handler. If the statement returns true, the data will be submitted. In the same fashion, you can prevent a Reset button from working with an onReset event handler.

Scripting Form Elements

The most important property of the form object is the elements array, which contains an object for each of the form elements. You can refer to an element by its own name or by its index in the array. For example, the following two expressions both refer to the first element in the order form, the name1 text field:

```
document.order.elements[0]
```

```
document.order.name1
```

> Both forms and elements can be referred to by their own names or as indices in the forms and elements arrays. For clarity, the examples in this hour use individual form and element names rather than array references. You'll also find it easier to use names in your own scripts.

If you do refer to forms and elements as arrays, you can use the length property to determine the number of objects in the array: document.forms.length is the number of forms in a document, and document.form1.elements.length is the number of elements in the form1 form.

Text Fields

Probably the most commonly used form elements are text fields. You can use them to prompt for a name, address, or any information. With JavaScript, you can display text in the field automatically. The following is an example of a simple text field:

```
<INPUT TYPE="TEXT" NAME="text1" VALUE="hello" SIZE="30">
```

This defines a text field called text1. The field is given a default value of "hello" and allows up to 30 characters to be entered. JavaScript treats this field as a text object with the name text1.

Text fields are the simplest to work with in JavaScript. Each text object has have the following properties:

- `name` is the name given to the field. This is also used as the object name.
- `defaultValue` is the default value and corresponds to the VALUE attribute. This is a read-only property.
- `value` is the current value. This starts out the same as the default value, but can be changed, either by the user or by JavaScript functions.

When you work with text fields, most of the time you will use the `value` attribute to read the value the user has entered or to change the value. For example, the following statement changes the value of a text field called `username` in the `order` form to `"John Q. User"`:

```
document.order.username.value = "John Q. User"
```

Text Areas

Text areas are defined with their own tag, `<TEXTAREA>`, and are represented by the `textarea` object. There is one major difference between a text area and a text field: Text areas allow the user to enter more than just one line of information. Here is an example of a text area definition:

```
<TEXTAREA NAME="text1" ROWS="2" COLS="70">
This is the content of the TEXTAREA tag.
</TEXTAREA>
```

This HTML defines a text area called `text1`, with 2 rows and 70 columns available for text. In JavaScript, this would be represented by a text area object called `text1` under the `form` object.

The text between the opening and closing `<TEXTAREA>` tags is used as the initial value for the text area. You can include line breaks within the default value.

Working with Text in Forms

The `text` and `textarea` objects also have a few methods you can use:

- `focus()` sets the focus to the field. This positions the cursor in the field and makes it the current field.
- `blur()` is the opposite; it removes the focus from the field.
- `select()` selects the text in the field, just as a user can do with the mouse. All of the text is selected; there is no way to select part of the text.

You can also use event handlers to detect when the value of a text field changes. The `text` and `textarea` objects support the following event handlers:

14

- The onFocus event happens when the text field gains focus.
- The onBlur event happens when the text field loses focus.
- The onChange event happens when the user changes the text in the field and then moves out of it.
- The onSelect event happens when the user selects some or all of the text in the field. Unfortunately, there's no way to tell exactly which part of the text was selected. (If the text is selected with the select() method described above, this event is not triggered.)

If used, these event handlers should be included in the <INPUT> tag declaration. For example, the following is a text field including an onChange event that displays an alert:

```
<INPUT TYPE="TEXT" NAME="text1" onChange="window.alert('Changed.');">
```

Buttons

The final type of form element is a button. Buttons use the <INPUT> tag and can use one of three different types:

- type=SUBMIT is a Submit button. This button causes the data in the form fields to be sent to the CGI script.
- type=RESET is a Reset button. This button sets all the form fields back to their default value, or blank.
- type=BUTTON is a generic button. This button performs no action on its own, but you can assign it one using a JavaScript event handler.

All three types of buttons include a NAME attribute to identify the button and a VALUE that indicates the text to display on the button's face. A few buttons were used in the examples in Hour 13, "Using Windows and Frames." As another example, the following defines a Submit button with the name sub1 and the value "Click Here":

```
<INPUT TYPE="SUBMIT" NAME="sub1" VALUE="Click Here">
```

If the user presses a Submit or Reset button, you can detect it with the onSubmit or onReset event handlers, described earlier in this hour. For generic buttons, you can use an onClick event handler.

Check Boxes

A check box is a form element that looks like a small box. Clicking on the check box switches between the checked and unchecked states, which is useful for indicating Yes or No choices in your forms. You can use the <INPUT> tag to define a check box. Here is a simple example:

```
<INPUT TYPE="CHECKBOX" NAME="check1" VALUE="Yes" CHECKED>
```

Again, this gives a name to the form element. The VALUE attribute assigns a meaning to the check box; this is a value that is returned if the box is checked. The default value is "on." The CHECKED attribute can be included to make the box checked by default.

A check box is simple: It has only two states. Nevertheless, the checkbox object in JavaScript has four different properties:

- name is the name of the check box and also the object name.
- value is the "true" value for the check box—usually on. This value is used by the server to indicate that the check box was checked. In JavaScript, you should use the checked property instead.
- defaultChecked is the default status of the check box, assigned by the CHECKED attribute.
- checked is the current value. This is a Boolean value: true for checked and false for unchecked.

To manipulate the check box or use its value, you use the checked attribute. For example, this statement turns on a check box called same in the order form:

```
document.order.same.checked = true;
```

The check box has a single method, click(). This method simulates a click on the box. It also has a single event, onClick, which occurs whenever the check box is clicked. This happens whether the box was turned on or off, so you'll need to examine the checked property to see what happened.

Radio Buttons

Another element for decisions is the radio button, using the <INPUT> tag's RADIO type. Radio buttons are similar to check boxes, but they exist in groups and only one button can be checked in each group. They are used for a multiple-choice or "one of many" input. Here's an example of a group of radio buttons:

```
<INPUT TYPE="RADIO" NAME="radio1" VALUE="Option1" CHECKED> Option 1
<INPUT TYPE="RADIO" NAME="radio1" VALUE="Option2"> Option 2
<INPUT TYPE="RADIO" NAME="radio1" VALUE="Option3"> Option 3
```

These statements define a group of three radio buttons. The NAME attribute is the same for all three (which is what makes them a group). The VALUE attribute is the value passed to a script or CGI program to indicate which button is selected—be sure you assign a different value to each button.

14

Radio buttons are named for their similarity to the buttons on old pushbutton radios. Those buttons used a mechanical arrangement so that when you pushed one button in, the others popped out.

As for scripting, radio buttons are similar to check boxes, except that an entire group of them shares a single name and a single object. You can refer to the following properties of the radio object:

- name is the name common to the radio buttons.
- length is the number of radio buttons in the group.

To access the individual buttons, you treat the radio object as an array. The buttons are indexed, starting with 0. Each individual button has the following properties:

- value is the value assigned to the button. (This is used by the server.)
- defaultChecked indicates the value of the CHECKED attribute and the default state of the button.
- checked is the current state.

For example, you can check the first radio button in the radio1 group on the form1 form with this statement:

```
document.form1.radio1[0].checked = true;
```

However, if you do this, be sure you set the other values to false as needed. This is not done automatically. You can use the click method to do both of these in one step.

Like a check box, radio buttons have a click() method and an onClick event handler. Each radio button can have a separate statement for this event.

Drop-Down Lists

A final form element is also useful for multiple-choice selections. The <SELECT> HTML tag is used to define a *selection list*, or a drop-down list of text items. The following is an example of a selection list:

```
<SELECT NAME="select1" SIZE=40>
<OPTION VALUE="choice1" SELECTED>This is the first choice.
<OPTION VALUE="choice2">This is the second choice.
<OPTION VALUE="choice3">This is the third choice.
</SELECT>
```

Each of the OPTION tags defines one of the possible choices. The VALUE attribute is the name that is returned to the program, and the text outside the OPTION tag is displayed as the text of the option.

An optional attribute to the SELECT tag, MULTIPLE, can be specified to allow multiple items to be selected. Browsers usually display a single-selection SELECT as a drop-down list and a multiple-selection list as a scrollable list.

The object for selection lists is the select object. The object itself has the following properties:

- name is the name of the selection list.
- length is the number of options in the list.
- options is the array of options. Each selectable option has an entry in this array.
- selectedIndex returns the index value of the currently selected item. You can use this to check the value easily. In a multiple-selection list, this indicates the first selected item.

The options array has a single property of its own, length, which indicates the number of selections. In addition, each item in the options array has the following properties:

- index is the index into the array.
- defaultSelected indicates the state of the SELECTED attribute.
- selected is the current state of the option. Setting this property to true selects the option. You can select multiple options if the MULTIPLE attribute is included in the <SELECT> tag.
- name is the value of the NAME attribute. This is used by the server.
- text is the text that is displayed in the option. In Netscape 3.0 or later, you can change this value.

The select object has two methods, blur() and focus(), which perform the same purposes as the corresponding methods for text objects. The event handlers are onBlur, onFocus, and onChange, also similar to other objects.

You can change selection lists dynamically—for example, choosing a product in one list could control which options are available in another list. You can also add and delete options from the list.

Reading the value of a selected item is a two-step process. You first use the selectedIndex property, then use the value property to find the value of the selected choice. Here's an example:

```
ind = document.navform.choice.selectedIndex;
val = document.navform.choice.options[ind].value;
```

14

This uses the `ind` variable to store the selected index, then assigns the `val` variable to the value of the selected choice. You'll see an example script that uses this technique in Hour 22, "Improving a Web Page with JavaScript."

Displaying Data from a Form

As a simple example of using forms, Listing 14.1 shows a form with name, address, and phone number fields, as well as a JavaScript function that displays the data from the form in a pop-up window.

LISTING 14.1 A FORM THAT DISPLAYS DATA IN A POP-UP WINDOW.

```
1    <HTML>
2    <HEAD>
3    <TITLE>Form Example</TITLE>
4    <SCRIPT LANGUAGE="JavaScript">
5    function display() {
6       DispWin = window.open('','NewWin',
          'toolbar=no,status=no,width=300,height=200')
7       message = "<UL><LI><B>NAME: </B>" + document.form1.yourname.value;
8       message += "<LI><B>ADDRESS: </B>" + document.form1.address.value;
9       message += "<LI><B>PHONE: </B>" + document.form1.phone.value +
          "</UL>";
10      DispWin.document.write(message);
11   }
12   </SCRIPT>
13   </HEAD>
14   <BODY>
15   <H1>Form Example</H1>
16   Enter the following information. When you press the Display button,
17   the data you entered will be displayed in a pop-up window.
18   <FORM name="form1">
19   <B>Name:</B> <INPUT TYPE="TEXT" LENGTH="20" NAME="yourname">
20   <P>
21   <B>Address:</B> <INPUT TYPE="TEXT" LENGTH="30" NAME="address">
22   <P>
23   <B>Phone: </B> <INPUT TYPE="TEXT" LENGTH="15" NAME="phone">
24   <P>
25   <INPUT TYPE="BUTTON" VALUE="Display" onClick="display();">
26   </FORM>
27   </BODY>
28   </HTML>
```

Here is a breakdown of how this HTML document and script work:

- Lines 5–11 define a function called `display` that opens a new window (as described in Hour 13) and displays the information from the form.

- Line 18 is the form definition. Because this form is handled entirely by JavaScript, no form action is needed.

- Lines 19–26 define a simple form with three fields: `yourname`, `address`, and `phone`. Line 25 defines the Display button, which is set to run the `display` function.

Figure 14.1 shows this form in action. The Display button has been pressed, and the pop-up window shows the results.

FIGURE 14.1

Displaying data from a form in a pop-up window.

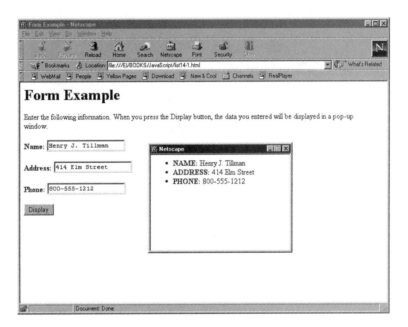

Sending Form Results by Email

One easy way to use a form is to send the results by email. You can do this without using any JavaScript, although you could use JavaScript to validate the information entered (as you'll learn later in this hour).

To send a form's results by email, you use the `mailto:` action in the form's ACTION attribute. Listing 14.2 is a modified version of the name and address form from Listing 14.1 that sends the results by email.

14

LISTING 14.2 SENDING A FORM'S RESULTS BY EMAIL.

```
 1: <HTML>
 2: <HEAD>
 3: <TITLE>Form Example</TITLE>
 4: </HEAD>
 5: <BODY>
 6: <H1>Form Example</H1>
 7: Enter the following information. When you press the Display button,
 8: the data you entered will be sent by email.
 9: <FORM NAME="form1" action="mailto:user@host.com" enctype="text/plain">
10: <B>Name:</B> <INPUT TYPE="TEXT" LENGTH="20" NAME="yourname">
11: <P>
12: <B>Address:</B> <INPUT TYPE="TEXT" LENGTH="30" NAME="address">
13: <P>
14: <B>Phone: </B> <INPUT TYPE="TEXT" LENGTH="15" NAME="phone">
15: <P>
16: <INPUT TYPE="SUBMIT" VALUE="Submit">
17: </FORM>
18: </BODY>
19: </HTML>
```

To use this form, change user@host.com to your email address. Notice the enctype=text/plain attribute in the <FORM> tag. This ensures that the information in the email message will be in a readable format.

Workshop: Validating a Form

JavaScript's single most useful purpose is probably validating forms. This means using a script to verify that the information entered is valid—for example, that no fields are blank and that the data is in the right format.

You can use JavaScript to validate a form whether it's submitted by email or to a CGI script or is simply used by a script. Listing 14.3 is a version of the name and address form that includes validation.

LISTING 14.3 A FORM WITH A VALIDATION SCRIPT.

```
1    <HTML>
2    <HEAD>
3    <TITLE>Form Example</TITLE>
4    <SCRIPT LANGUAGE="JavaScript">
5    function validate() {
6        if (document.form1.yourname.value.length < 1) {
7            alert("Please enter your full name.");
8            return false;
```

```
 9          }
10          if (document.form1.address.value.length < 3) {
11              alert("Please enter your address.");
12              return false;
13          }
14          if (document.form1.phone.value.length < 3) {
15              alert("Please enter your phone number.");
16              return false;
17          }
18          return true;
19      }
20      </SCRIPT>
21      </HEAD>
22      <BODY>
23      <H1>Form Example</H1>
24      Enter the following information. When you press the Display button,
25      the data you entered will be validated, then sent by email.
26      <FORM NAME="form1" action="mailto:user@host.com" enctype="text/plain"
27      onSubmit="validate();">
28      <B>Name:</B> <INPUT TYPE="TEXT" LENGTH="20" NAME="yourname">
29      <P>
30      <B>Address:</B> <INPUT TYPE="TEXT" LENGTH="30" NAME="address">
31      <P>
32      <B>Phone: </B> <INPUT TYPE="TEXT" LENGTH="15" NAME="phone">
33      <P>
34      <INPUT TYPE="SUBMIT" VALUE="Submit">
35      </FORM>
36      </BODY>
37      </HTML>
```

This form uses a function called validate to check the data in each of the form fields. Each if statement in this function checks a field's length. If the field is long enough to be valid, the form can be submitted; otherwise, the submission is stopped and an alert message is displayed.

The <FORM> tag on line 26 uses an onSubmit event handler to call the validate function. The return keyword ensures that the value returned by validate will determine whether the form is submitted.

You can also use the onChange event handler in each form field to call a validation routine. This allows the field to be validated before the Submit button is pressed.

14

Figure 14.2 shows this script in action, as displayed by Netscape. The form has been filled out except for the name, and a dialog box indicates that the name needs to be entered.

FIGURE 14.2

The form validation example in action.

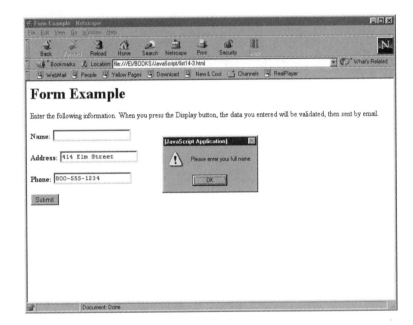

Summary

During this hour, you learned all about HTML forms and how they can be used with JavaScript. You learned about the form object and the objects for the various form elements and used them in several example scripts.

You also learned how to submit a form by email and how to use JavaScript to validate a form before it is submitted.

While JavaScript allows you to create such businesslike things as forms, it also has uses that are a bit more fun. In the next hour, you'll learn how to use JavaScript to work with graphics and create simple animations.

Q&A

Q If I use JavaScript to add validation and other features to my form, can users with non-JavaScript browsers still use the form?

A Yes, if you're careful. Be sure to use a Submit button rather than the submit action. Also, the CGI script may receive nonvalidated data, so be sure to include validation in the CGI script. Non-JavaScript users will be able to use the form, but won't receive instant feedback about their errors.

Q Can I add new form elements "on the fly" or change them—for example, change a text box into a password field?

A No. The form elements are set by the HTML code. There are ways to work around this, such as updating the form in a separate frame or layer.

Q Is there any way to create a large number of text fields without dealing with different names for all of them?

A Yes. If you use the same name for several elements in the form, their objects will form an array. For example, if you defined 20 text fields with the name member, you could refer to them as member[0] through member[19]. This also works with other types of form elements.

Q Why doesn't JavaScript recognize my form elements when I use a table to lay them out?

A Some versions of JavaScript do not deal well with forms or scripts within tables when <TABLE> tags are nested. For now, the only solution is to avoid using nested tables.

Q Is there a way to place the cursor on a particular field when the form is loaded, or after my validation routine displays an error message?

A Yes. You can use the field's focus() method to send the cursor there. To do this when the page loads, you can use the onLoad method in the <BODY> tag. However, there is no way to place the cursor in a particular position within the field.

Quiz

1. Which of these attributes of a <FORM> tag determines where the data will be sent?

    a. ACTION

    b. METHOD

    c. NAME

14

2. Where do you place the onSubmit event handler to validate a form?

   a. In the <BODY> tag.

   b. In the <FORM> tag.

   c. In the <INPUT> tag for the Submit button.

3. What can JavaScript do with forms that a CGI script can't?

   a. Cause all sorts of problems.

   b. Give the user instant feedback about errors.

   c. Submit the data to a server.

Answers

1. a. The ACTION attribute determines where the data is sent.

2. b. You place the onSubmit event handler in the <FORM> tag.

3. b. JavaScript can validate a form and let the user know about errors immediately, without waiting for a response from a server. (If you use server-side JavaScript, you can also submit the data to the server, but that's another story.)

Exercises

If you want to study the form objects further, perform these exercises:

- Change the validate function in Listing 14.3 so that after a message is displayed indicating that a field is wrong, the cursor is moved to that field. (Use the focus method for the appropriate form element.)

- Add a text field to the form in Listing 14.3 for an email address. Add a feature to the validate function that verifies that the email address is at least five characters and that it contains the @ symbol.

Hour 15

Using Graphics and Animation

One of the most challenging—and rewarding—uses of a programming language is creating graphic applications and games. In this hour, you'll look at some techniques you can use for graphic pages—or to add excitement to any Web page.

Of course, JavaScript is a relatively simple language and this is a relatively simple book, so you won't be learning how to write your own version of Quake in JavaScript. Nevertheless, JavaScript can perform some useful features with graphics and can even do simple animations.

In this hour, you'll learn how to use graphics and animation in JavaScript. You will cover the following topics:

- Using image maps with JavaScript
- How JavaScript uses objects to represent images
- Creating rollover images
- Loading images into the cache
- Creating a simple JavaScript animation

Using Image Maps with JavaScript

Image maps are a popular way to provide navigation for a site. They're images that are divided into a number of "hot spots," or areas that act as links. Using JavaScript, you can perform script commands when an area of the image is clicked.

 There are two types of image maps: client-side and server-side. Client-side maps define the linked areas of the image within the HTML document, and thus can be used with JavaScript. Server-side maps require a separate map definition file and are handled by Web servers.

As an example of using a client-side image map with JavaScript, let's create a simple image map menu for a fictional company. (The company's name isn't important, but it's obviously not a graphic design company.)

To create a client-side map, you need to do three things:

- Use your favorite graphics application to create the actual graphic as a GIF or JPEG image. (The sample image used in this example is available at this book's Web site, www.jsworkshop.com.)
- Create a MAP definition that describes areas in the image.
- Include the image map in the document, using the USEMAP attribute to point to the map definition.

Listing 15.1 shows the example client-side image map definition.

LISTING 15.1   USING A CLIENTSIDE IMAGE MAP WITH JAVASCRIPT.

```
1     <HTML>
2     <HEAD>
3     <TITLE>Image Map Example</TITLE>
4     <SCRIPT LANGUAGE="JavaScript">
5     function update(text) {
6         document.form1.text1.value = text;
7     }
8     </SCRIPT>
9     </HEAD>
10    <BODY>
11    <MAP NAME="map1">
12    <AREA SHAPE=RECT COORDS="14,15,151,87"
        HREF="javascript:update('service');"
13    onMouseOver="window.status='Service Department'; return true;">
14    <AREA SHAPE=RECT COORDS="162,16,283,85"
        HREF="javascript:update('sales');"
```

```
15    onMouseOver="window.status='Sales Department'; return true;">
16    <AREA SHAPE=RECT COORDS="294,15,388,87"
       HREF="javascript:update('info');"
17    onMouseOver="window.status='Information'; return true;">
18    <AREA SHAPE=RECT COORDS="13,98,79,178"
       HREF="javascript:update('email');"
19    onMouseOver="window.status='Email Us'; return true;">
20    <AREA SHAPE=RECT COORDS="92,97,223,177"
       HREF="javascript:update('products');"
21    onMouseOver="window.status='Products'; return true;">
22    <AREA SHAPE=RECT COORDS="235,98,388,177"
       HREF="javascript:update('our staff');"
23    onMouseOver="window.status='Our Staff'; return true;">
24    <AREA SHAPE=default HREF="javascript:update('No item selected.');"
25    onMouseOver="window.status='Please select an item.'; return true;">
26    </MAP>
27    <H1>Client-Side Image Map Example</H1>
28    <HR>
29    The image map below uses JavaScript functions in each of its areas.
30    Moving over an area will display information about it in the status
31    line. Clicking on an area places the name of the area in the text
32    field below the image map.
33    <HR>
34    <IMG SRC="imagemap.gif" USEMAP="#map1">
35    <HR>
36    <FORM NAME="form1">
37    <B>Clicked Item:</B>
38    <INPUT TYPE="text" NAME="text1" VALUE="Please select an item.">
39    </FORM>
40    <HR>
41    </BODY>
42    </HTML>
```

This script uses both javascript: links and event handlers to perform functions. Rather than link to an actual page, clicking on the areas will display a message in a text field (see Figure 15.1). In addition, the onMouseOver event handlers display a description in the status line for each area.

This program uses a single JavaScript function called update(), which simply places an item in the text field form1.text1. The text is sent directly by the link in each area definition.

FIGURE 15.1

*An image map in
JavaScript.*

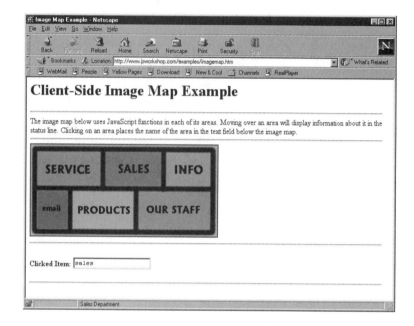

Using Dynamic Images in JavaScript

One of the most useful features of JavaScript is the capability to dynamically change images. This means you can create images that "magically" change, which could be used for clocks, image rollovers (images that change when you move the mouse over them), or even simple animations.

The images in a Web page are reflected in an array, just like form elements. By modifying the properties of the array items, you can replace the image with a different one. This enables you to create dynamically changing content on the page without even using frames or layers.

This technique isn't perfect for all applications. Before you get started, note the following limitations:

- You can only change existing images in the page—you can't add new ones or remove an image entirely.
- You can replace an image with a larger or smaller image, but this may not look good because the text won't be reformatted to match.
- Any image you use will have to be loaded from the server. This makes this technique impractical for complicated animations or large images.

Dynamic images are part of JavaScript 1.1, supported in Netscape 3.0 and later. Internet Explorer 4.0 and later also support this feature.

Working with the `images` Array

You can change images dynamically by using the `images` array. This array contains an item for each of the images defined on the page. Each image can also have a name. In the object hierarchy, each `image` object is a child of the `document` object.

Each `image` object has the following properties:

- `border` represents the `BORDER` attribute of the `<IMG>` tag. This defines whether a border is drawn around a linked image.

- `complete` is a flag that tells you whether the image has been completely loaded. This is a Boolean value (true or false).

- `height` and `width` reflect the corresponding image attributes. This is for information only; you can't change an image's size dynamically.

- `hspace` and `vspace` represent the corresponding image attributes, which define the image's placement on the page. Again, this is a read-only attribute.

- `name` is the image's name. You can define this with the `NAME` attribute in the image definition.

- `lowsrc` is the value of the `LOWSRC` attribute. This is a Netscape-specific attribute that enables you to specify a low-resolution image to be loaded before the "real" image.

- `src` is the image's source, or URL. You can change this value to change images dynamically.

For most purposes, the `src` attribute is the only one you'll use. However, you can also change the `lowsrc` attribute. This defines a low-resolution image to load first and will be used only when you change the `src` attribute.

The `image` object has no methods. It does have three event handlers you can use:

- The `onLoad` event occurs when the image finishes loading. (Since the `onLoad` event for the entire document is triggered when all images have finished loading, it's usually a better choice.)

- The `onAbort` event occurs if the user aborts the page before the image is loaded.

- The `onError` event occurs if the image file is not found or corrupt.

Preloading Images

Although you can't add an image to the page dynamically, you can create an independent image object. This enables you to specify an image that will be loaded and placed in the cache, but will not be displayed on the page.

This may sound useless, but it's a great way to work with modem-speed connections. Once you've preloaded an image, you can replace any of the images on the page with that image—and because it's already cached, the change happens instantly.

You can cache an image by creating a new image object, using the new keyword. Here's an example:

```
Image2 = new Image();
Image2.src = "arrow1.gif";
```

> You learned about the new keyword and its other uses for object-oriented programming in Hour 11, "Creating Custom Objects."

Creating Rollovers

The most common use of JavaScript's dynamic image feature is to create *rollovers*, which are images that change when you move the mouse pointer over them.

Rollovers are usually used for images that are links. Using this feature, you can highlight the current link with a different color or a border, or even by changing the image entirely.

You can turn an image into a rollover by adding an onMouseOver event handler that replaces the image with a highlighted version and an onMouseOut handler that returns the original image. Listing 15.2 shows an example that uses four images as rollovers.

LISTING 15.2 AN EXAMPLE OF ROLLOVERS.

```
1    <HTML>
2    <HEAD>
3    <TITLE>Roll Over, Spot. Good Dog.</TITLE>
4    </HEAD>
5    <BODY>
6    <H1>An Example of Rollovers</H1>
7    <HR>
8    The images below will change when you move the mouse over them.
9    <P>
10   <A HREF="home.html"
11   onMouseOver="document.images[0].src='home1.gif';"
12   onMouseOut="document.images[0].src='home.gif';">
13   <IMG src="home.gif" width=192 height=47 alt="" border="0">
```

```
14      </A>
15      <BR>
16      <A HREF="links.html"
17      onMouseOver="document.images[1].src='links1.gif';"
18      onMouseOut="document.images[1].src='links.gif';">
19      <IMG src="links.gif" width=93 height=42 alt="" border="0">
20      </A>
21      <BR>
22      <A HREF="guest.html"
23      onMouseOver="document.images[2].src='guest1.gif';"
24      onMouseOut="document.images[2].src='guest.gif';">
25      <IMG src="guest.gif" width=195 height=42 alt="" border="0">
26      </A>
27      <BR>
28      <A HREF="email.html"
29      onMouseOver="document.images[3].src='email1.gif';"
30      onMouseOut="document.images[3].src='email.gif';">
31      <IMG src="email.gif" width=185 height=42 alt="" border="0">
32      </A>
33      </BODY>
34      </HTML>
```

In this example, two versions of each image are used. For example, guest.gif is the guest book graphic, and guest1.gif is the same graphic with a border around it. Each link includes onMouseOver and onMouseOut handlers that change the image. Figure 15.2 shows Netscape Navigator's display of this script.

FIGURE 15.2

Using JavaScript for image rollovers.

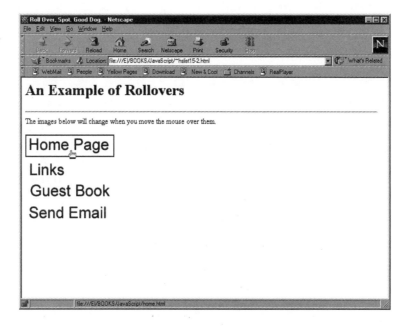

> You can highlight your images in other ways—for example, change their color. Another method is to place a smaller image to the side of each image that starts out as blank and changes to an arrow or other symbol when the mouse cursor is over the link image.

Workshop: Creating a Simple Animation

Although rollovers are undoubtedly the most practical use for JavaScript's dynamic images, you can also use the feature for simple animations. JavaScript isn't always the best way to do animations, but it's very useful in cases where you want to control the animation from a script.

> If you just want an animated image that repeats over and over, an animated GIF image is often a better choice. Many graphic software packages are available that automate the process of creating animated GIF images.

As a simple example of JavaScript animation, you will now create a script that moves an animated character across the browser display.

Creating the Images

The first step in creating a JavaScript animation is to create the images themselves. For this example, you will make an animated mouse move across the page. (You could use anything, of course, but this mouse is the only thing I can draw.)

The mouse animation uses a series of eight images, shown in Figure 15.3. To create these images, draw the mouse in a 100×100 square and then shift it to the left and right to create the various steps in the animation.

Call these images mouse1.gif through mouse8.gif. You will also need a blank image for those times when the mouse isn't there; call that mouse0.gif. All of these files are available on this book's Web site (www.jsworkshop.com), so you can try the example yourself.

FIGURE 15.3

The eight images for the mouse animation.

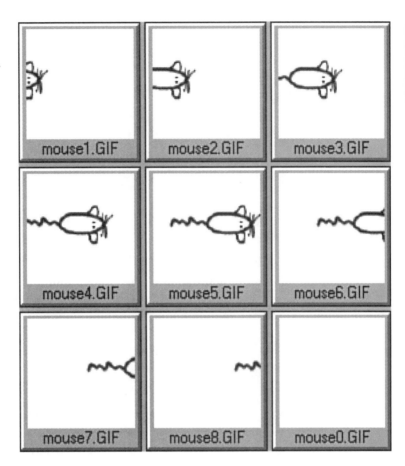

15

Creating the HTML Document

Next, you'll need to create the HTML document for the animation. You will animate the mouse through five adjacent images on the page so it appears to move from one end to the other. Here is the basic HTML to lay out the graphics:

```
<H1>Animation in JavaScript</H1>
<HR>
<CENTER>
<IMG src="mouse0.gif" width=100 height=100 alt="" border="0">
<IMG src="mouse0.gif" width=100 height=100 alt="" border="0">
<IMG src="mouse0.gif" width=100 height=100 alt="" border="0">
<IMG src="mouse0.gif" width=100 height=100 alt="" border="0">
<IMG src="mouse0.gif" width=100 height=100 alt="" border="0">
</CENTER>
```

At this point, all five of the images on the page are displaying the `mouse0.gif` image and are therefore invisible. Because these are the first five images on the page, the script will be able to access them as `images[0]` through `images[4]`.

Defining the Variables

To begin the actual script, define some global variables. Here is the beginning of the script:

```
var cbox=0;
var nbox=1;
var cimage=0;
var nimage=0;
```

The `cbox` variable will store a value from 0 to 4, indicating which of the five images the mouse is currently running through. Part of the mouse may protrude into the next image, so use the `nbox` variable to store the position of the right half of the mouse, if required.

The `cimage` variable will store the value of the image (from 1 to 8) in the current box. Similarly, `nimage` will store the value of the image for the part of the mouse that protrudes into the next box, if needed.

Stepping Through the Animation

Next, create the actual animation. You'll use a function called `next` to move the mouse to its next position and use the `setTimeout` method to call this function regularly.

The first step in the `next` function is to increment the image in the current box. Here is the function definition and the increment statement:

```
function next() {
cimage += 1;
```

After incrementing the value of `cimage`, the script needs to make sure it hasn't gone past 8, because there are eight images. The next part of the script checks for values greater than 8:

```
if (cimage > 8) {
        cimage = 4;
        document.images[cbox].src = "mouse0.gif";
        cbox = (cbox + 1) % 5;
        nbox = (cbox + 1) % 5;
}
```

If the current image has a value over 8, this code increments the value of `cbox` and assigns `nbox` to the next value. Both of these statements use the modulo (%) operator, which prevents the position from reaching a value greater than 4. Instead, the mouse will start over at the left side of the page.

The preceding script also resets cimage to 4. (Because the current box was previously the next box, it's already moved through images 1, 2, and 3.)

Next, the script needs to calculate the image for the next box, if any:

```
nimage = cimage - 5;
if (nimage <= 0) nimage = 0;
```

The first statement here assigns nimage to five less than cimage. If you look at the images in Figure 15.3, you'll notice that images 6, 7, and 8 match up with images 1, 2, and 3, respectively, to form a complete mouse. If the subtraction results in a negative value, there shouldn't be a next image, so assign 0 to nimage.

Finally, the end of the next function assigns the images indicated by cimage and nimage to the locations indicated by cbox and nbox:

```
document.images[cbox].src = "mouse" + cimage + ".gif";
document.images[nbox].src = "mouse" + nimage + ".gif";
window.setTimeout("next();",100);
}
```

The final statement here sets a timeout so that the next function will be called again in a tenth of a second. (You can increase or decrease this value to change the mouse's speed.)

Putting It All Together

You now have all of the components of a working animation script. Listing 15.3 shows the complete HTML document and script. The <BODY> tag includes an onLoad event handler that calls the next function after a timeout to get the animation started.

LISTING 15.3   THE COMPLETE ANIMATION EXAMPLE.

```
1     <HTML>
2     <HEAD>
3     <TITLE>Primitive Animation in JavaScript</TITLE>
4     <SCRIPT LANGUAGE="JavaScript">
5     var cbox=0;
6     var nbox=1;
7     var cimage=0;
8     var nimage=0;
9
10    function next() {
11    cimage += 1;
12    if (cimage > 8) {
13            cimage = 4;
14            document.images[cbox].src = "mouse0.gif";
15    cbox = (cbox + 1) % 5;
16    nbox = (cbox + 1) % 5;
17        }
```

continues

LISTING 15.3   CONTINUED

```
18    nimage = cimage - 5;
19    if (nimage <= 0) nimage = 0;
20    document.images[cbox].src = "mouse" + cimage + ".gif";
21    document.images[nbox].src = "mouse" + nimage + ".gif";
22    window.setTimeout("next();",100);
23    }
24    </SCRIPT>
25    </HEAD>
26    <BODY onLoad="next();">
27    <H1>Animation in JavaScript</H1>
28    <HR>
29    <CENTER>
30    <IMG src="mouse0.gif" width=100 height=100 alt="" border="0">
31    <IMG src="mouse0.gif" width=100 height=100 alt="" border="0">
32    <IMG src="mouse0.gif" width=100 height=100 alt="" border="0">
33    <IMG src="mouse0.gif" width=100 height=100 alt="" border="0">
34    <IMG src="mouse0.gif" width=100 height=100 alt="" border="0">
35    </CENTER>
36    <HR>
37    </BODY>
38    </HTML>
```

To test the script, load it into a browser. Be sure the HTML document is in the same directory as the mouse0 through mouse8 image files. If everything works, you should see a little mouse scurrying across the screen, as shown in Figure 15.4.

FIGURE 15.4

The animation example in action.

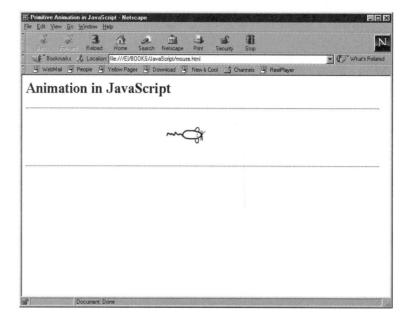

You may notice a slight gap between the five images as the mouse moves across the screen. To remedy this, remove the spaces and carriage returns between the <IMG> tags on lines 30–34, making them into one long line.

Summary

In this hour, you learned how to use JavaScript to work with graphics. JavaScript can work with image maps and can be used to create image rollovers and simple animations.

In the final hour of Part IV, you'll learn more techniques that are helpful in creating scripts for the Web: detecting browser versions and creating scripts that work on multiple browsers.

Q&A

Q I created an onMouseOver event handler for rollovers, and it works in Internet Explorer but not Netscape. What's wrong?

A This is probably because you used the onMouseOver handler in the <IMG> tag. This is supported only by Internet Explorer. For Netscape, you need to make the image a link and use event handlers in the <A> tag. (This will also work in Internet Explorer.)

Q Can I use rollovers in an image map?

A No, you'll need to replace the entire map image to do this. Usually, it's easier and faster to divide the map image into a number of sections and use those as the rollovers.

Q I need to eliminate an image entirely, rather than changing its source. Is there a way to do this?

A Not officially; you can't remove an image. However, you can replace it with a blank image of the same size, which should produce the same effect—and a one-color GIF is a very small file. Remember, you can't do anything that would change the layout of the text.

Q I created a JavaScript program on a page with images, and my event handlers don't seem to be working. What's wrong?

A JavaScript requires you to use HEIGHT and WIDTH attributes on all <IMG> tags. Adding them will most likely make the event handlers work properly. See Hour 21, "Debugging JavaScript Applications," for other debugging techniques.

Quiz

1. Which two event handlers are used for a rollover?

   a. onMouseOver and onClick

   b. onMouseOver and onMouseUnder

   c. onMouseOver and onMouseOut

2. Which types of image maps can be used with JavaScript?

   a. Server-side image maps.

   b. Client-side image maps.

   c. Both types.

3. What is the JavaScript object for the second image on a page?

   a. image[2]

   b. images[2]

   c. images[1]

Answers

1. c. You create rollovers with the onMouseOver and onMouseOut event handlers.

2. b. Client-side image maps can be used with JavaScript.

3. c. The second image on a page is represented by images[1].

Exercises

If you want to study JavaScript graphics further, perform these exercises:

- Change the image map example in Listing 15.1 to link to HTML documents rather than display alert messages.

- In the rollover example in Listing 15.2, try adding a third image that is displayed while the mouse is clicked. You can use the onMouseDown event handler.

- The animated mouse in Listing 15.3 may get off to a rough start if it's used over an Internet connection, because the images won't all load immediately. Add a function to preload the images using the technique you learned earlier in this hour.

HOUR 16

Creating Browser-Specific Scripts

Welcome to the fourth hour of Part IV. Up until now, most of the scripts you've written will work in the latest versions of either of today's most popular browsers: Netscape Navigator and Internet Explorer (IE). Between these two, your scripts will work for a vast majority of the Web audience.

As you move to Part V, however, you'll start working with topics that aren't so compatible. The latest features, such as channels and layers, tend to work differently on different browsers, and some features are specific to one or the other.

Although you may be tempted to take the easy way out and make your pages require Netscape, there is another solution. Using JavaScript, you can differentiate between browsers, allowing you to support all of them—either in the same or separate pages.

Hour 16 covers the following topics:

- Using JavaScript to get browser information
- Displaying browser details with JavaScript
- Making a page browser specific
- Dealing with browsers without JavaScript support
- Creating a script for multiple browser support

Reading Browser Information

In Hour 10, "Working with Browser Objects," you learned about the various objects (such as `window` and `document`) that represent portions of the browser window and the current Web document. JavaScript also includes an object called `navigator` that you can use to read information about the user's browser.

The `navigator` object isn't part of Netscape's object hierarchy, so you can refer to it directly. It includes a number of properties, each of which tells you something about the browser. These include the following:

- `navigator.appCodeName` is the browser's internal code name, usually `"Mozilla"`.
- `navigator.appName` is the browser's name, usually `"Netscape"` or `"Microsoft Internet Explorer"`.
- `navigator.appVersion` is the version of Netscape being used—for example, `"4.0(Win95;I)"`.
- `navigator.userAgent` is the user-agent header, a string that the browser sends to the Web server when requesting a Web page. It includes the entire version information, for example `"Mozilla/4.0(Win95;I)"`.
- `navigator.language` is the language (such as English or Spanish) of the browser. This is stored as a two-letter code, such as `"en"` for English. If you create pages in multiple languages, you can use this property to display the correct page for the user's language.
- `navigator.platform` is the computer platform of the current browser. This is a short string, such as `"Win16"`, `"Win32"`, or `"MacPPC"`. You can use this to enable any platform-specific features (for example, ActiveX components).

You will usually use these properties in an `if` statement. For example, the following statement sends the user to a different URL if he is not using Netscape 4.*x*:

```
if (navigator.userAgent.indexOf("Mozilla/4") == -1)
    window.location="non_netscape.html";
```

As you might have guessed, the navigator object is named after Netscape Navigator, the browser that originally supported JavaScript. Fortunately, this object is also supported by Internet Explorer.

Displaying Browser Information

As an example of how to read the navigator object's properties, Listing 16.1 shows a script that displays a list of the properties and their values for the current browser.

LISTING 16.1   A SCRIPT TO DISPLAY INFORMATION ABOUT THE BROWSER.

```
1    <HTML>
2    <HEAD>
3    <TITLE>Browser Information</TITLE>
4    </HEAD>
5    <BODY>
6    <H1>Browser Information</H1>
7    <HR>
8    <P>
9    The <B>navigator</B> object contains the following information
10   about the browser you are using.
11   </P>
12   <UL>
13   <SCRIPT LANGUAGE="JavaScript">
14   document.write("<LI><B>Code Name:</B> " + navigator.appCodeName);
15   document.write("<LI><B>App Name:</B> " + navigator.appName);
16   document.write("<LI><B>App Version:</B> " + navigator.appVersion);
17   document.write("<LI><B>User Agent:</B> " + navigator.userAgent);
18   document.write("<LI><B>Language:</B> " + navigator.language);
19   document.write("<LI><B>Platform:</B> " + navigator.platform);
20   </SCRIPT>
21   </UL>
22   <HR>
23   </BODY>
24   </HTML>
```

This script includes a basic HTML document. A script is used within the body of the document (lines 13 to 20) to display each of the properties of the navigator object using the document.write statement.

To try this script, load it into the browser of your choice. If you have more than one browser or browser version handy, try it in each one. Netscape's display of the script is shown in Figure 16.1.

FIGURE 16.1

FIGURE 16.1

*Netscape displays
the browser
information script.*

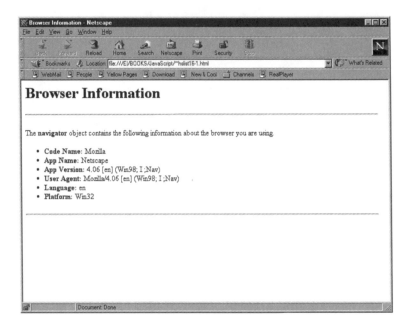

Dealing with Dishonest Browsers

If you ran the browser information script in Listing 16.1 using Internet Explorer, you
probably got a surprise. Figure 16.2 shows how Internet Explorer displays the script.

FIGURE 16.2

*Internet Explorer
displays the browser
information script.*

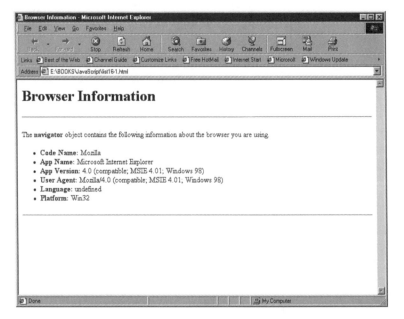

16

There are two unexpected things about this display. First of all, the `navigator.language` property is listed as undefined. This isn't much of a surprise because this property isn't yet supported by Internet Explorer.

More importantly, you'll notice that the word `Mozilla` appears in the code name and user agent fields. The full user agent string reads as follows:

```
Mozilla/4.0 (compatible; MSIE 4.01; Windows 98)
```

What is this? Some sort of secret endorsement of Netscape by Microsoft? Some sort of government conspiracy? Is Netscape's mythical monster, Mozilla, hiding somewhere under Microsoft's Redmond campus?

As it turns out, Microsoft did have a good reason for this. At the height of the browser wars, about the time Netscape 3.0 and IE 3.0 came out, it was becoming common to see "Netscape only" pages. Some Webmasters who used features such as frames and JavaScript set their servers to turn away browsers without `Mozilla` in their user agent string. The problem with this was that most of these features were also supported by Internet Explorer.

Microsoft solved this problem by making IE's user agent read `Mozilla`, with the word `compatible` in parentheses. This allows IE users to view those pages, but still includes enough details to tell Web servers which browser is in use.

Many Web servers keep statistics about which browsers people use to access them. When Microsoft changed IE's user agent string, many of the statistics programs were not aware of the change. As a result, they counted a visit by IE as a visit by Netscape. Ironically, Microsoft's move to make their browser more compatible caused Netscape's market share statistics to improve, at least for a while.

Although this is an interesting episode in the annals of the browser wars, what does it mean to you? Well, you'll need to be careful when your scripts are trying to differentiate between IE and Netscape. For example, the following statement was presented earlier in this hour as an example of the `navigator` properties:

```
if (navigator.userAgent.indexOf("Mozilla/4") == -1)
   window.location="non_netscape.html";
```

As it turns out, this statement checks for the string `Mozilla/4`—which will actually allow either Netscape 4.*x* or Internet Explorer 4.*x*. This isn't necessarily a bad thing, but what if your page definitely requires Netscape 4.0? In that case, you can be more specific:

```
if (navigator.appName.indexOf("Netscape") == -1)
|| (navigator.appVersion.indexOf("4.0") == -1)
window.location="non_netscape.html";
```

This longer if statement first checks the navigator.appName property, which will contain the appropriate value of Netscape or Microsoft. Next, it checks the navigator.appVersion property. If the name isn't Netscape or the version isn't 4.0, it sends the user to another page.

> This example uses the indexOf string method, which searches for a string within another string. To refresh your memory about this and other string functions, see Hour 6, "Using Strings and Arrays."

Supporting Browsers with JavaScript

If you're using features that are on the cutting edge and require a particular browser or version, there are several ways of using JavaScript to steer users in the right direction. The following sections explain three different methods.

Creating a Browser-Specific Page

The easiest solution—and the least polite—is to pick a browser version to support and kick out everyone who isn't using it. This is easy to do with a script in the header or body of the page. Listing 16.2 shows a simple example.

LISTING 16.2 CREATING A BROWSER-SPECIFIC PAGE.

```
1    <SCRIPT>
2    if (navigator.appName.indexOf("Netscape") == -1)
     || (navigator.appVersion.indexOf("4.5") == -1)
     window.alert("Download Netscape now, or else.");
3    window.location = "http://www.netscape.com/";
4    </SCRIPT>
```

If you're using a non-Netscape browser or a version of Netscape earlier than 4.5, this script displays a rude message and sends you to Netscape's Web page. Needless to say, there are more polite ways of saying this.

If you must make a page browser specific, be sure you have a good reason to do so. If other browsers can display the page's content—even if your cute buttons or animations don't work—you should support them. Few users are willing to download a new browser just for your page, so you'll be losing a good part of your audience.

Branching to Separate Pages

In most cases, it's not hard to support more than one browser. If you want to fine-tune your pages to display perfectly on both Netscape and Internet Explorer, one convenient way is to create a separate version of the page for each browser. You can then use JavaScript to send the user to the appropriate page.

Listing 16.3 shows a script that could be placed on the introductory page of a site. After detecting the browser version, it sends the user to the appropriate page.

LISTING 16.3 SENDING BROWSERS TO SPECIFIC PAGES.

```
1    <SCRIPT>
2    if (navigator.appName.indexOf("Netscape") > -1)
       && (navigator.appVersion.indexOf("4") > -1)
       window.location = "netscape.html";
3    if (navigator.appName.indexOf("Microsoft") > -1)
       && (navigator.appVersion.indexOf("4") > -1)
       window.location = "ie.html";
4    window.location = "default.html";
5    </SCRIPT>
```

This script sends the user to one of three pages: `netscape.html` for Netscape 4.*x*, `ie.html` for Internet Explorer 4.*x*, or `default.html` for any other browser.

You might have noticed that there is no third if statement in Listing 16.3. The statement to send the user to default.html is unconditional. This works because if either of the if statements were true, the browser would have been sent to a different page, immediately aborting the current script. The only browsers that make it to the last line are those that aren't detected specifically.

Making a Multiple-Browser Page

The third alternative is to make a single page that supports more than one type of browser. You can use a script in the page to detect the browser, and then use script commands to include different HTML codes in the document, depending on the browser.

This method uses only one document, but you might find that it transforms a long, complicated page into a long, *impossibly* complicated page. A short example of a page that does this is included in the "Workshop: Scripting for Multiple Browsers" section of this hour.

 Some more sophisticated techniques for dealing with multiple browsers are presented in Hour 19, "Creating Cross-Browser Scripts."

Supporting Non-JavaScript Browsers

What about browsers that don't support JavaScript at all? You can't detect them with a script because they won't even *run* the script. However, there are ways of dealing with these browsers.

With 99% of Web users using a recent copy of Netscape or IE, where are the non-JavaScript browsers? First, there are still some older browsers out there, and text browsers such as Lynx don't support scripting. Second, and more importantly, many Netscape and IE users have JavaScript support turned off, either due to security concerns or just to avoid watching scrolling messages in the status line.

In the last year or two, a wide variety of new browsers has also emerged. Palmtop computers, such as 3Com's PalmPilot and the Windows CE platform, support Web browsing, as do some cellular phones and other appliances. Since none of these support JavaScript, it's even more important to provide an alternative when possible.

One way to be friendly to non-JavaScript browsers is to use the <NOSCRIPT> tag. Supported in Netscape 3.0 and later, this tag displays a message to non-JavaScript browsers. Browsers that support JavaScript ignore the text between the <NOSCRIPT> tags, while others display it. Here is a simple example:

```
<NOSCRIPT>
This page requires JavaScript. You can either download a copy
of Netscape from <A HREF="http://www.netscape.com/"> their page,
or switch to the <A HREF="nojs.html">Non-JavaScript</A> version of
this page.
</NOSCRIPT>
```

The main problem with using <NOSCRIPT> is that Netscape 2.0 will display the text between the tags, even though it does support some JavaScript. There's a way to solve this problem, but it's a bit tricky. Listing 16.4 shows a script that can detect non-JavaScript browsers and display a message.

LISTING 16.4 DETECTING NON-JAVASCRIPT BROWSERS.

```
1   <SCRIPT LANGUAGE='JavaScript'>
2       <!-- //hide from old browsers
3       ...script commands go here...
4       /* (start JavaScript comment, end HTML comment)
5       -->
6       You're using a non-JavaScript browser! Shame on you.
7       <!-- */ // -->
8   </SCRIPT>
```

This uses the HTML comment tags (<!-- and -->) to hide the script commands from old browsers. It then uses JavaScript comment tags (/* and */) to enclose the message for non-JavaScript browsers, so it will be disregarded by browsers that support JavaScript.

An easier alternative is to send users with JavaScript support to another page. This can be accomplished with a single JavaScript statement:

```
<SCRIPT LANGUAGE="JavaScript">
window.location="JavaScript.html";
</SCRIPT>
```

This simply sends the user to a different page. If the browser doesn't support JavaScript, of course, the script won't be executed.

The final alternative is to simply make your scripts unobtrusive. Use comments to hide them from other browsers, as described in Hour 4, "How JavaScript Programs Work," and be sure they're not essential to navigate or read the page.

Workshop: Scripting for Multiple Browsers

As an example of the techniques you learned in this chapter, you can create a script that works on multiple browsers. Suppose you have a MIDI music file that you want to play in the background while users look at your page.

16

MIDI stands for *Musical Instrument Digital Interface*, and is a standard that lets computers talk to musical instruments, such as synthesizers. It's also a common format for music files that can be played by computers.

Internet Explorer 3.0 supports the <BGSOUND> HTML tag, which you can use to play a MIDI file in the background. Netscape doesn't support this tag, but browsers with the proper plug-in installed can play a MIDI file using the <EMBED> tag. Internet Explorer 4.0 also supports <EMBED>.

Using JavaScript, you can make a document that automatically includes the appropriate tag for the browser in use. Listing 16.5 shows the multiple-browser document.

LISTING 16.5   USING BACKGROUND MUSIC ON MULTIPLE BROWSERS.

```
 1    <HTML>
 2    <HEAD>
 3    <TITLE>Background Music for Multiple Browsers</TITLE>
 4    </HEAD>
 5    <BODY>
 6    <H1>Background Music</H1>
 7    <P>This document includes a background music file. It will play on
 8    Internet Explorer 3.0, or on Netscape or IE4 with the appropriate
 9    plug-in.</P>
10    <SCRIPT LANGUAGE="JavaScript">
11    if (navigator.appName.indexOf("Microsoft") > -1)
         && (navigator.appVersion.indexOf("3") > -1)
12        document.write("<BGSOUND SRC='polka.mid'>");
13    if (navigator.appVersion.indexOf("4") > -1)
14        document.write("<EMBED SRC='polka.mid'>");
15    </SCRIPT>
16    </BODY>
17    </HTML>
```

The script begins on line 9. Lines 10 and 11 check for Internet Explorer 3.0 and use `document.write` to include the <BGSOUND> tag in the document. Lines 12 and 13 check for a 4.0 browser and include the <EMBED> tag instead. For browsers that don't match either `if` statement, no extra tag is included.

Summary

In this hour, you learned various ways to use JavaScript to read information about the user's browser and to accommodate multiple browsers.

You've reached the end of Part IV and are well on your way to becoming a JavaScript expert. In the next four hours, you'll learn some of the cutting-edge browser features that can be used with JavaScript—style sheets, layers, channels, and plug-ins.

16

Q&A

Q What if my page requires a particular plug-in? Is there a way to detect that with JavaScript?

A Yes, the `navigator` object includes properties for detecting plug-ins. These are described in Hour 20, "Working with Multimedia and Plug-Ins." However, this method doesn't work in Internet Explorer.

Q Can I detect the user's email address using the `navigator` object or another technique?

A No, there is no reliable way to detect users' email addresses using a non-signed script. (If there was, you would get hundreds of advertisements in your mailbox every day from companies that detected your address as you browsed their pages.) You can use a signed script to obtain the user's email address, but this requires the user's permission.

Q Do I need to worry about browsers besides Netscape and Internet Explorer, since they don't support JavaScript anyway?

A Actually, there is a Windows browser called Opera that supports JavaScript, and you never know when a new browser may come out. It's always best to support all of them if you can.

Quiz

1. Which of the following `navigator` object properties is the same in both Netscape and IE?

   a. `navigator.appCodeName`

   b. `navigator.appName`

   c. `navigator.appVersion`

2. Which of the following is something you *can't* do with JavaScript?

   a. Send users of Netscape to a different page.

   b. Send users of IE to a different page.

   c. Send users of non-JavaScript browsers to a different page.

3. What does the <NOSCRIPT> tag do?

   a. Encloses text to be displayed by non-JavaScript browsers.

   b. Prevents scripts on the page from executing.

   c. Describes certain low-budget movies.

Answers

1. a. The navigator.appCodeName property is the same (Mozilla) in the latest Netscape and Microsoft browsers.

2. c. You can't use JavaScript to send users of non-JavaScript browsers to a different page because the script won't be executed at all.

3. a. The <NOSCRIPT> tag encloses text to be displayed by non-JavaScript browsers.

Exercises

If you want to gain more experience detecting browsers in JavaScript, perform these exercises:

- Create a script (similar to Listing 16.3) that sends users of IE 4.0 or Netscape 4.0 to one page and users of IE 3.0 and Netscape 3.0 to a different page.

- The example in Listing 16.5 checks for Microsoft or Netscape browsers, but IE 2.0 and Netscape 2.0 don't support MIDI files. Change the if statements to also check for the right version.

PART V

Scripting Advanced Web Features

Hour

Hour **17**

Working with Style Sheets

Welcome to Part V! In the next four hours, you'll learn how to use some of the more recent additions to the Web developer's arsenal and how to use JavaScript to control these features.

Hour 17 begins with an introduction to style sheets, which you can use to take more control over how the browser displays your document. You can also use JavaScript with style sheets to change the display dynamically.

Hour 17 covers the following topics:

- The components of Dynamic HTML
- Why style sheets are needed
- How to define Cascading Style Sheets (CSS)
- How to use a style sheet in a document
- Using an external style sheet file
- Defining style sheets with JavaScript
- Using JavaScript to change styles

Introducing Dynamic HTML

Dynamic HTML, or DHTML, is a standard, supported to some extent by Netscape and Microsoft browsers, for several cutting-edge Web features. These include the following:

- *Style sheets* allow you to control the appearance of a Web page and its elements.
- *Layers* allow you to position portions of pages.
- *Dynamic fonts* allow you to define a downloadable font to be used to display a page. While the font is used to display the document, it is not copied to the user's computer.

In this hour, you'll learn how to define and use style sheets, and how to use JavaScript to work with styles. In Hour 18, "Creating Dynamic Pages with Layers," you'll learn about layers.

Style and Substance

If you've ever tried to make a really good-looking Web page, you've probably encountered some problems. First of all, HTML doesn't give you very much control over a page's appearance. For example, you can't change the amount of space between words—in fact, you can't even use two spaces between words because they'll be converted to a single space.

Second, even when you do your best to make a perfect-looking document using HTML, you will find that it doesn't necessarily display the same way on all browsers—or even on different computers running the same browser.

The reason for these problems is simple: HTML was never meant to handle such things as layout, justification, and spacing. HTML deals with a document's *structure*—in other words, how the document is divided into paragraphs, headings, lists, and other elements.

This isn't a bad thing. In fact, it's one of the most powerful features of HTML. You only define the structure of the document, so it can be displayed in all sorts of different ways without changing its meaning. For example, a well-written HTML document can be displayed in Netscape or Internet Explorer, which generally treat elements the same way—there is a space between paragraphs, headings are in big, bold text, and so on.

Because HTML only defines the structure, the same document can be displayed in a text-based browser, such as Lynx. In this case, the different elements will be displayed differently, but you can still tell which text is a heading, which is a list, and so on.

Text-based browsers aren't the only alternate way of displaying HTML. Browsers designed for the blind can read a Web page using a speech synthesizer, with different voices or sounds that indicate the different elements.

As you should now understand, HTML is very good at its job—defining a document's structure. Not surprisingly, using this language to try to control the document's *presentation* will only drive you crazy.

Fortunately, the World Wide Web Consortium (W3C) realized that Web authors need to control the layout and presentation of documents. This resulted in the *Cascading Style Sheets (CSS)* recommendation.

CSS adds a number of features to standard HTML to control style and appearance. More importantly, it does this without affecting HTML's ability to describe document structures. While style sheets still won't make your document look 100% identical on all browsers and all platforms, it is certainly a step in the right direction.

17

Let's look at a real-world example. If you're browsing the Web with a CSS-supported browser and come across a page that uses CSS, you'll see the document exactly as it was intended. You can also turn off your browser's support for style sheets if you'd rather view all of the pages in the same consistent way.

Defining and Using CSS Styles

To use styles on a page, you first need to define the styles, using the <STYLE> tag, and then indicate the styles that should be used with various HTML elements.

The main HTML tag you'll use to define style sheets is the <STYLE> tag, which starts a listing of styles. The initial <STYLE> tag specifies the type of style sheet, and the </STYLE> tag ends the style definitions. For example, the following tag starts a style definition using CSS:

```
<STYLE TYPE="text/css">
```

Rather than using a style sheet defined in the document header, you can specify a style for an individual element only. For example, the following HTML tag represents a level 1 header colored blue:

```
<H1 STYLE="color: blue">This is a blue header.</H1>
```

You should place the <STYLE> tags in the <HEAD> section of the HTML document. In the following sections, you'll learn how to create style rules and about the various parameters you can set using CSS.

Creating Rules

Each line within the `<STYLE>` tags is called a *rule*. To create a rule, you specify the HTML elements that it will affect, as well as a list of properties and values that control the appearance of those elements. We'll look at the properties later in this section.

As a simple example, the following style sheet contains a single rule—all level 1 headings are blue:

```
<STYLE TYPE="text/css">
H1 {color: blue}
</STYLE>
```

You can also specify multiple HTML tags to affect, as well as multiple styles. For example, the following style sheet specifies that all headers are blue, italic, and centered:

```
<STYLE TYPE="text/css">
H1,H2,H3,H4,H5,H6 {color: blue;
                   font-style: italic;
                   text-align: center }
</STYLE>
```

You can specify any HTML element in a rule, and you can even affect large portions of the page with a single rule. If you make a rule that sets the style of the `<BODY>` tag, it will affect the entire document. This becomes the default rule for the document; you can override it with the styles of elements within the body of the page.

Aligning Text

One of the most useful features of style sheets is the capability to change the spacing and alignment of text. Most of these features aren't available using standard HTML. You can use the following properties to change the alignment and spacing of text:

- `letter-spacing`—Specifies the spacing between letters. (Internet Explorer 4 only)
- `text-decoration`—Allows you to create lines over, under, or through the text, or to choose blinking text.
- `vertical-align`—Allows you to move the element up or down to align with other elements on the same line. (Internet Explorer 4 only)
- `text-align`—Specifies the justification of text. This can be `left`, `right`, `center`, or `justify`.
- `text-transform`—Changes the capitalization of text. `capitalize` makes the first letter of each word uppercase; `uppercase` makes *all* letters uppercase; and `lowercase` makes all letters lowercase.

- `text-indent`—Allows you to specify the amount of indentation for paragraphs and other elements.

- `line-height`—This allows you to specify the distance between the top of one line of text and the top of the next.

Changing Colors and Background Images

You can also use style sheets to gain more control over the colors and background images used on your Web page. CSS includes the following properties for this purpose:

- `color`—Specifies the text color of an element. This is useful for emphasizing text or for using a specific color scheme for the document.

- `background-color`—Specifies the background color of an element. By setting this value, you can make paragraphs, table cells, and other elements with unique background colors.

- `background-image`—Specifies a GIF format image to be used as the background for the element.

- `background-repeat`—Specifies whether the background image is repeated (tiled). The image can be repeated horizontally, vertically, or both. (Internet Explorer 4 only)

- `background-attachment`—Controls whether the background image scrolls when you scroll through the document. `fixed` means that the background image stays still while the document scrolls; `scroll` means the image scrolls with the document (like background images on normal Web documents). Currently, this feature is supported only by Internet Explorer 4.

- `background-position`—Allows you to offset the position of the background image. (Internet Explorer 4 only)

- `background`—This provides a quick way to set all of the background elements in this list. You can specify all of the attributes in a single `background` rule.

Working with Fonts

Style sheets also allow you to control the fonts used on the Web document and how they are displayed. You can use the following properties to control fonts:

- `font-family`—Specifies the name of a font, such as `arial` or `helvetica`, to use with the element. Because not all users have the same fonts installed, you can list several fonts. The CSS specification also supports several generic font families that are guaranteed to be available: `serif`, `sans-serif`, `cursive`, `fantasy`, and `mono-space`.

17

- `font-style`—Specifies the style of a font, such as `normal`, `italic`, or `oblique`.

- `font-variant`—This value is `normal` for normal text, and `small-caps` to display lowercase letters as small capitals.

- `font-weight`—Allows you to specify normal or bold text. You can also specify a numeric font weight for a specific amount of boldness.

- `font-size`—The point size of the font.

- `font`—This is a quick way to set all of the font properties in this list. You can list all of the values in a single `font` rule.

Margins and Borders

Last but not least, you can use style sheets to control the general layout of the page. The following properties affect margins, borders, and the width and height of elements on the Web page:

- `margin-top, margin-bottom, margin-left, margin-right`—These properties specify the margins of the element. You can specify the margins as an exact number or as a percentage of the page's width.

- `margin`—Allows you to specify a single value for all four of the margins.

- `width`—Specifies the width of an element, such as an image.

- `height`—Specifies the height of an element.

- `float`—Allows the text to flow around an element. This is particularly useful with images or tables.

- `clear`—Specifies that the text should stop flowing around a floating image.

> Along with these features, CSS style sheets allow you to create sections of the document that can be positioned independently. This feature is described in Hour 18.

Creating a Simple Style Sheet

As an example of CSS, you can now create a Web page that uses a wide variety of styles:

- For the entire body, the text is blue.

- Paragraphs are centered and have a wide margin on either side.

- Levels 1, 2, and 3 headings are red.

- Bullet lists are boldface and green by default.

Listing 17.1 shows the CSS style sheet to define these properties, using the <STYLE> tags.

LISTING 17.1   A SIMPLE CSS STYLE SHEET.

```
1    <STYLE>
2    BODY {color: blue}
3    P {text-align: center;
4        margin-left:20%;
5        margin-right:20%}
6    H1, H2, H3 {color: red}
7    UL {color: green;
8        font-weight: bold}
9    </STYLE>
```

Here's a rundown of how this style sheet works:

- Lines 1 and 9 are the <STYLE> tags that enclose the style sheet.
- Line 2 sets the body's default text color to blue.
- Lines 3, 4, and 5 define the style for paragraphs.
- Line 6 defines the style for H1, H2, and H3 tags.
- Lines 7 and 8 define a style for bullet lists.

To show how this style sheet works, Listing 17.2 shows a document that includes this style sheet and a few examples of overriding styles for particular elements. Figure 17.1 shows Netscape Communicator's display of this example.

LISTING 17.2   AN EXAMPLE OF A DOCUMENT USING CSS STYLE SHEETS.

```
1    <HTML>
2    <HEAD><TITLE>Style Sheet Example</TITLE>
3    <STYLE>
4    BODY {color: blue}
5    P {text-align: center;
6        margin-left:20%;
7        margin-right:20%}
8    H1, H2, H3 {color: red}
9    UL {color: green;
10       font-weight: bold}
11   </STYLE>
12   </HEAD>
13   <BODY>
14   <H1>Welcome to this page</H1>
15   <P>The above heading is red, since we specified that H1-H3 headers
```

continues

17

LISTING 17.2   CONTINUED

```
16    are red. This paragraph is blue, which is the default color for
17    the entire body. It's also centered and has 20% margins, which we
18    specified as the default for paragraphs.
19    </P>
20    <P STYLE="color:black">This paragraph has black text, because it
21    overrides the default color in the paragraph tag. We didn't override
22    the centering, so this paragraph is also centered.</P>
23    <UL>
24    <LI>This is a bullet list.
25    <LI>It's green and bold, because we specified those defaults for
        bullet lists.
26    <LI STYLE="color:red">This item is red, overriding the default.
27    <LI>This item is back to normal.
28    </UL>
29    <P>This is another paragraph with the default paragraph style.</P>
30    </BODY>
31    </HTML>
```

FIGURE 17.1

The style sheet example as displayed by Netscape.

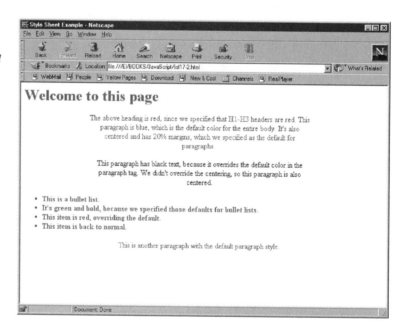

Using External Style Sheets

The preceding example only changes a few aspects of the HTML document's appearance, but it adds about 10 lines to its length. If you were trying to make a very stylish page and had defined new styles for all of the attributes, you would end up with a very long and complicated document.

For this reason, you can use a CSS style sheet from a separate file in your document. This makes your document short and to the point. More importantly, it allows you to define a single style sheet and use it to control the appearance of all of the pages on your site.

To define an external style sheet, place the commands you would normally use between the <STYLE> tags in a separate file. You can then refer to that file using the <LINK> tag in the header of one or more documents:

```
<LINK REL=STYLESHEET TYPE="text/css" HREF="style.css">
```

This tag refers to an external CSS-type style sheet stored in the style.css file.

Using JavaScript Style Sheets

Netscape also supports an alternate type of style sheet syntax called *JavaScript style sheets*, or *JSS*. For the most part, JSS style sheets can use the same styles as CSS style sheets, but they use a JavaScript-based syntax. This type of style sheet is not supported by Internet Explorer.

To begin a JSS style sheet, use this tag:

```
<STYLE TYPE="text/javascript">
```

Within the <STYLE> tags, you specify each element as an object. Netscape supports three basic objects: tags, which includes all of the HTML tags, classes, which includes classes you define, and ids, which includes ID codes for individual elements. All of these are children of the document object.

To change the style for an HTML tag using JavaScript syntax, you specify the tag as an object. For example, the following statement changes the color of H1 headings to blue:

```
document.tags.H1.color = "blue";
```

17

Workshop: Creating Dynamic Styles

Using the JavaScript style sheet objects, you can create a page that allows you to control the colors used in displaying a frame. You will create a document with two frames: a top frame with a form to control the colors, and a bottom frame with the text that will be displayed in the selected colors.

To begin, you'll need a document to define the frames. Listing 17.3 shows a basic frame definition.

LISTING 17.3   THE FRAMESET DOCUMENT FOR THE DYNAMIC STYLES EXAMPLE.

```
1: <HTML>
2: <HEAD>
3: <TITLE>Dynamic Styles</TITLE>
4: </HEAD>
5: <FRAMESET ROWS="*,*">
6: <FRAME NAME="topframe" SRC="top.html">
7: <FRAME NAME="botframe" SRC="bottom.html">
8: </FRAMESET>
9: </HTML>
```

This example is also a good example of communicating between frames in scripts. See Hour 13, "Using Windows and Frames," for details about frame objects.

Next, Listing 17.4 shows the HTML document for the upper frame. You should save this document as top.html so that the preceding frameset document can refer to it.

LISTING 17.4   THE TOP FRAME OF THE DYNAMIC STYLES EXAMPLE.

```
 1    <HTML>
 2    <HEAD>
 3    <TITLE>Controlling Styles with JavaScript</TITLE>
 4    </HEAD>
 5    <BODY>
 6    <H1>Controlling Styles with JavaScript</H1>
 7    <HR>
 8    Select the color for paragraphs and headings, then press the Reload
 9    button. The colors you specified will be used in the document
10    displayed below.
11    <FORM NAME="form1">
12    <B>Body text color: </B>
```

```
13    <SELECT name="body">
14       <option value="red">Red</option>
15       <option value="blue">Blue</option>
16       <option value="green">Green</option>
17       <option value="yellow">Yellow</option>
18       <option value="black">Black</option>
19    </SELECT>
20    <BR>
21    <B>Heading color: </B>
22    <SELECT name="heading">
23       <option value="red">Red</option>
24       <option value="blue">Blue</option>
25       <option value="green">Green</option>
26       <option value="yellow">Yellow</option>
27       <option value="black">Black</option>
28    </SELECT>
29    <INPUT TYPE="BUTTON" VALUE="Reload"
30    onClick="parent.botframe.location.reload();">
31    </FORM>
32    </BODY>
33    </HTML>
```

17

This document includes a form with two drop-down lists to select the heading and body colors. On line 30, a single JavaScript statement is used to reload the bottom document. The script in the bottom document will handle the changing of styles.

Finally, Listing 17.5 shows the bottom frame document, which you should save as bottom.html. This uses a script to get the current value of the two selection lists and assign the values to the body and heading 1 color properties. The selected colors are also displayed in the body of the document.

LISTING 17.5   THE BOTTOM FRAME FOR THE DYNAMIC STYLES EXAMPLE.

```
 1: <HTML>
 2: <HEAD>
 3: <TITLE>Controlling Styles with JavaScript</TITLE>
 4: <STYLE TYPE="text/javascript">
 5: i = parent.topframe.document.form1.heading.selectedIndex;
 6: headcolor = parent.topframe.document.form1.heading.options[i].value;
 7: document.tags.H1.color = headcolor;
 8: i = parent.topframe.document.form1.body.selectedIndex;
 9: doccolor = parent.topframe.document.form1.body.options[i].value;
10: document.tags.BODY.color = doccolor;
11: </STYLE>
12: </HEAD>
13: <BODY>
```

continues

LISTING 17.5   CONTINUED

```
14: <H1>This is a heading. It is
15: <SCRIPT LANGUAGE="JavaScript">
16: document.write(" " + headcolor + ".");
17: </SCRIPT>
18: </H1>
19: <P>This is a paragraph of regular text. Blah, blah, blah.
20: Blah blah, blah blah blah. The end.</P>
21: <P>This is the second paragraph.
22: <SCRIPT LANGUAGE="JavaScript">
23: document.write(" The regular text is " + doccolor + ".");
24: </SCRIPT>
25: </P>
26: </BODY>
27: </HTML>
```

After you've prepared all three of these documents, load Listing 17.3 into the browser. Select the colors and press the Reload button. Figure 17.2 shows a typical display of this document after the colors have been changed.

FIGURE 17.2

The dynamic styles example in action.

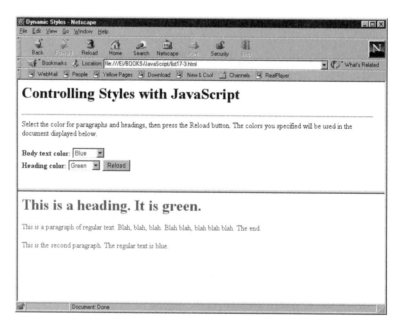

The example in Listing 17.3 is Netscape specific, due to the way it refers to style sheet elements. See Hour 19, "Creating Cross-Browser Scripts," for an explanation of how to make this script work in Internet Explorer.

Summary

In this hour, you used style sheets to control the appearance of Web documents. You learned the CSS and JavaScript syntax for style sheets and used JavaScript to control the styles of a document.

In Hour 18, you will move on to layers, another component of Dynamic HTML.

Q&A

Q What's the difference between changing the appearance of text with traditional tags, such as `<B>` and `<I>`, and using a style sheet?

A Functionally, there is no difference. If you're only using simple boldface, italics, and such, it's probably best to avoid style sheets. On the other hand, if you need to use more specific formatting, style sheets are ideal.

Q What happens if two style sheets affect the same text?

A The CSS specification is designed to allow style sheets to overlap, or cascade. Thus, you can specify a style for the body of the document and override it for specific elements, such as headings and paragraphs. You can even go one step further and override the style for one particular instance of an element.

Q What if users don't like the styles I use in my pages?

A This is another distinct advantage style sheets have over browser-specific tags. When style sheets are fully supported, users will be able to choose a default style sheet of their own and override any properties they wish.

Quiz

1. Which tag do you use to begin a CSS style sheet?

   a. `<STYLE>`

   b. `<STYLE TYPE="text/css">`

   c. `<STYLE TYPE="text/javascript">`

2. Why isn't the normal HTML language very good at defining layout and presentation?

   a. Because it was designed by programmers.

   b. Because magazines feared the competition.

   c. Because its main purpose is to describe document structure.

3. Which type of style sheet allows you to use JavaScript statements to change styles?

   a. CSS

   b. JSS

   c. Both types

Answers

1. b. You begin a CSS style sheet with the tag `<STYLE TYPE="text/css">`.

2. c. HTML is primarily intended to describe the structure of documents.

3. b. JSS style sheets allow you to change styles with JavaScript statements.

Exercises

If you want to gain more experience using style sheets, try the following exercises:

- Convert the CSS style sheet in Listing 17.1 to JSS style sheet syntax.

- Modify Listing 17.4 to include a separate form element to select the color of level 2 headings. Modify Listing 17.5 to include a level 2 heading, and apply the appropriate style to both H1 and H2 elements.

Hour **18**

Creating Dynamic Pages with Layers

In Hour 13, "Using Windows and Frames," you learned that JavaScript can support separate browser windows and frames dividing a single window.

The CSS specification includes a proposed way of creating positionable blocks or *layers*, which provide a more sophisticated way to deal with multiple windows. Layers are similar to frames but can appear anywhere on a page. Additionally, they can be moved, displayed, and hidden using JavaScript.

During the next hour, you'll learn to use layers with JavaScript. Hour 18 covers the following topics:

- The two methods of defining layers
- Creating layers with the <DIV> tag
- Dealing with browsers that don't support layers
- Creating a simple layered document
- Using JavaScript to show, hide, and move layers
- Using layers for animation

How Layers Work

Using layers is a new way to make Web pages dynamic. A *layer* is a section of a Web page that can be treated as a separate entity—it can be updated, repositioned on the screen, and made to appear and disappear easily. Multiple layers can appear at once and can even overlap, with background layers showing through transparent foreground layers.

Layers are similar to frames, but more dynamic—they aren't restricted to the same area of the page, and they don't necessarily have to be displayed at all. Each layer has its own properties, such as background color and images, to make its appearance unique.

Layers are also known as *positionable elements* and are part of the Cascading Style Sheets (CSS) specification. This feature is currently supported by Netscape Navigator and Microsoft Internet Explorer, although there are differences in implementation between the two.

 Other aspects of the CSS standard were described in Hour 17, "Working with Style Sheets."

In the remainder of this hour, you'll learn the syntax to create layers and use JavaScript to control the layers you've created.

The Two Layer Standards

When layers were introduced, they were supported by a Netscape-only tag called <LAYER>. You enclosed the content of a layer between <LAYER> and </LAYER> tags.

Although this method still works in Netscape Navigator, it is no longer the best way to create layers—a new standard has emerged. The positioning feature of CSS provides the same functionality as the <LAYER> tag, and it's supported by both Netscape (4.0 and later) and Internet Explorer (4.0 and later).

Except in rare cases, CSS positioning is the best way to implement layers. You can make your document work in both browsers with this method. Additionally, because it's a standard, it should remain supported in future browsers.

 Although CSS positioning is supported by both Netscape and Internet Explorer, there are differences in implementation between the two, especially where scripting is concerned. Hour 19, "Creating Cross-Browser Scripts," explores these differences.

Creating CSS Layers

CSS layers use style-sheet attributes to define layers, similar to the attributes introduced in Hour 17. You can define layers in a number of ways, but the most popular is to use the <DIV> tag.

 The <DIV> tag is part of the HTML 3.0 standard. It defines an arbitrary section of the HTML document, and by itself it does not specify any formatting for the text it contains. This makes it the ideal choice for implementing styles and layers.

To create a layer with <DIV>, enclose the content of the layer between the two division tags and specify the layer's properties in the STYLE attribute of the <DIV> tag. Here's a simple example:

```
<DIV ID="layer1" STYLE="position:absolute; left:100; top:100">
This is the content of the layer.
</DIV>
```

This code defines a layer with the name layer1. This is a moveable layer that's 100 pixels down and 100 pixels to the right of the upper-left corner of the browser window. You'll learn more details about the layer properties in the next section.

18

Setting Layer Properties

You can use various properties in the STYLE attribute of the <DIV> tag when you define a layer to set its position, visibility, and other features. The following properties are available:

- position is the main positioning attribute and can affect the properties listed below. The position property can have one of three values:
  - static defines items that are laid out in normal HTML fashion and cannot be moved. This is the default.
  - absolute specifies that an item will be positioned using coordinates you specify.
  - relative defines an item that is offset a certain amount from the static position, where the element would normally have been laid out within the HTML page.
- left and top specify offsets for the position of the item. For absolute positioning, this is relative to the main browser window or a containing item. For relative positioning, it's relative to the usual static position.
- width and height are similar to the standard HTML WIDTH and HEIGHT attributes and specify a width and height for the item.

- clip specifies the clipping rectangle for an item. Only the portion of the item inside this rectangle is displayed.

- overflow indicates whether the clipping rectangle cuts off the item or a scrollbar allows viewing the rest of the item. Values include none, clip, and scroll.

- z-index specifies how items overlap. Normally indexes start with 1 and go up with each layer added "on top" of the page. By changing this value, you can specify which item is on top. You can manipulate this value with JavaScript to provide a feature similar to Netscape's layers.

- visibility specifies whether an item is visible. Values include visible (default), hidden, and inherit. A value of inherit means the item inherits the visibility of any item it appears within (such as a table or paragraph).

- background-color specifies the color for the background of any text in the layer.

- layer-background-color specifies the background color for the entire layer (whether it contains text or not).

- background-image specifies a background image for any text in the layer.

- layer-background-image specifies the background image for the entire layer (whether it contains text or not).

Supporting Older Browsers

As with frames and JavaScript, it's best to support users of older browsers when you can. Netscape includes a <NOLAYER> tag for this purpose. This tag encloses a block of HTML tags and text that will be ignored by layer-capable browsers.

As a simple example, this HTML code displays a message to users without layer-capable browsers:

```
<NOLAYER>
This page uses layers, which require Netscape 4.0 or IE 4.0.
Please switch browsers, or link to the <A href="nolayer.html">
Non-layer version</A> of the page.
</NOLAYER>
```

Creating a Layered Document

You'll now create a simple example of a layered Web page. This page uses four layers:

- A static layer, displayed with the normal text but with a different background color.

- The first layer, displayed at the right side of the page.

- The last layer, displayed at the left side of the page.
- A hidden layer, which is not displayed.

Listing 18.1 is the HTML for the layers example. Figure 18.1 shows the output of this example, as displayed in Navigator.

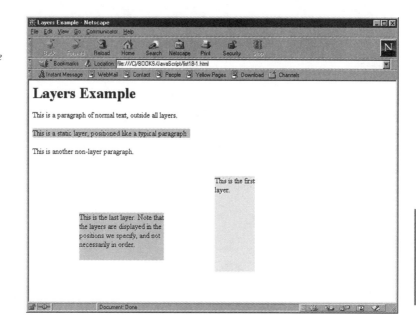

LISTING 18.1 AN EXAMPLE OF LAYER POSITIONING.

```
 1:    <HTML>
 2:    <HEAD><TITLE>Layers Example</TITLE>
 3:    </HEAD>
 4:    <BODY>
 5:    <H1>Layers Example</H1>
 6:    <P>This is a paragraph of normal text, outside all layers.</P>
 7:    <DIV ID="layer1" style="position:static;
 8:     background-color:lightgreen">
 9:    This is a static layer, positioned like a typical paragraph.
10:    </DIV>
11:    <P>This is another non-layer paragraph.</P>
12:    <DIV ID="layer2" style="position:absolute; LEFT:400; TOP:200;
13:     WIDTH:100; HEIGHT:200; background-color:yellow">
14:        This is the first layer.
15:    </DIV>
16:    <DIV ID="layer3" style="position:absolute; LEFT:50;
17:     TOP:200; VISIBILITY:hidden">
```

continues

LISTING **18.1**   CONTINUED

```
18:      This layer is not shown.
19:     </DIV>
20:     <DIV ID="layer4" style="position:relative; LEFT:100; TOP:100;
21:      background-color:lightblue; WIDTH:200; HEIGHT:100">
22:      This is the last layer. Note that the layers are displayed in the
23:      positions we specify, and not necessarily in order.
24:     </DIV>
25:     </BODY>
26:     </HTML>
```

Using the `layer` Object

JavaScript includes a `layer` object that allows you to work with layers. This is part of the browser object hierarchy described in Hour 10, "Working with Browser Objects."

Each layer in the document is represented by a `layer` object, which is a child of the main `document` object. The `layer` object is similar to the `window` object and can contain a `document` object to display HTML content.

> Netscape treats layers the same way whether they are created with the `<DIV>` tag or the `<LAYER>` tag. Both are represented by `layer` objects.

The `layer` objects are all part of the `layers` array, which contains one entry for each layer in the window. As with the `frames` and `forms` arrays, you can use `layers.length` to find the number of layers on the page.

You can access layers with JavaScript by either using an index into the `layers` array or using their names, which you define with the `ID` attribute of the `<DIV>` tag. For example, if a page contains exactly one positionable layer called `mainlayer`, you could refer to it with either of these objects:

```
document.layers[0]
document.mainlayer
```

Each `layer` object has properties for each of the attributes you specified in the `<DIV>` tag, such as `visibility`, `width`, and `height`. You can manipulate these properties dynamically with JavaScript, as you'll see in the next example.

In Internet Explorer's object model, layers are treated a bit differently. `layer` objects are stored under the `document.all` object, and the layer properties are stored under the `style` property of the `layer` object. These differences are explained in detail in Hour 19.

Controlling Layers with JavaScript

One of the most powerful features of Dynamic HTML is that you can combine it with JavaScript to make features such as layers interactive.

As an example of this feature, you can make a script to work with layers. This example is based on the layers example in Listing 18.1, and it allows you to control the layer that starts out hidden with JavaScript buttons.

Listing 18.2 is the HTML document. The second layer is controlled by the buttons at the bottom of the page. These buttons manipulate the `visibility` attribute of the `layer` object, which controls whether the layer is visible. A function, `showOrHide`, is used for this purpose. Figure 18.2 shows Netscape Communicator's display of this example.

18

FIGURE 18.2

The JavaScript and layers example shown in Netscape.

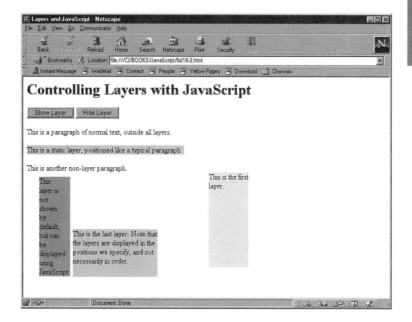

The showOrHide function checks the document.layers property to determine which object to use, and thus supports both Netscape Navigator and Internet Explorer. See Hour 19 for more examples of cross-browser scripting.

LISTING **18.2**   CONTROLLING LAYERS WITH JAVASCRIPT.

```
 1:   <HTML>
 2:   <HEAD><TITLE>Layers and JavaScript</TITLE>
 3:   <SCRIPT LANGUAGE="JavaScript">
 4:   function showOrHide(value) {
 5:      if (value==0) {
 6:          if (document.layers)
 7:             document.layers["layer3"].visibility='hide';
 8:          else
 9:             document.all["layer3"].style.visibility='hidden';
10:      }
11:      else if (value==1) {
12:          if (document.layers)
13:             document.layers["layer3"].visibility='show';
14:          else
15:             document.all["layer3"].style.visibility='visible';
16:      }
17:   }
18:   </SCRIPT></HEAD>
19:   <BODY>
20:   <H1>Controlling Layers with JavaScript</H1>
21:   <FORM NAME="form1">
22:   <INPUT TYPE="button" VALUE="Show Layer"
23:    onClick="showOrHide(1);">
24:   <INPUT TYPE="button" VALUE="Hide Layer"
25:    onClick="showOrHide(0);">
26:   </FORM>
27:   <P>This is a paragraph of normal text, outside all layers.</P>
28:   <DIV ID="layer1" style="position:static;
29:    background-color:lightgreen">
30:   This is a static layer, positioned like a typical paragraph.
31:   </DIV>
32:   <P>This is another non-layer paragraph.</P>
33:   <DIV ID="layer2" style="position:absolute; LEFT:400; TOP:200;
34:   WIDTH:100; HEIGHT:200; background-color:yellow">
35:       This is the first layer.
36:   </DIV>
37:   <DIV ID="layer3" style="position:absolute; LEFT:35; TOP:210;
38:    background-color:orange; width:50; height:50;
39:    visibility:hidden">
40:    This layer is not shown by default, but can be displayed using
41:    JavaScript.
42:   </DIV>
43:   <DIV ID="layer4" style="position:relative; LEFT:100; TOP:100;
```

```
44:     background-color:lightblue; WIDTH:200; HEIGHT:100">
45:      This is the last layer. Note that the layers are displayed in the
46:      positions we specify, and not necessarily in order.
47:     </DIV>
48:     </BODY>
49:     </HTML>
```

Workshop: Using Layers for Animation

One of the most common uses for positioning is to create animation. In Hour 15, "Using Graphics and Animation," you used JavaScript to create a simple animation. Using a layer, you can animate the mouse from Hour 15 using a simpler approach.

Just to make things more fun (and because mice are still the only thing I can draw), you will animate three mice at a time using Dynamic HTML. Using layers to accomplish the animation provides smoother animation and is easier to program. Listing 18.3 shows the Dynamic HTML animation script.

LISTING 18.3   THE DYNAMIC HTML ANIMATION SCRIPT.

18

```
1:      <HTML>
2:      <HEAD>
3:      <TITLE>Animation with Dynamic HTML</TITLE>
4:      <SCRIPT LANGUAGE="JavaScript">
5:      var pos1=-95;
6:      var pos2=-95;
7:      var pos3=-95;
8:      var speed1 = Math.floor(Math.random()*10)+2;
9:      var speed2 = Math.floor(Math.random()*10)+2;
10:     var speed3 = Math.floor(Math.random()*10)+2;
11:     function next() {
12:        pos1 += speed1;
13:        pos2 += speed2;
14:        pos3 += speed3;
15:        if (pos1 > 795) pos1 = -95;
16:        if (pos2 > 795) pos2 = -95;
17:        if (pos3 > 795) pos3 = -95;
18:        if (document.layers) {
19:           document.layers[0].left = pos1;
20:           document.layers[1].left = pos2;
21:           document.layers[2].left = pos3;
22:        }
23:        else {
24:           mouse1.style.left = pos1;
25:           mouse2.style.left = pos2;
```

continues

LISTING 18.3   CONTINUED

```
26:          mouse3.style.left = pos3;
27:      }
28:      window.setTimeout("next();",10);
29:  }
30:  </SCRIPT>
31:  </HEAD>
32:  <BODY onLoad="next();">
33:  <H1>Animation with Dynamic HTML</H1>
34:  <HR>
35:  <DIV ID="mouse1" STYLE="position:absolute; left:0; top:100;
36:  width:100; height:100; visibility:show">
37:  <img src="mouse5.gif" width=100 height=100 alt="" border="0">
38:  </DIV>
39:  <DIV ID="mouse2" STYLE="position:absolute; left:0; top:200;
40:  width:100; height:100; visibility:show">
41:  <IMG src="mouse5.gif" width=100 height=100 alt="" border="0">
42:  </DIV>
43:  <DIV ID="mouse3" STYLE="position:absolute; left:0; top:300;
44:  width:100; height:100; visibility:show">
45:  <IMG src="mouse5.gif" width=100 height=100 alt="" border="0">
46:  </DIV>
47:  </BODY>
48:  </HTML>
```

This HTML document creates three layers with the <DIV> tag, each with a copy of the mouse image (mouse5.gif). Because you are animating with Dynamic HTML, only one image is necessary.

Lines 5–7 define variables to store the current position of each mouse. Lines 8–10 choose a random speed for each mouse. The next function in lines 11–30 performs the animation by changing the layer positions.

The next function is started when the document is loaded by the onLoad event handler. This function checks the document.layers property to determine whether to support Netscape or IE. At the end of the next function, it sets a timeout to start itself again in 10 milliseconds.

To try this yourself, load Listing 18.3 into Netscape Navigator 4.0 or later. As always, you can download the HTML file and graphics for this example from this book's Web site at http://www.jsworkshop.com/.

Summary

In this hour, you've learned how to use positionable elements, also known as layers, to create separate elements on a Web page. These elements can be positioned independently, overlap each other, and be moved, shown, or hidden by JavaScript statements.

You also created a simple layered document and used JavaScript to control a layer's visibility. Finally, you used layers to create smooth animation across a page.

You may have noticed that the examples in this hour behave differently in Internet Explorer than they do in Netscape Navigator. In Hour 19, you will learn ways of making layers and other features work consistently in both browsers.

Q&A

Q Rather than show a layer that was defined as hidden, can I use JavaScript to create an entirely new layer?

A Yes. JavaScript includes a `Layer()` function that allows you to create new layers. This works similarly to other objects you can create (such as `String` and `Date`). This technique does not work in Internet Explorer, however.

Q Can I create a layer inside another layer?

A Yes, layers can be nested by including a `<DIV>` tag within another layer's definition. The inner layer becomes a child object of the outer layer.

Q Can I use JavaScript to write to a layer?

A Yes. Each layer includes a `document` object. You can write to it with commands such as `layer1.document.write("Test.")`. You can also use the `open` and `close` document methods. These are described in Hour 10.

Quiz

1. Which type of layers is supported by both Netscape and Internet Explorer?
    a. The `<LAYER>` tag
    b. CSS positioning
    c. Both of these

2. Which attribute controls a layer's left-to-right position?
    a. `left`
    b. `right`
    c. `lrpos`

18

3. Which tag should you use to display a message to browsers that don't support layers?

    a. `<NOSCRIPT>`

    b. `<NOLAYER>`

    c. `<NOSTYLE>`

Answers

1. b. The CSS positioning features are supported by both Netscape and Internet Explorer.

2. a. The `left` attribute controls a layer's left-to-right positioning.

3. b. Use the `<NOLAYER>` tag to display a message to browsers that don't support layers.

Exercises

If you want to gain more experience using positionable layers with JavaScript, try these exercises:

- Modify Listing 18.2 to include a button that moves the `layer1` layer to a different part of the screen.

- Modify Listing 18.3 to make one of the mice run the race from right to left instead of left to right. (For the full effect, use a reversed version of the graphic.)

HOUR 19

Creating Cross-Browser Scripts

In Hour 18, "Creating Dynamic Pages with Layers," you learned how to use positionable layers, a function of Dynamic HTML, to show, hide, and move areas within a Web page. You might have noticed that the scripts in that hour had to use extra code to ensure that they worked in both Netscape Navigator and Internet Explorer (IE).

This is just one of the many areas where differences in the object models of IE and Netscape can cause problems with your scripts. In this hour, you'll learn some of the major differences between the latest Netscape and Microsoft browsers, and how to compensate for them.

Hour 19 covers the following topics:

- How the IE4 and Netscape object models differ
- Creating scripts for multiple browsers
- How Dynamic HTML works in different browsers
- Converting Dynamic HTML scripts for cross-browser use

Basic Differences Between Browsers

With the release of Internet Explorer 4.0, Microsoft added support for JavaScript 1.1 and much of JavaScript 1.2. In most cases, scripts written to the JavaScript 1.2 standard will work in both browsers. For the most part, IE4 does not support the new JavaScript 1.3 features.

> This hour focuses on the differences between the 4.0 versions of IE and Netscape Navigator. Earlier versions of the two have a greater number of differences, as do the upcoming (5.0) versions.

The greatest differences between the browsers is in their object models. The document object model (DOM) is the hierarchy that organizes browser objects. The basics of the Netscape object model (most of which are also supported by IE4) are described in Hour 10, "Working with Browser Objects." The following sections describe some of the major differences between the Netscape and Microsoft object models.

> Netscape's object model is described in Hour 10.

Windows and Documents

The basic features of the window object are similar in both browsers. Here are a few of the differences:

- IE includes a window.navigate method that loads a new URL. Netscape does not support this method, but you can assign the URL to the window.location object, which works in both browsers.

- Netscape includes window.back and window.forward methods, which are similar to the browser's Back and Forward buttons. These are not supported by IE. In most cases, you can use history.back and history.forward to accomplish the same effect.

- The classes, ids, and tags properties of the document object, introduced in Hour 18, are exclusive to Netscape. IE4 stores these items under the document.all array instead, as explained later in this hour.

Forms

Form objects and the various form element objects are supported in nearly the same way on both browsers. The only possible incompatibility is with the `method`, `target`, and `action` properties of the `form` object. These cannot be changed in IE 3.0; IE 4.0 corrects this problem.

Events

The available event handlers for various objects also differ between IE4 and Netscape. Here are some of the major differences:

- Netscape includes `onMove` and `onDragDrop` events for the `window` object. These are not supported by IE.

- The `event` object, which stores information about an event that has occurred, is supported by both browsers. However, its properties are completely different in different browsers.

Techniques for Cross-Browser Scripting

Although it's beyond the scope of this hour to provide a detailed list of all of the differences between IE4 and Netscape 4.0, you'll undoubtedly run into many differences if you test your scripts on both browsers.

Why script for both? The answer is simple. Although you may be a fan of one browser or the other, each one currently has close to 50% of the browser market. This figure varies with each browser release, but you could be losing as much as half of your audience by scripting for only one browser.

Once you know the differences between browsers that will affect your script, there are different ways of compensating for them. Several techniques for creating cross-browser scripts are described in the following sections.

19

Detecting Browser Versions

First of all, your script will need to figure out which browser is being used. As you learned in Hour 16, "Creating Browser-Specific Scripts," you can do this with the `navigator` object.

Because your script will probably do several things that need to be done differently in different browsers, a good strategy is to detect the browser at the beginning of the script and set a variable that can be checked by later script commands.

For example, the following statements check the browser and assign the value "ie" or
"netscape" to the browser variable:

```
1:   if ((navigator.appVersion.charAt(0) == "4")
2:   ||(navigator.appVersion.charAt(0) == "5")) {
3:      if (navigator.appName == "Netscape")
4:         browser="netscape";
5:      if (navigator.appName=="Microsoft Internet Explorer")
6:         browser="ie";
7:   }
```

As an alternate approach, you can check for the existence of the document.layers object
for Netscape 4.0 or later, and the document.all object for IE 4.0 or later. The examples
in Hour 18 use this technique.

This example first checks for a version 4.0 or 5.0 browser. Next, it checks the
navigator.appName property to assign either "netscape" or "ie" to the browser
variable. You can then check this variable later in the script.

If the browser is version 3.0 or earlier, or it is neither Netscape nor Internet
Explorer, this example does not assign a value to the browser variable. You
might want to take this into account in your scripts.

Using Separate Script Commands

Once you know which browser is in use, a simple strategy is to use a separate block of
commands for each browser. Here is a basic structure you can use:

```
if (browser == "ie") {
// place IE-specific statements here
}
if (browser == "netscape") {
// place Netscape-specific statements here
}
```

Creating Pointers to Objects

A more concise strategy is to set a variable as a pointer to an object. If the browsers use
different objects, you can use this pointer as a universal substitute.

For example, playing an embedded sound called sound1 uses the
document.sound1.play() method in Netscape and the document.sound1.run() method
in Internet Explorer. You can set a pointer that will work with either browser:

```
if (browser == "ie")
   noise = document.sound1.run;
```

```
else
   noise = document.sound1.play;
noise();
```

This sets the `noise` variable to the appropriate method. After these statements, the simple command `noise()` will play the sound regardless of the browser.

> You'll learn more about embedded sounds in Hour 20, "Working with Multimedia and Plug-Ins."

Avoiding Problems

Of course, one way to deal with multiple-browser issues is to avoid using any browser-specific features. This is a simple approach and will still allow you to use most JavaScript 1.1 commands. Of course, using this approach rules out Dynamic HTML, sounds, and a host of other relatively new features.

Often, a cross-browser function is equivalent to a browser-specific one. For example, the `window.location` object can be used to send either browser to a different URL. Using this rather than the IE4-specific `window.navigate` method lets you support both browsers without any special effort.

Testing and Debugging Scripts

If you're trying to write cross-browser scripts (and you should), it's important that you test the scripts in both browsers. Although it may eat up disk space, you should have the latest versions of both browsers installed on your development system.

> You may also want to keep some older versions of browsers installed, or use them on a separate machine. IE 3.0 and Netscape 3.0 are still widely used.

19

Creating Dynamic HTML for Both Browsers

Dynamic HTML is a relatively new feature, and as such is supported in wildly different ways by Netscape 4.0 and IE4. You can use the browser-detection methods described earlier in this hour to create cross-platform Dynamic HTML.

Because Dynamic HTML is not supported by anything earlier than the 4.0 browsers, you don't need to worry about supporting early browsers (except, of course, providing a non-Dynamic HTML alternative for them).

Style Sheets

As you learned in Hour 17, "Working with Style Sheets," you can use JavaScript to dynamically change style sheet properties. Hour 17 used the Netscape method; IE uses an entirely different model for style sheet objects.

Rather than the `tags`, `ids`, and `classes` objects supported by Netscape Navigator, IE4 supports the `document.all` object, which stores all of the tags in the array. IE4 also supports the `document.stylesheets` object, which stores defined styles.

Here is a simple cross-browser example that changes the color of all `H1` tags, using the `browser` variable (as defined earlier in this hour) to decide which format to use:

```
<STYLE ID="iestyle" TYPE="text/css">
</STYLE>
if (browser=="ie")
    document.styleSheets["iestyle"].addRule("H1","color:blue");
if (browser=="netscape")
    document.tags.h1.color = blue;
```

Positionable Layers

Netscape and IE also handle positionable elements (layers) differently. Netscape stores layer objects under the `document` object and their style properties directly under the layer.

In IE4, you can refer to layer objects using the `all` object, as in `document.all.layer1`. You can also refer to them directly within the HTML document, as in `layer1`. The style properties are stored under a `style` object under the layer. For example, this statement makes a layer visible in Netscape:

```
document.layer1.visibility="visible";
```

In IE4, this statement performs the same function:

```
document.all.layer1.styles.visibility="visible";
```

Workshop: Adding Cross-Browser Support

As an example of the techniques you've learned in this hour, you can modify the style sheet example from Hour 17 (Listing 17.5) to work in either Netscape or Internet Explorer.

Detecting the Browser

First, you'll need to add a browser-detection routine to the script. Listing 19.1 shows a simple routine to do this.

LISTING 19.1 DETECTING THE CURRENT BROWSER.

```
1:    if ((navigator.appVersion.charAt(0) == "4")
2:    ||(navigator.appVersion.charAt(0) == "5")) {
3:       if (navigator.appName == "Netscape")
4:          browser="netscape";
5:       else if (navigator.appName=="Microsoft Internet Explorer")
6:          browser="ie";
7:       else alert("This document requires a 4.0 or later browser.");
8:    }
```

These statements detect the browser and assign a value to the browser variable, as described earlier in this hour. Additionally, lines 1 and 2 check for version 4.x or 5.x browsers and display an alert if the browser is not compatible.

Implementing Browser-Specific Code

Next, you can implement the browser-specific statements. Because the statements that change the color of the style sheet elements are the only ones that are incompatible with IE, you can accomplish this with a simple if statement, as shown in Listing 19.2.

LISTING 19.2 IMPLEMENTING DIFFERENT CODE FOR EACH BROWSER.

```
1:    if (browser=="netscape") {
2:        document.tags.BODY.color = dc;
3:        document.tags.H1.color = hc;
4:    }
5:    if (browser=="ie") {
6:        hc1 = "color:" + hc;
7:        dc1 = "color:" + dc;
8:        document.styleSheets["iestyle"].addRule("H1",hc1);
9:        document.styleSheets["iestyle"].addRule("BODY",dc1);
10:   }
```

19

Lines 2–3 are the statements from the original script. The if statement uses the browser variable to decide between them and the IE-specific statements in lines 6–9.

Putting It All Together

Listing 19.3 shows the style sheet script with added cross-browser support.

LISTING 19.3   CROSS-BROWSER STYLE SHEETS IN JAVASCRIPT.

```
 1:   <HTML>
 2:   <HEAD>
 3:   <TITLE>Controlling Styles with JavaScript</TITLE>
 4:   <STYLE ID="iestyle" TYPE="text/css">
 5:   </STYLE>
 6:   <SCRIPT LANGUAGE="JavaScript">
 7:     if ((navigator.appVersion.charAt(0) == "4")
 8:     ||(navigator.appVersion.charAt(0) == "5")) {
 9:        if (navigator.appName == "Netscape")
10:           browser="netscape";
11:        else if (navigator.appName=="Microsoft Internet Explorer")
12:           browser="ie";
13:        else alert("This document requires a 4.0 or later browser.");
14:     }
15:     i = parent.topframe.document.form1.heading.selectedIndex;
16:     hc = parent.topframe.document.form1.heading.options[i].value;
17:     i = parent.topframe.document.form1.body.selectedIndex;
18:     dc = parent.topframe.document.form1.body.options[i].value;
19:     if (browser=="netscape") {
20:        document.tags.BODY.color = dc;
21:        document.tags.H1.color = hc;
22:     }
23:     if (browser=="ie") {
24:        hc1 = "color:" + hc;
25:        dc1 = "color:" + dc;
26:        document.styleSheets["iestyle"].addRule("H1",hc1);
27:        document.styleSheets["iestyle"].addRule("BODY",dc1);
28:     }
29:   </SCRIPT>
30:   </HEAD>
31:   <BODY>
32:   <H1>This is a heading. It is
33:   <SCRIPT LANGUAGE="JavaScript">
34:   document.write(" " + hc + ".");
35:   </SCRIPT>
36:   </H1>
37:   <P>This is a paragraph of regular text. Blah, blah, blah.
38:   Blah blah, blah blah blah. The end.</P>
39:   <P>This is the second paragraph.
40:   <SCRIPT LANGUAGE="JavaScript">
41:   document.write(" The regular text is " + dc + ".");
42:   </SCRIPT>
43:   </P>
44:   </BODY>
45:   </HTML>
```

With these changes, the script will work equally well in Netscape 4.x and IE4. As proof, Figure 19.1 shows the style sheet example as displayed by IE4.

FIGURE 19.1

IE4 displaying the cross-browser style sheet example.

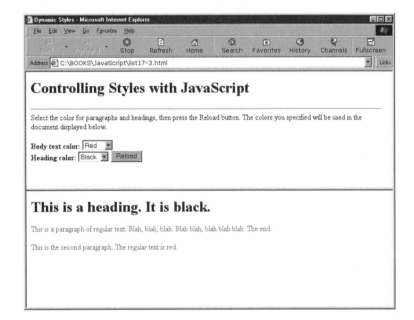

Summary

In this hour, you learned some of the major differences between Microsoft's and Netscape's browsers, and you learned techniques for making scripts work in both browsers. Finally, you created a Dynamic HTML animation script that works in both browsers.

You're nearing the end of Part V. In the last hour of this part, you will explore techniques for working with sounds and plug-ins using JavaScript.

Q&A

Q Are these all of the differences between IE and Netscape?

A By no means—this hour just summarized the major issues. Additionally, because both browsers are continually being updated, writing cross-browser scripts requires a constant eye on the latest developments. See Appendix A, "Other JavaScript Resources," for some sources of current news.

19

Q Where can I learn about more of the specific IE4 and Netscape Dynamic HTML properties?

A See Netscape and Microsoft's Web pages. Also, Appendix A includes a list of books that may be helpful.

Quiz

1. Which property can be used to determine whether a browser is version 4.0?

    a. `navigator.codeName`

    b. `navigator.appVersion`

    c. `navigator.version`

2. Which browser supports the `document.all` object?

    a. Internet Explorer 4.0

    b. Netscape 4.5

    c. FSC Browser 4.7

3. Which of the following objects has the fewest differences between browser versions?

    a. `tags`

    b. `layer`

    c. `form`

Answers

1. b. You can test browser versions with the `navigator.appVersion` property.

2. a. The `document.all` property is specific to Internet Explorer 4.0 or later.

3. c. The `form` object has few differences between browsers.

Exercises

If you want to gain more experience creating cross-browser JavaScript programs, try this exercise:

- Modify the style sheet example in Listing 19.3 to test for `document.all` and `document.layer` instead of using the `navigator` object to check browser versions.

Hour **20**

Working with Multimedia and Plug-Ins

Welcome to the last hour of Part V. In the last three hours, you've learned some of JavaScript's most advanced features: style sheets, layers, and Dynamic HTML. In Hour 20, you'll learn how to use JavaScript with plug-ins.

Plug-ins are browser add-ons that allow you to use additional types of information in the browser: sounds, videos, and so forth. You can use JavaScript to control the behavior of these plug-ins, allowing your scripts to do just about anything.

Hour 20 covers the following topics:

- How LiveConnect connects JavaScript, Java, and plug-ins
- Detecting plug-ins with JavaScript
- Checking available MIME types
- Scripting objects in plug-ins
- Creating an application using sounds

Introducing Plug-Ins and LiveConnect

Plug-ins were introduced by Netscape in Navigator 3.0. Rather than adding support directly to the browser for media types such as formatted text, video, and audio, Netscape created a modular architecture that allows programmers to write their own browser add-ons for these features.

There are now hundreds of plug-ins available. Here are a few of the most popular:

- Macromedia's ShockWave and Flash plug-ins support animation and video.
- Adobe's Acrobat plug-in supports precisely formatted, cross-platform text.
- RealPlayer supports streaming audio and video.
- Headspace's Beatnik plug-in supports music in Web pages.

You can download these plug-ins from their manufacturers. The Navigator browser installation includes several basic plug-ins:

- The QuickTime plug-in for inline movies
- The LiveAudio plug-in for audio and MIDI (music) files
- Bundled versions of the RealPlayer, ShockWave, and Beatnik plug-ins

Because these are included with Navigator, you can assume that at least half of your Web page's audience will have them. The Workshop section of this hour will use the LiveAudio plug-in to play sounds.

 Microsoft Internet Explorer also supports plug-ins, but usually requires a different version of a plug-in. Additionally, some plug-ins are available for only one platform, such as Windows or Macintosh. All of the examples in this hour use plug-ins that are available for all platforms, but they do require Netscape Navigator 3.0 or later.

You can include a file that uses a plug-in in a Web document with the <EMBED> tag. This tag specifies the filename for the content and any parameters required by the plug-in.

Understanding MIME Types

Multipurpose Internet Mail Extensions (MIME) is a standard for classifying different types of files and transmitting them over the Internet. The different types of files are known as *MIME types*.

You've already worked with a few MIME types: HTML (MIME type `text/html`), text (MIME type `text/plain`), and GIF images (MIME type `image/gif`). Although Web browsers don't normally support many more than these types, external applications and plug-ins can provide support for additional types.

When a Web server sends a document to a browser, it includes that document's MIME type in the heading. If the browser supports that MIME type, it displays the file. If not, you're asked what to do with the file (such as when you click on a .zip or .exe file to download it).

How LiveConnect Works

So far, you've learned how useful plug-ins can be to a browser, but you haven't seen how they work with JavaScript. That's where LiveConnect comes in. LiveConnect is a Netscape standard that allows JavaScript, Java, and plug-ins to communicate.

LiveConnect allows plug-ins to make parameters available as objects. These objects are stored as part of the `browser` object hierarchy and are available to JavaScript and Java programs.

> You can also use LiveConnect to use Java commands from within a JavaScript program, or to communicate between Java and JavaScript programs. See Netscape's Web site for more detail:
>
> `http://developer.netscape.com/docs/manuals/liveconnect.html`

Working with Plug-In Objects

The JavaScript `navigator` object, which you learned about in Hour 10, "Working with Browser Objects," includes a child object called `plugins`. This object is an array, with one entry for each plug-in installed on the browser.

20

Each plug-in has an entry in the array. Each entry has the following properties:

- `name` is the name of the plug-in.
- `filename` is the executable file that was loaded to install the plug-in.
- `description` is a description of the plug-in, supplied by the developer.
- `mimeTypes` is an array with one entry for each MIME type supported by the plug-in.

You can use these properties in a script to find out about the installed plug-ins, as you'll see in the next section.

The `navigator` object also has a child object called `mimeTypes`, which includes an array element for each MIME type supported by the browser or one of its plug-ins.

Checking for Plug-Ins

What if you want to use a hot new plug-in on your pages, but you know that not everyone has the plug-in installed? One of the handiest uses for JavaScript is to detect a plug-in before loading the page that contains that plug-in's content.

For example, Listing 20.1 shows a simple script that checks for the QuickTime plug-in (or any other plug-in that handles QuickTime movies). If a plug-in is found, the script writes the <EMBED> tag to include a movie in the document. If not, it displays a still image.

LISTING 20.1   CHECKING FOR THE QUICKTIME PLUG-IN.

```
1: test=navigator.mimeTypes["video/quicktime"];
2: if (test)
3:    document.writeln("<EMBED SRC='quick.mov' HEIGHT=100 WIDTH=100>");
4: else
5:    document.writeln("<IMG SRC='quick.gif' HEIGHT=100 WIDTH=100>");
```

If your script does not detect the appropriate plug-in, you can provide a link to the download location for the plug-in or to a non-plug-in version of the page.

Listing Plug-Ins

As another example of the `plugins` array, you can use JavaScript to list the plug-ins supported by your browser. Listing 20.2 shows a script that lists the plug-ins in a table, with filenames and descriptions.

LISTING 20.2   LISTING PLUG-INS WITH JAVASCRIPT.

```
1:    <HTML>
2:    <HEAD>
3:    <TITLE>List of Plug-Ins</TITLE>
4:    </HEAD>
5:    <BODY>
6:    <H1>List of Plug-Ins</H1>
```

```
 7:   <HR>
 8:   The following is a list of the plug-ins installed in this
 9:   copy of Netscape, generated using the JavaScript
10:   navigator.plugins object:
11:   <HR>
12:   <TABLE BORDER>
13:   <TR><TH>Plug-in Name</TH>
14:   <TH>Filename</TH>
15:   <TH>Description</TH>
16:   </TR>
17:   <SCRIPT LANGUAGE="JavaScript">
18:   for (i=0; i<navigator.plugins.length; i++) {
19:      document.write("<TR><TD>");
20:      document.write(navigator.plugins[i].name);
21:      document.write("</TD><TD>");
22:      document.write(navigator.plugins[i].filename);
23:      document.write("</TD><TD>");
24:      document.write(navigator.plugins[i].description);
25:      document.write("</TD></TR>");
26:   }
27:   </SCRIPT>
28:   </TABLE>
29:   </BODY>
30:   </HTML>
```

The action of the script is performed by lines 18–26. Line 18 begins a for loop that loops from 0 to the number of plug-ins (the length property of the plugins array).

The document.write statements in lines 19–25 display the properties for a single plugin object, along with some HTML tags to make the table. This script's output in Navigator is shown in Figure 20.1.

Using Objects in Plug-Ins

You now know how to use the navigator object's properties to detect plug-ins. Thanks to LiveConnect, you can also use objects to manipulate plug-ins themselves.

Each embedded object in a document is represented by an element in the embeds array, which is a child of the document array. For example, if a document contains a single embedded object, it is represented by document.embeds[0].

The properties and methods of the embed object depend on the plug-in in use. For example, the LiveAudio plug-in includes play and stop methods for controlling audio output. Some plug-ins may not be scriptable at all.

20

FIGURE 20.1

The list of plug-ins as displayed by Navigator.

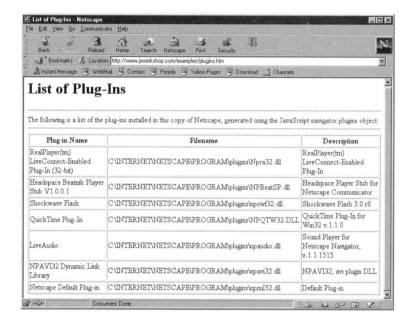

Workshop: Playing Music with the Mouse

As an example of controlling a plug-in with JavaScript, you will now create a script to play sounds. I've created some graphics that vaguely resemble a piano keyboard and audio files for each note. Your script can detect mouse clicks on the keys and play the appropriate notes.

You can download the audio files and graphics used in this example from this book's Web site at http://www.jsworkshop.com/.

Embedding the Sounds

For this example, I've created sound files in WAV format for each of the 13 notes in a single octave of a piano keyboard. Each file is named after the note it contains. Your HTML document will need to include these sounds using the <EMBED> tag.

Normally, when you embed a sound, it plays as soon as the page loads. You don't want all 13 notes to play at once (and that wouldn't work anyway), so use the AUTOSTART=false parameter to prevent the sounds from playing.

Also include the HIDDEN=true parameter to prevent the browser from displaying cute little control panels for each of the sounds. The <EMBED> tag for a single note (the bottom C) would look like this:

```
<EMBED SRC="C0.wav" HIDDEN=true AUTOSTART=false>
```

Because the HTML document will include a tag like this for each sound, the 13 sounds will be loaded (but not played) immediately. This will prevent the browser from having to communicate with the server to load a file each time you click on a piano key.

Displaying the Keyboard

For the keyboard display, I've created two GIF graphics: a white key and a black key. The HTML document simply needs to include whitekey.gif and blackkey.gif in the right combination to display the 13 keys.

For a better-looking keyboard, you could use an image map. The script in this hour's workshop sticks to linked graphics for simplicity; see this book's Web site for a fancier version. Here's the HTML link tag for a single piano key:

```
<A HREF="#" onClick="playnote(0);">
   <IMG border=0 SRC="whitekey.gif" ALIGN=TOP></A>
```

This displays the white key graphic. It is linked with "#" as a target (which will prevent the browser from loading a different page), and the onClick event handler runs a JavaScript function to play the note.

Playing the Sounds

The playnote function handles the playing of the appropriate sound. It accepts a parameter, note (a number from 0 to 11 representing one of the embedded sounds) and uses the play method to play the sound. Here's the function:

```
function playnote(note) {
document.embeds[note].play();
}
```

Putting It All Together

20

Listing 20.3 shows the complete HTML document for the piano. This listing may look long, but most of the lines are just repeated forms of the ones in previous sections: 13 <EMBED> tags and 13 links and images for the keyboard display. Each link sends a different parameter to the play function to play the appropriate note.

LISTING 20.3   THE COMPLETE HTML AND SCRIPT FOR THE PIANO EXAMPLE.

```
 1:    <HTML>
 2:    <HEAD>
 3:    <TITLE>JavaScript Piano</TITLE>
 4:    <SCRIPT LANGUAGE="JavaScript">
 5:    function playnote(note) {
 6:    document.embeds[note].play();
 7:    }
 8:    </SCRIPT>
 9:    </HEAD>
10:    <BODY>
11:    <EMBED SRC="C0.wav" HIDDEN=true AUTOSTART=false>
12:    <EMBED SRC="cs0.wav" HIDDEN=true AUTOSTART=false>
13:    <EMBED SRC="d0.wav" HIDDEN=true AUTOSTART=false>
14:    <EMBED SRC="ds0.wav" HIDDEN=true AUTOSTART=false>
15:    <EMBED SRC="e0.wav" HIDDEN=true AUTOSTART=false>
16:    <EMBED SRC="f0.wav" HIDDEN=true AUTOSTART=false>
17:    <EMBED SRC="fs0.wav" HIDDEN=true AUTOSTART=false>
18:    <EMBED SRC="g0.wav" HIDDEN=true AUTOSTART=false>
19:    <EMBED SRC="gs0.wav" HIDDEN=true AUTOSTART=false>
20:    <EMBED SRC="a0.wav" HIDDEN=true AUTOSTART=false>
21:    <EMBED SRC="as0.wav" HIDDEN=true AUTOSTART=false>
22:    <EMBED SRC="b0.wav" HIDDEN=true AUTOSTART=false>
23:    <EMBED SRC="c1.wav" HIDDEN=true AUTOSTART=false>
24:    <H1>The JavaScript Piano</H1>
25:    <HR>
26:    Click on the funny-looking piano keys below to play a melody.
27:    <HR>
28:    <A HREF="#" onClick="playnote(0);">
29:       <IMG border=0 SRC="whitekey.gif" ALIGN=TOP></A>
30:    <A HREF="#" onClick="playnote(1);">
31:       <IMG border=0 SRC="blackkey.gif" ALIGN=TOP></A>
32:    <A HREF="#" onClick="playnote(2);">
33:       <IMG border=0 SRC="whitekey.gif" ALIGN=TOP></A>
34:    <A HREF="#" onClick="playnote(3);">
35:       <IMG border=0 SRC="blackkey.gif" ALIGN=TOP></A>
36:    <A HREF="#" onClick="playnote(4);">
37:       <IMG border=0 SRC="whitekey.gif" ALIGN=TOP></A>
38:    <A HREF="#" onClick="playnote(5);">
39:       <IMG border=0 SRC="whitekey.gif" ALIGN=TOP></A>
40:    <A HREF="#" onClick="playnote(6);">
41:       <IMG border=0 SRC="blackkey.gif" ALIGN=TOP></A>
42:    <A HREF="#" onClick="playnote(7);">
43:       <IMG border=0 SRC="whitekey.gif" ALIGN=TOP></A>
44:    <A HREF="#" onClick="playnote(8);">
45:       <IMG border=0 SRC="blackkey.gif" ALIGN=TOP></A>
46:    <A HREF="#" onClick="playnote(9);">
47:       <IMG border=0 SRC="whitekey.gif" ALIGN=TOP></A>
48:    <A HREF="#" onClick="playnote(10);">
```

```
49:       <IMG border=0 SRC="blackkey.gif" ALIGN=TOP></A>
50:   <A HREF="#" onClick="playnote(11);">
51:       <IMG border=0 SRC="whitekey.gif" ALIGN=TOP></A>
52:   <A HREF="#" onClick="playnote(12);">
53:       <IMG border=0 SRC="whitekey.gif" ALIGN=TOP></A>
54:   <HR>
55:   </BODY>
56:   </HTML>
```

To try out the piano, put the HTML document in the same directory as the required
graphic and sound files, either on your local computer or a Web server. You can then load
the document and begin playing the piano. (You can't play chords, but that's life.)

Figure 20.2 shows Navigator's display of the piano keyboard. Books aren't nearly as
multimedia ready as the Web, so you'll have to try the script yourself to hear the sounds.

FIGURE 20.2

*Netscape displays the
piano keyboard script.*

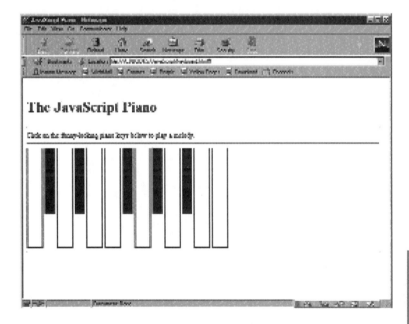

20

Summary

In this hour, you learned about the JavaScript features that work with plug-ins. You
learned how to detect or list plug-ins with JavaScript and how to use LiveConnect to control plug-ins. Finally, you created a script that uses a plug-in to play sounds.

You've reached the end of Part V and are nearing the end of this book. In the final four hours, you'll learn how to debug programs and apply the various techniques you've learned throughout this book to create several JavaScript applications.

Q&A

Q Is there a way to play sounds in Internet Explorer?

A Yes, and it can also be scripted. The method for embedding and scripting sounds in Internet Explorer is described in Hour 19, "Creating Cross-Browser Scripts."

Q Can I force the browser to download a plug-in automatically to support my document?

A No, although a future version of Netscape may support this feature. If the user does download and install the plug-in, you can use the `navigator.plugins.reload` method to refresh the list of plug-ins.

Q Where can I find a list of the exact properties and methods supported by a plug-in?

A Check the plug-in vendor's Web site. For the plug-ins that are bundled with Netscape, you can find information on Netscape's site.

Quiz

1. Which feature of Netscape allows JavaScript to control a plug-in?

    a. Java

    b. LiveConnect

    c. LiveAudio

2. The `plugins` object is a child of which browser object?

    a. `document`

    b. `window`

    c. `navigator`

3. Which plug-in for playing sounds is included with Netscape Navigator?

    a. LiveConnect

    b. LiveAudio

    c. No plug-in is included; you must make the sounds with your mouth

Answers

1. b. LiveConnect enables JavaScript to control plug-ins.

2. c. The `plugins` object is a child of the `navigator` object.

3. b. The LiveAudio plug-in is included with Navigator.

Exercises

If you want to gain more experience using JavaScript with plug-ins, try these exercises:

- Modify Listing 20.1 to detect a plug-in and display a message with a link to the plug-in vendor's site if it is not supported.

- Expand the piano keyboard in Listing 20.3 to include another octave of notes. (Audio files for all 88 keys of a piano are available at this book's Web site, if you want to go all out.)

20

Part VI
Putting It All Together

Hour

HOUR 21

Debugging JavaScript Applications

Welcome to Part VI. In the final three hours of this book, you'll use the JavaScript features and techniques you've learned to create some complete applications. Before you move on to this, it's important to know how to deal with problems in your scripts.

In this hour, you'll learn a few pointers on keeping your scripts bug-free, and you'll look at the tools and techniques you can use to find and eliminate bugs when they occur. Hour 21 covers the following topics:

- Using good programming practices to avoid bugs
- Tips for debugging with the JavaScript Console
- Using alert messages and status messages to debug scripts
- Using the JavaScript Debugger
- Debugging an actual script

Avoiding Bugs

A bug is an error in a program that prevents it from doing what it should do. If you've tried writing any scripts on your own, you've probably run into one or more bugs. If not, you will—no matter how careful you are.

 Currently, the most famous bug of them all is the Year 2000 bug, which you learned about in Hour 2, "Creating a Simple Script." The Y2K bug is not actually a single bug, but a collective term for similar problems shared by thousands of programs. Needless to say, this makes it difficult to fix.

Although you'll undoubtedly run into a few bugs if you write a complex script, you can avoid many others by carefully writing and double-checking your script.

Using Good Programming Practices

There's not a single programmer out there whose programs always work the first time, without any bugs. However, good programmers share a few habits that help them avoid some of the more common bugs. Here are a few good habits you can develop to improve your scripts:

- Format your scripts neatly and try to keep them readable. Use consistent spacing and variable names that mean something. It's hard to determine what's wrong with a script when you can't even remember what a particular line does.

- Similarly, use JavaScript comments liberally to document your script. This will help if you need to work on the script after you've forgotten the details of how it works—or if someone else inherits the job.

- End all JavaScript statements with semicolons. Although this is optional, it makes the script more readable. Additionally, it may help the browser to produce meaningful error messages.

- Declare all variables with the var keyword. This is optional in most cases, but it will help make sure you really mean to create a new variable and will avoid problems with variable scope.

- Divide complicated scripts into functions. This will make the script easier to read, and it will also make it easy to pinpoint the cause of a problem.

- Write a large script in several phases and test the script at each phase before adding more features. This way, you can avoid having several problems happen at once.

Avoiding Common Mistakes

Along with following scripting practices, you should also watch for common mistakes in your scripts. Different people make different mistakes in JavaScript programming, but the following sections explore some of the most common ones.

Syntax Errors

A syntax error is an incorrect keyword, operator, punctuation mark, or other item in a script. Most often, it's caused by a typing error.

Syntax errors are usually obvious—both to you when you look at the script and to the browser's JavaScript interpreter when you load the script. These errors usually result in an error message and can easily be corrected.

Assignment and Equality

One of the most common syntax errors made by beginning JavaScript programmers is confusing the assignment operator (=) with the equality operator (==). This can be a hard error to spot because it may not result in an error message.

If you're confused about which operator to use, follow this simple rule: use = to change the value of a variable and == to compare two values. Here's an example of a statement that confuses the two:

```
If (a = 5) alert("found a five.");
```

The statement looks logical enough, but a = 5 will actually assign the value 5 to the a variable rather than comparing the two. Netscape usually detects this type of error and displays an error message in the JavaScript Console, but the opposite type of error (using == when you mean =) may not be detected.

Local and Global Variables

Another common mistake is confusing local and global variables, such as trying to use the value of a variable that was declared in a function outside the function. If you actually need to do this, you should either use a global variable or return a value from the function.

Hour 5, "Using and Storing Values," describes the differences between local and global variables in detail.

21

Using Objects Correctly

Another common error is referring to JavaScript objects incorrectly. It's important to use the correct object names and to remember when to explicitly name the parent of an object.

For example, you can usually refer to the `window.alert` method as simply `alert`. However, there are some cases when you must use `window.alert`, such as in some event handlers. If you find that `alert` or another method or property is not recognized by the browser, try specifying the `window` object.

Another common mistake is to assume that you can omit the `document` object's name, such as using `write` instead of `document.write`. This won't work because most scripts have a `window` object as their scope.

Basic Debugging Tools

If checking your script for common mistakes and obvious problems doesn't fix things, it's time to start debugging. This is the process of finding errors in a program and eliminating them. Some basic tools for debugging scripts are described in the following sections.

The JavaScript Console

The first thing you should do if your script doesn't work is check for error messages. In Netscape 4.5 and later, the messages are not displayed by default, but are logged to the JavaScript Console.

To access the console, type `javascript:` in Netscape's Location field. The console displays the last few error messages that have occurred, as shown in Figure 21.1.

Along with reading the error messages, you can use the console to type a JavaScript command or expression and see its results. This is useful if you need to make sure a line of your script uses the correct syntax.

Making the Console Display Automatically

After you've spent a while dealing with JavaScript errors, you'll find yourself frequently typing `javascript:` to access the console. Fortunately, Netscape (version 4.5 or later) includes an option to display the console automatically each time an error occurs.

This setting is not available in the Preferences dialog. To change the setting, you'll need to edit your Netscape Preferences file. This file is stored in your user preferences directory (usually named with your initials) under the Netscape installation directory. The filename is `prefs.js`.

FIGURE 21.1

*The JavaScript
Console displays
recent error messages.*

To make the change, open the `prefs.js` file in a text editor. This file consists of a number of JavaScript commands to set your user preferences. To make the console display automatically, add this line to the end of the file:

```
user_pref("javascript.console.open_on_error", true);
```

After you've made the change, save the file and start Netscape. Now, when the JavaScript interpreter encounters an error, the console will pop up automatically and display the error.

Netscape rewrites the contents of the `prefs.js` file each time it runs, so you cannot edit the file while Netscape is running. Exit all browser windows before editing the file.

Alert Messages and the Status Line

If you're lucky, the error messages in the console will tell you how to fix your script. However, your script may not generate any error messages at all—but still fail to work correctly. In this case, the real debugging process begins.

One useful debugging technique is to add temporary statements to your script to let you know what's going on. For example, you can use an alert message to display the value of

21

a variable. Once you understand what's happening to the variable, you can figure out what's wrong with the script.

> You can also display debugging information on the status line or in a separate browser window. You can use document.write in some cases, but this works only when the document hasn't finished loading yet.

Netscape's JavaScript Debugger

Although you can use alert messages and a little common sense to quickly find a bug in a simple script, larger scripts can be difficult to debug. Netscape's JavaScript Debugger is a powerful tool you can use to debug scripts.

Installing the Debugger

The Debugger is a Java-based program that runs within the Netscape browser. You can download the current version of the Debugger from Netscape's Web site:

```
http://developer.netscape.com/software/jsdebug.html
```

> The Debugger installs using Netscape's SmartUpdate feature. Because of this, you must use the latest version of the Navigator browser to perform the download and installation.

To install the Debugger, follow the instructions on the site to reach the download link. The software will be downloaded and installed automatically.

The Debugger Window

Once you've installed the Debugger, you can begin to use it. To load the Debugger, enter the location of the local Debugger page, jsdebugger.html. This page is stored under the Netscape directory on your computer.

The first time you run the Debugger, you'll be presented with a number of security warnings. The Debugger uses a number of features that are allowed only with authorization; you can safely grant it these privileges.

After the security warnings, the Debugger window is displayed. Once it is displayed, you can leave it open while you run scripts in the Navigator window you already have open.

The Debugger keeps track of the scripts you load after it starts running. To open a script for debugging, first load its HTML document into the browser. Next, click the Open button on the Debugger toolbar. A list of recently opened documents is displayed; select the appropriate one. The script is then displayed in the Debugger window, as shown in Figure 21.2.

FIGURE 21.2

The Debugger window displays the current script.

Once the script is loaded into the Debugger, you can begin the debugging process. The following sections describe the basic features of the Debugger. For more details about its operation, see Netscape's Web site at the URL mentioned earlier in this section.

21

Setting Breakpoints and Interrupts

After the Debugger is loaded, it monitors the currently running script in the browser window. One useful feature is the capability to freeze the execution of the script at a certain point. The statement where you want to stop the script is called a *breakpoint*.

To set a breakpoint, click to the left of the statement in the Debugger window. A red dot will appear to indicate a breakpoint. You can place as many breakpoints as you need. When the script reaches the statement where you have placed a breakpoint, it pauses and the Debugger takes control. You can then check variables or other aspects of the script.

If you want the script to stop executing as soon as possible, use the Interrupt button on the Debugger toolbar. This will stop the script as soon as it is able (usually when the current statement finishes) and return control to the Debugger.

BThe script will also stop executing and return control to the Debugger if it encounters a JavaScript error.

Watching Values

Usually, the main reason to interrupt the execution of the script is to see what the current values of your variables are. You can easily keep track of one or more variables by adding them to the Debugger's watch list.

To add a variable to the list, select its name in the Debugger window and then choose Copy to Watch from the Edit menu. The values of any variables you've set to watch will be displayed in the console in the lower-right corner of the Debugger window.

Stepping Through a Script

Once the script has been interrupted and you've learned what you need to know, you will probably want to continue the execution of the script. The easiest way to do this is to use the Run button in the Debugger toolbar. This continues the script where it stopped and keeps running it until the next breakpoint or interrupt.

You can also execute the script one step at a time. To do this, use the Step Into command from the Control menu. This will execute the current statement and then return control to the Debugger.

You can also step through an entire function in one step with the Debugger's Step Over command. For information about other options, see Netscape's Debugger documentation.

Workshop: Debugging a Script

You should now have a good understanding of what can go wrong with JavaScript programs and the tools you have available to diagnose these problems. You can now try your hand at debugging a script.

Listing 21.1 shows a script I wrote to play the classic "Guess a Number" game. The script picks a number between 1 and 100 and then allows the user 10 guesses. If a guess is incorrect, it provides a hint as to whether the target number is higher or lower.

This is a relatively simple script with a twist: It includes at least one bug and doesn't work at all in its present form.

LISTING 21.1 THE NUMBER GUESSER SCRIPT, COMPLETE WITH BUGS.

```
1:   <HTML>
2:   <HEAD>
3:   <TITLE>Guess a Number</TITLE>
4:   <SCRIPT LANGUAGE="JavaScript">
5:   var num = Math.random() * 100 + 1;
6:   var tries = 0;
7:   function guess() {
8:   var guess = document.form1.guess1.value;
9:   tries++;
10:  status = "Tries: " + tries;
11:  if (guess < num)
12:      document.form1.hint.value = "No, guess higher.";
13:  if (guess > num)
14:      document.form1.hint.value = "No, guess lower.";
15:  if (guess == num) {
16:      window.alert("Correct! You guessed it in " + tries + " tries.");
17:      location.reload();
18:      }
19:  if (tries == 10) {
20:      window.alert("Sorry, time's up. The number was: " + num);
21:      location.reload();
22:      }
23:  }
24:  </SCRIPT>
```

21

continues

LISTING 21.1   CONTINUED

```
25:  </HEAD>
26:  <BODY>
27:  <H1>Guess a Number</H1>
28:  <HR>
29:  <P>I'm thinking of a number between 1 and 100. Try to guess
30:  it in less than 10 tries.</P>
31:  <FORM NAME="form1">
32:  <INPUT TYPE="text" SIZE=25 NAME="hint" VALUE="Enter your Guess.">
33:  <BR>
34:  <B>Guess:</B>
35:  <INPUT TYPE="text" NAME="guess1" SIZE="5">
36:  <INPUT TYPE="BUTTON" VALUE="Guess"  onClick="guess();">
37:  </FORM>
38:  </BODY>
39:  </HTML>
```

Here's a summary of how this script should work:

- Line 5 picks a random number and stores it in the num variable.
- The guess function in lines 7–23 is called each time the user enters a guess.
- Within the guess function, several if statements test the user's guess. If it is incorrect, a hint is displayed in the text box. If the guess is correct, the script displays an alert message to congratulate the user.

Testing the Program

To test this program, load the HTML document into your browser. It appears to load correctly and does not immediately cause any errors. However, when you enter a guess and press the Guess button, a JavaScript error occurs.

According to the JavaScript Console, the error message is this:

```
guess is not a function.
```

Fixing the Error

As the error message indicates, there must be something wrong with the function call to the guess function. This might happen if the names of the function definition and the function call didn't match, but they do in this case.

Upon further examination, you'll notice that the first two lines of the function are as follows:

```
function guess() {
var guess = document.form1.guess1.value;
```

Although this looks correct at first glance, there's a problem here: The function and the variable definition use the same name, guess. As a result, the variable definition overwrites the function. Thus, when the event handler tries to call the function, it finds a variable called guess instead. Sure enough, as the error message reported, guess is not a function.

This is easy to fix. Simply change the name of the function from guess to a unique name, guessit. Make the same change in both the function definition (line 7) and the event handler (line 36).

Testing the Script Again

Now that you've fixed the error, try the script again. This time it loads without an error, and you can enter a guess without an error. The hints about guessing higher or lower are even displayed correctly.

However, to truly test the script, you'll need to play the game all the way through. When you do, you'll discover that there's still another problem in the script: You can't win, no matter how hard you try.

After your 10 guesses are up, an alert message informs you that you've lost the game. Coincidentally, this alert message also tells you what's wrong with the script. Figure 21.3 shows how the browser window looks after a complete game, complete with this dialog.

FIGURE 21.3

The number guesser script's display after a game is finished.

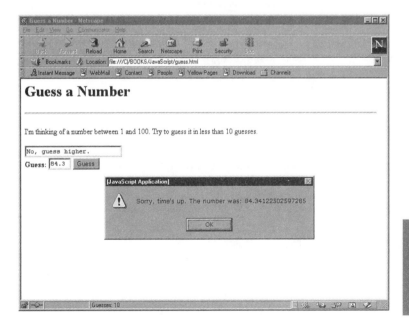

21

As you can see from the alert message, it's no wonder you didn't win: The random number the computer picked includes more than 10 decimal places, and you've been guessing integers. There's nothing stopping you from guessing decimal numbers, but you'll need a whole lot more than 10 guesses. The game starts to lose its simplicity and charm.

To fix this problem, look at the statement that generates the random number:

```
5:  var num = Math.random() * 100 + 1;
```

This uses the `Math.random` method, which results in a random number between 0 and 1. The number is then multiplied and incremented to result in a number between 1 and 100.

This statement does indeed produce a number between 1 and 100, but not an integer. To fix the problem, you can add the `Math.floor` method to chop off the decimal portion of the number. Here's a corrected statement:

```
var num = Math.floor(Math.random() * 100) + 1;
```

To fix the script, make this change and then test it again. If you play a game or two, you'll find that it works just fine. Listing 20.2 shows the complete, debugged script.

LISTING 21.2 THE COMPLETE, DEBUGGED NUMBER GUESSER SCRIPT.

```
 1:  <HTML>
 2:  <HEAD>
 3:  <TITLE>Guess a Number</TITLE>
 4:  <SCRIPT LANGUAGE="JavaScript">
 5:  var num = Math.floor(Math.random() * 100) + 1;
 6:  var tries = 0;
 7:  function guessit() {
 8:  var guess = document.form1.guess1.value;
 9:  tries++;
10:  status = "Tries: " + tries;
11:  if (guess < num)
12:      document.form1.hint.value = "No, guess higher.";
13:  if (guess > num)
14:      document.form1.hint.value = "No, guess lower.";
15:  if (guess == num) {
16:      window.alert("Correct! You guessed it in " + tries + " tries.");
17:      location.reload();
18:      }
19:  if (tries == 10) {
20:      window.alert("Sorry, time's up. The number was: " + num);
21:      location.reload();
22:      }
23:  }
```

```
24:  </SCRIPT>
25:  </HEAD>
26:  <BODY>
27:  <H1>Guess a Number</H1>
28:  <HR>
29:  <P>I'm thinking of a number between 1 and 100. Try to guess
30:  it in less than 10 tries.</P>
31:  <FORM NAME="form1">
32:  <INPUT TYPE="text" SIZE=25 NAME="hint" VALUE="Enter your Guess.">
33:  <BR>
34:  <B>Guess:</B>
35:  <INPUT TYPE="text" NAME="guess1" SIZE="5">
36:  <INPUT TYPE="BUTTON" VALUE="Guess"  onClick="guessit();">
37:  </FORM>
38:  </BODY>
39:  </HTML>
```

Summary

In this hour, you learned how to debug JavaScript programs. You got some tips for producing scripts with a minimum of bugs and learned about some tools that will help you find bugs in scripts. Finally, you tried your hand at debugging a script.

Congratulations—you're nearing the final hours of your JavaScript education. In the last three hours, you will use the scripting commands and techniques you've learned to create some complete applications.

Q&A

Q Can I debug a script using Internet Explorer instead of Netscape?

A Yes. In fact, you should test your script in both browsers if at all possible. Internet Explorer displays its error messages immediately when an error happens, and it does not include a JavaScript Console or debugger.

Q Why are some errors displayed after the script runs for a time, while others are displayed when the script loads?

A The JavaScript interpreter looks at scripts in the body or heading of the document, such as function definitions, when the page loads. Event handlers aren't checked until the event happens. Additionally, a statement might look fine when the page loads, but will cause an error because of the value of a variable it uses later.

21

Q **What is the purpose of the `location.reload` statements in the number guesser script?**

A This is an easy way to start a new game because reloading the page reinitializes the variables. This results in a new number being picked, and the default "Guess a Number" message is displayed in the hint field.

Quiz

1. If you mistype a JavaScript keyword, which type of error is the result?

    a. Syntax error

    b. Function error

    c. Pilot error

2. The process of dealing with errors in a script or program is known as:

    a. Error detection

    b. Frustration

    c. Debugging

3. Which Netscape JavaScript Debugger feature stops the script's execution when a specific statement is reached?

    a. An interrupt

    b. A watch

    c. A breakpoint

Answers

1. a. A syntax error can result from a mistyped JavaScript keyword.

2. c. Debugging is the process of finding and fixing errors in a program.

3. c. A breakpoint causes the script to stop at a specific statement.

Exercises

If you want to gain more experience debugging JavaScript programs, try these exercises:

- Although the number guesser script in Listing 20.2 avoids JavaScript errors, it is still vulnerable to user errors. Add a statement to verify that the user's guess is between 1 and 100. If it isn't, display an alert message and make sure that the guess doesn't count toward the total of 10 guesses.

- Load Listing 20.1, the number guesser script with bugs, into the JavaScript Debugger. Try using the watch and breakpoint features to quickly diagnose the problem.

HOUR **22**

Improving a Web Page with JavaScript

You should now know quite a bit about JavaScript's features and how to write and debug JavaScript programs. In the last three hours of this book, you will be applying this knowledge by creating some complete applications.

You will start with a simple application: an ordinary Web page with a few JavaScript features to make it friendlier and easier to navigate. Hour 22 covers the following topics:

- Creating a basic HTML document
- Adding a drop-down navigation bar
- Adding status-line descriptions for links
- Adding graphic links and rollovers
- Combining these features into a complete Web page

Creating the HTML Document

For this example, you'll start with the Web page of a small (and hopeless) software company known as Fictional Software Company (FSC). Their Web page is rather unimpressive, but you've got to start somewhere.

The main FSC Web page is shown in Figure 22.1. It includes a logo at the top, three paragraphs of information, and a simple bulleted list of links to the various subpages. This page is defined using the HTML in Listing 22.1.

FIGURE 22.1

A simple Web page using only HTML.

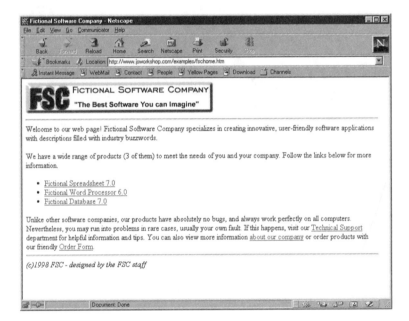

LISTING 22.1 THE HTML DOCUMENT FOR THE INITIAL FSC WEB PAGE.

```
 1:  <HTML>
 2:  <HEAD><TITLE>Fictional Software Company</TITLE></HEAD>
 3:  <BODY>
 4:  <IMG SRC="fsclogo.gif" alt="Fictional Software Company">
 5:  <HR>
 6:  Welcome to our Web page! Fictional Software Company
 7:  specializes in creating innovative, user-friendly software
 8:  applications with descriptions filled with industry
 9:  buzzwords.
10:  <P>We have a wide range of products (3 of them) to meet
11:  the needs of you and your company. Follow the links
12:  below for more information.
13:  <P>
```

```
14: <UL>
15: <LI><A HREF="spread.html">Fictional Spreadsheet 7.0</A>
16: <LI><A HREF="word.html">Fictional Word Processor 6.0</A>
17: <LI><A HREF="data.html">Fictional Database 7.0</A>
18: </UL>
19: <P>
20: Unlike other software companies, our products have
21: absolutely no bugs, and always work perfectly on all
22: computers. Nevertheless, you may run into problems in
23: rare cases, usually your own fault. If this happens,
24: visit our <A HREF="support.html">Technical Support</A>
25: department for helpful information and tips. You can
26: also view more information <A HREF="company.html">about
27: our company</A> or order products with our friendly
28: <a href="order.html">Order Form</A>.
29: <HR>
30: <I>(c)1998 FSC - designed by the FSC staff</I>
31: </BODY>
32: </HTML>
```

The various links on the page send you to the company's other pages. One describes all of the company's products, another contains information about the company, and another gives technical support information. There's also a link to an order form.

Using Drop-Down Lists for Navigation

More recently, FSC decided to add more detailed information to its pages. The main page remains the same, but each product's page is now a menu of links to subpages with various categories of information.

As it is, the pages can be difficult to navigate. For example, if you want to view the system requirements for the Fictional Word Processor product, you must select the product name from the main page, wait for the page to load, and then select the System Requirements link.

With JavaScript, you can create a friendly interface to all the pages on the main page without taking up much space. Let's use one drop-down list to choose a product and another drop-down list to choose the type of information to view about the product.

Naming the Pages

In writing a program, the programming isn't always the hardest part. You should define the task the program will perform and the data it will use in advance, simplifying the actual task of writing the program.

In order to make programming the navigation bar easier, choose simple, meaningful names for the subpages. Construct their names based on the value of the selection lists. Assign a one-letter code to each product: w for the word processor, s for the spreadsheet, and d for the database. Then follow that with an underscore and a word indicating the type of information.

Here are the categories of information and their corresponding codes:

- tech—Technical support for the product
- sales—Sales and availability information
- feat—A list of features
- price—Pricing information for the product
- tips—Tips for getting the most out of the product

For example, s_feat.html is the features list for the spreadsheet program. Meaningful names like this make it easier to maintain HTML pages. When you're automating with JavaScript, meaningful names can make a big difference.

To try this example yourself, you'll need all the individual HTML files. You can download them from this book's Web site at http://www.jsworkshop.com/.

Creating the Data Structures and HTML

Before you write the function to navigate the pages, you need to store the needed data. In this case, you need to store the three codes for the software products and the five codes for the types of pages. You could create an array for each list, but that isn't necessary in this case.

Rather than creating an array, you can simply place the information in the HTML page itself and it will be stored in the properties of the form object by the JavaScript interpreter. You will use the codes as the VALUE attribute of each option.

You will need to define an HTML selection list for each of the lists of information. In addition, the user needs a way to visit the page after selecting it. You can do this with a Go button next to the drop-down lists.

Listing 22.2 shows the HTML to add to the main page. You'll include it toward the end of the page, but it's generally self-contained and could be placed anywhere.

LISTING 22.2   THE HTML TO DEFINE THE TABLE OF CONTENTS.

```
1:    <FORM name="navform">
2:    <SELECT name="program">
3:    <OPTION VALUE="x" SELECTED>Select a Product
4:    <OPTION VALUE="w">Fictional Word Processor
5:    <OPTION VALUE="s">Fictional Spreadsheet
6:    <OPTION VALUE="d">Fictional Database
7:    </SELECT>
8:    <SELECT name="category">
9:    <OPTION VALUE="x" SELECTED>Select a Category
10:   <OPTION VALUE="tech">Technical Support
11:   <OPTION VALUE="sales">Sales and Availability
12:   <OPTION VALUE="feat">List of Features
13:   <OPTION VALUE="price">Pricing Information
14:   <OPTION VALUE="tips">Tips and Techniques
15:   </SELECT>
16:   <INPUT TYPE="button" NAME="go" VALUE="Go to Page"
17:   onClick="Navigate();">
18:   </FORM>
```

In addition to the categories discussed, there's an additional option with the value x in each selection list. These are the default options and display instructions until another selection is made. Selecting the Go button while one of these options is selected does nothing.

Creating the Function for the Navigation Bar

You defined an onClick event handler for the Go button, which calls the Navigate() function. Next, you need to create this function. It will read the current value of both selection lists, construct a filename, and then load that file into the browser.

Listing 22.3 shows the Navigate() function. Next you will look at the features of this function in detail.

LISTING 22.3   THE FUNCTION FOR NAVIGATING BASED ON THE SELECTION LISTS.

```
1: function Navigate() {
2:     prod = document.navform.program.selectedIndex;
3:     cat = document.navform.category.selectedIndex;
4:     prodval = document.navform.program.options[prod].value;
5:     catval = document.navform.category.options[cat].value;
6:     if (prodval == "x" || catval == "x") return;
7:     window.location = prodval + "_" + catval + ".html";
8:  }
```

To begin, this function sets two variables, prod and cat, to hold the currently selected index for each selection list. Next, prodval and catval are assigned to the corresponding value properties.

The if statement checks both lists for the x value, meaning that the user hasn't yet selected an item. If no value has been selected in either list, it returns without doing anything.

Finally, the new document filename is constructed by concatenating the two codes, the underscore (_), and the html suffix. This value is assigned to the window.location property, which causes the new page to be loaded.

> Because changing the location property loads the new document, you can't do anything more in the current JavaScript program. In fact, the Navigate() function never returns. However, you could include JavaScript functions on the next page.

Adding Link Descriptions

Some users will undoubtedly prefer traditional hyperlinks to the navigation bar. To make these links more friendly, you can display descriptions of them on the status line when the user moves the mouse pointer over them.

You can accomplish this easily with onMouseOver event handlers. When the user moves the mouse over a link, this event will call a function to display the appropriate message on the status line. For example, the following HTML defines a link with a friendly status line:

```
<A HREF="order.html"
onMouseOver="window.status='Allows you to order products';return true;"
onMouseOut="window.status='';">

Order form</A>
```

This sets the value of window.status to display the message. In addition, the true value is returned; this is necessary to override the normal action (displaying the URL) for the status line. The onMouseOut event handler can be used to clear the status line when the mouse pointer moves off the link.

You learned the basics of window objects, including the `window.status` object, in Hour 10, "Working with Browser Objects." Event handlers are described in Hour 12, "Responding to Events."

Listing 22.4 shows the result of adding onMouseOver functions to the links in the original version of the FSC Software page. The page is shown in action in Figure 22.2, with the mouse pointer currently over the Order Form link.

LISTING 22.4   HTML LINKS WITH JAVASCRIPT DESCRIPTIONS.

```
 1:  <UL>
 2:  <LI><A HREF="spread.html"
 3:  onMouseOver="window.status='Spreadsheet Information';return true;"
 4:  onMouseOut="window.status='';">
 5:  Fictional Spreadsheet 7.0</A>
 6:  <LI><A HREF="word.html"
 7:  onMouseOver="window.status='Word Processor Info';return true;"
 8:   onMouseOut="window.status='';">
 9:  Fictional Word Processor 6.0</A>
10:  <LI><A HREF="data.html"
11:  onMouseOver="window.status='Database Information';return true;"
12:   onMouseOut="window.status='';">
13: Fictional Database 7.0</A>
14: </UL>
```

FIGURE 22.2

The HTML document with link descriptions.

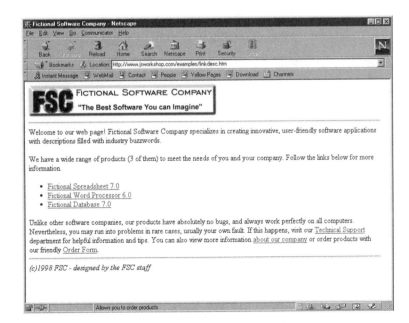

Adding Graphic Links

As an alternative to the drop-down navigation bar, you can use graphics in a navigation bar at the top of the page. You'll use rollovers to change the graphics when the mouse moves over them, as described in Hour 15, "Using Graphics and Animation."

Creating the Graphics

To begin creating the rollovers, you will need to create graphics for the links. For each one, you'll need a highlighted and an unhighlighted version. The highlighting can be a different color, an added line or circle, or anything you want.

For this example, I've created graphics for the major links: Spreadsheet, Word Processor, Database, and Order Form. The highlighted versions are negatives of the normal graphics. For simplicity, call the standard graphics `spread.gif`, `word.gif`, `data.gif`, and `order.gif`. The highlighted versions will have an added numeral 2, as in `order2.gif`.

 When you're creating graphics for rollovers, remember that the highlighted and unhighlighted versions of an image must be the same size. Otherwise, the images may be distorted or may not be replaced correctly.

Creating Event Handlers

Once you've created the graphics, you simply need to add the graphic links with `onMouseOver` and `onMouseOut` event handlers. Listing 22.5 shows the HTML for the graphics, including the event handlers.

LISTING 22.5   THE ROLLOVER EVENT HANDLERS.

```
 1:  <A HREF="spread.html"
 2:     onMouseOver="document.images[1].src='spread2.gif';"
 3:     onMouseOut ="document.images[1].src='spread.gif';">
 4:  <IMG BORDER=0 SRC="spread.gif" height=28 width=173></A>
 5:  <A HREF="word.html"
 6:     onMouseOver="document.images[2].src='word2.gif';"
 7:     onMouseOut ="document.images[2].src='word.gif';">
 8:  <IMG BORDER=0 SRC="word.gif" height=28 width=225></A>
 9:  <A HREF="data.html"
10:     onMouseOver="document.images[3].src='data2.gif';"
11:     onMouseOut ="document.images[3].src='data.gif';">
12:  <IMG BORDER=0 SRC="data.gif" height=28 width=121></A>
13:  <A HREF="order.html"
```

```
14:        onMouseOver="document.images[4].src='order2.gif';"
15:        onMouseOut ="document.images[4].src='order.gif';">
16:     <IMG BORDER=0 SRC="order.gif" height=28 width=152></A>
```

In this case, all of the code for the rollover is included in the HTML event handler, rather than in a separate function. Each link's event handlers change the source of the appropriate image when the mouse enters or exits the area.

> To ensure that image rollovers work quickly and reliably, you should preload any images that are not initially displayed on the page, as described in Hour 15. The full script in the next section includes this feature.

Workshop: Putting It All Together

Over the course of this hour, you've added three different navigational tools to the FSC Web page: ordinary links with status-line descriptions, a drop-down navigation bar, and graphic links that change when the mouse moves over them.

Each of these methods has its advantages and disadvantages. For the best of all three worlds, you can add all of these features to the same Web page. Listing 22.6 is the original Web document combined with the functions for the navigation bar, rollovers, and status-line messages.

LISTING 22.6   THE COMPLETE HTML DOCUMENT.

```
1:     <HTML>
2:     <HEAD>
3:     <TITLE>Fictional Software Company</TITLE>
4:     <SCRIPT LANGUAGE="JavaScript1.1">
5:     o2 = new Image();
6:     o2.src = "order2.gif";
7:     d2 = new Image();
8:     d2.src = "data2.gif";
9:     w2 = new Image();
10:    w2.src = "word2.gif";
11:    s2 = new Image();
12:    s2.src = "spread2.gif";
13:     function Navigate() {
14:        var prod = document.navform.program.selectedIndex;
15:        var cat = document.navform.category.selectedIndex;
16:        var prodval = document.navform.program.options[prod].value;
17:        var catval = document.navform.category.options[cat].value;
18:        if (prodval == "x" || catval == "x") return;
```

continues

LISTING 22.6   CONTINUED

```
19:        window.location = prodval + "_" + catval + ".html";
20:    }
21:    </SCRIPT>
22:    </HEAD>
23:    <BODY>
24:    <IMG SRC="fsclogo.gif" alt="Fictional Software Company"
25:    width=405 height=65>
26:    <HR>
27:    <A HREF="spread.html"
28:       onMouseOver="document.images[1].src='spread2.gif';"
29:       onMouseOut ="document.images[1].src='spread.gif';">
30:    <IMG BORDER=0 SRC="spread.gif" height=28 width=173></A>
31:    <A HREF="word.html"
32:       onMouseOver="document.images[2].src='word2.gif';"
33:       onMouseOut ="document.images[2].src='word.gif';">
34:    <IMG BORDER=0 SRC="word.gif" height=28 width=225></A>
35:    <A HREF="data.html"
36:       onMouseOver="document.images[3].src='data2.gif';"
37:       onMouseOut ="document.images[3].src='data.gif';">
38:    <IMG BORDER=0 SRC="data.gif" height=28 width=121></A>
39:    <A HREF="order.html"
40:       onMouseOver="document.images[4].src='order2.gif';"
41:       onMouseOut ="document.images[4].src='order.gif';">
42:    <IMG BORDER=0 SRC="order.gif" height=28 width=152></A>
43:    <P>Welcome to our web page! Fictional Software Company
44:    specializes in creating innovative, user-friendly software
45:    applications with descriptions filled with industry
46:    buzzwords.
47:    We have a wide range of products:
48:    </P>
49:    <UL>
50:    <LI><A HREF="spread.html"
51:    onMouseOver="window.status='Spreadsheet Information';return true;"
52:       onMouseOut="window.status='';">
53:    Fictional Spreadsheet 7.0</A>
54:    <LI><A HREF="word.html"
55:    onMouseOver="window.status=' Word Processor Info';return true;"
56:       onMouseOut="window.status='';">
57:    Fictional Word Processor 6.0</A>
58:    <LI><A HREF="data.html"    ~
59:    onMouseOver="window.status='Database Information';return true;"
60:       onMouseOut="window.status='';">
61:    Fictional Database 7.0</A>
62:    </UL>
```

22

```
63:    <P>
64:    Unlike other software companies, our products have
65:    absolutely no bugs, and always work perfectly on all
66:    computers. Nevertheless, you may run into problems in
67:    rare cases, usually your own fault. If this happens,
68:    visit our <A HREF="support.html"
69:    onMouseOver="window.status='Technical Support';return true;"
70:      onMouseOut="window.status='';">
71:    Technical Support</A>
72:    department for helpful information and tips. You can
73:    also view more information <A HREF="company.html"
74:    onMouseOver="window.status=' FSC Software Co.';return true;"
75:      onMouseOut="window.status='';">
76:    about our company</A> or order products with our friendly
77:    <A HREF="order.html"
78:    onMouseOver="window.status='Order products';return true;"
79:      onMouseOut="window.status='';">
80:    Order Form</A>.
81:    <FORM name="navform">
82:    <SELECT name="program">
83:    <OPTION VALUE="x" SELECTED>Select a Product
84:    <OPTION VALUE="w">Fictional Word Processor
85:    <OPTION VALUE="s">Fictional Spreadsheet
86:    <OPTION VALUE="d">Fictional Database
87:    </SELECT>
88:    <SELECT name="category">
89:    <OPTION VALUE="x" SELECTED>Select a Category
90:    <OPTION VALUE="tech">Technical Support
91:    <OPTION VALUE="sales">Sales and Availability
92:    <OPTION VALUE="feat">List of Features
93:    <OPTION VALUE="price">Pricing Information
94:    <OPTION VALUE="tips">Tips and Techniques
95:    </SELECT>
96:    <INPUT TYPE="button" NAME="go" VALUE="Go to Page"
97:    onClick="Navigate();">
98:    </FORM>
99:    <HR>
100:   <I>(c)1998 FSC - designed by the FSC staff</I>
101:   </BODY>
102:   </HTML>
```

Figure 22.3 shows this page as it appears in Netscape Navigator. Of course, on a page with this little actual content, all of these navigation features can make it look cluttered. This shouldn't be a problem if your page has more to say than this one.

FIGURE 22.3

The complete HTML document displayed by Netscape.

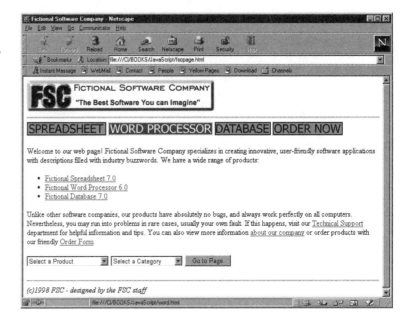

Summary

In this hour, you've used various JavaScript techniques you learned throughout this book to improve a Web page's appearance and user-friendliness.

In the next hour, you'll move on to a more complex JavaScript application: a shopping cart script that tracks orders from a Web page.

Q&A

Q Is there any way to use some kind of "floating hints" or "balloon help" with links instead of using the status bar?

A Not with JavaScript alone. However, you can use Dynamic HTML to achieve this effect.

Q Can the navigation bar in this hour be used with browsers that don't support JavaScript?

A Yes. You could easily modify it to send the selections to a CGI script, which could send the user to the correct page. This would be slower, but would still work.

22

Q Can I add status-line descriptions to the graphic links along with rollovers?

A Yes. Because this would lengthen the event handlers considerably, a function would simplify things in this case.

Quiz

1. In the navigation script, what does `document.navform.category.selectedIndex` refer to?

    a. The number of the currently selected option

    b. The text of the currently selected option

    c. An index to another document

2. When creating rollovers, which HTML tag should include the `onMouseOver` event handler?

    a. `<A>`

    b. `<IMG>`

    c. `<MOOSE>`

3. What's wrong with using the `onMouseOver="window.status='test';"` event handler for a link?

    a. It should include a better description of the link.

    b. It doesn't return a value of `true`.

    c. It should read `onMouseOut`.

Answers

1. a. This refers to the number of the currently selected index.

2. a. The event handler should be included with the link tag, `<A>`. Internet Explorer supports event handlers in the `<IMG>` tag, but Navigator does not.

3. b. The event handler should return a value of `true` to prevent the status line display from being erased.

Exercises

If you want to gain more experience in improving Web pages with JavaScript, try adding one of the following to the page in Listing 22.6:

- A scrolling message (Hour 6)
- Back and Forward buttons (Hour 10)

Hour **23**

Creating a Shopping Cart Script

In Hour 22, "Improving a Web Page with JavaScript," you used simple JavaScript techniques to add features to a Web page. In the last two hours of this book, you'll create some more complex applications with JavaScript.

In this hour, you will create a shopping cart and order form using JavaScript. Hour 23 covers the following topics:

- Planning the shopping cart script
- Creating a frameset
- Choosing variables for data storage
- Writing the script functions
- Submitting the order

Planning the Script

In the last year or so, Internet shopping has gone from something done only by computer junkies to a popular pastime. Web sites that offer products for sale typically use a *shopping cart*, which keeps track of the items ordered and offers a way to finalize the order.

Many shopping carts are created with CGI or Java programs, but you can create a perfectly good one using JavaScript. First, you will need to plan the layout of the Web page and the variables and objects that the shopping cart will use to store data.

 Security is an important consideration in any online ordering system. The shopping cart you will create in this hour is not secure, although it could be used with a secure server to ensure that all orders are valid.

Creating the Frameset Document

One popular way to implement a shopping cart uses frames. You will divide your Web page into two columns: a small shopping cart frame on the left and a frame with a list of products that can be ordered on the right. Listing 23.1 shows the frameset document to implement this.

LISTING 23.1   THE FRAMESET FOR THE SHOPPING CART.

```
1:   <HTML>
2:   <FRAMESET COLS="20%,80%">
3:   <FRAME NAME="cart" SRC="about:blank">
4:   <FRAME NAME="products" SRC="products.html">
5:   </FRAMESET>
6:   </HTML>
```

Notice that there is no HTML document for the shopping cart frame (line 3). This is because you will create that frame's document dynamically with a script, which will enable the frame to display an updated list of products in the cart.

The products.html document will be the focus of most of this hour. This document will include the scripts for displaying and managing the shopping cart. The body of the document will include product descriptions and links for ordering products. Here is a typical order link:

```
<A HREF="javascript:additem('WP 97', 399.95,1);">
<B>ORDER NOW</B></A>
```

This link calls a JavaScript function called `additem` and sends it a product description, price, and quantity. You will create the `additem` script later in this hour.

I've included sample product descriptions and links in the HTML document (presented later this hour) for products offered by FSC, the ill-fated software company introduced in Hour 22. However, this script could easily be used for any products you want to sell.

Choosing Variables

Next, you should plan how the shopping cart will store data. Because you will be dealing with ordered items, each with its own price, description, and quantity, an object will be helpful.

The script will use a simple object called `Item` that stores the description, quantity, and price as properties of the object. You will use an array, `items`, to store an `Item` object for each item in the shopping cart.

Listing 23.2 shows the object definition function for the `Item` object, as well as variable declarations for the `items` array and a counter, `numitems`, to track the number of items in the cart.

LISTING 23.2 VARIABLE DEFINITIONS FOR THE SHOPPING CART.

```
1:   var items = new Array(10);
2:   var numitems = 0;
3:   function Item(d,c,q) {
4:   this.desc = d;
5:   this.price = c;
6:   this.quantity = q;
7:   }
```

Creating Script Functions

Now that you've laid out the frames, HTML documents, and variables, you can begin scripting in earnest. The shopping cart will be managed by several JavaScript functions:

- A function to add an item to the cart
- A function to display the list of items in the shopping cart frame
- A function to update the cart list if an item's quantity is changed
- A function to complete the order

Adding Items to the Cart

The `additem` function adds a single item to the cart. This is the script that will be referred to by the links on the product description page. Listing 23.3 shows the `additem` function.

LISTING 23.3   THE FUNCTION TO ADD AN ITEM TO THE CART.

```
1:    function additem(desc, price,quantity) {
2:    items[++numitems] = new Item(desc,price,quantity);
3:    displaycart();
4:    }
```

This function accepts the description, price, and quantity as parameters from the link. Line 2 creates a new `Item` object, assigns it to the next element of the `items` array, and increments the `numitems` counter. As its last action, this script calls the `displaycart` function.

Listing the Items

The next script function you'll need is `displaycart`, which displays the list of items in the shopping cart frame. This function is called by the `additem` function. Additionally, it will be used when the page is first loaded and when the user changes an item's quantity.

LISTING 23.4   THE SCRIPT TO DISPLAY THE CART'S CONTENTS.

```
1:    function displaycart() {
2:       var totalcost=0;
3:       with (parent.cart.document) {
4:          open();
5:          write("<HTML><BODY>");
6:          write("<H1>Shopping Cart</H1><HR>");
7:          if (numitems==0) {
8:             write("No items ordered.");
9:             close();
10:            return;
11:         }
12:         write("<TABLE BORDER=1><FORM NAME='form1'>");
13:         for(i=1;i<=numitems;i++) {
14:            write("<TR><TD>");
15:            write("<INPUT NAME='qty' TYPE='TEXT' SIZE=2 VALUE=");
16:            write(items[i].quantity + ">");
17:            write("<TD>" + items[i].desc);
18:            write("<TD>" + items[i].price);
19:            write("<TD>" + (items[i].price * items[i].quantity));
```

```
20:                    write("</TR>\n");
21:                    totalcost += (items[i].price * items[i].quantity);
22:                }
23:            totalcost = Math.floor(totalcost*100) /100;
24:            write("<TR><TD COLSPAN=3><B>Total Cost:</B>");
25:            write("<TD>" + totalcost);
26:            write("</TABLE>");
27:            write("<INPUT TYPE=BUTTON VALUE='Update'");
28:            write("onClick='parent.products.updatecart();'>");
29:            write("<INPUT TYPE=BUTTON VALUE='Complete Order'");
30:            write("onClick='parent.products.complete();'>");
31:            write("</FORM></HTML>");
32:            close();
33:        }
34:    }
```

23

This function lists the items in a table in the shopping cart frame, with one added feature: It displays the quantity for each item in a text field so that it can be changed. This allows the user to order more than one of a product or change a quantity to 0 to cancel an item. Here's a breakdown of how the displaycart function works:

- Line 3 uses the with statement to make parent.cart.document the current object. This eliminates the need to type this object name in nearly every line of the function.

- Lines 4–6 open a document in the shopping cart frame and display an HTML header.

- Lines 7–11 check the number of items. If it is 0 (as it will be when the page is first loaded), the function returns, displaying only the header and a brief message.

- Lines 12–22 use a loop to display the quantity, description, price, and total price for each item in an HTML table.

- Lines 23–26 add a total cost and end the table.

- Lines 27–30 create two buttons: one to update the shopping cart and another to complete the order. These both call functions in the main (product list) frame.

- Lines 31–32 write some closing HTML tags and close the document.

Updating the Cart Contents

The shopping cart display uses text fields for the quantities for the ordered items. This allows the user to modify the quantity for an item or change it to zero to cancel the item. The next function, updatecart, is called when the user clicks the Update button displayed at the end of the cart listing. Listing 23.5 shows this function.

LISTING 23.5   THE SCRIPT TO UPDATE THE CART.

```
1:   function updatecart() {
2:      for (i=1; i<=numitems;i++) {
3:      if (numitems == 1)
4:         items[i].quantity = parent.cart.document.form1.qty.value;
5:      else
6:         items[i].quantity = parent.cart.document.form1.qty[i-1].value;
7:      }
8:      displaycart();
9:   }
```

This function reads the quantities from the text fields in the shopping cart document and updates the quantities in the `items` array. Finally, the `displaycart` function is called to update the display.

If you use the same name for several form elements, JavaScript treats them as an array with that name. This is how line 5 reads the quantity. However, if only one item was ordered, there is no array. In this case, lines 3 and 4 read the value as a simple property.

Completing the Order

The simplest function in the script is the `complete` function, which completes the order. This opens a new window, which loads the `complete.html` file. You will create this file later in this hour. Listing 23.6 shows the `complete` function.

LISTING 23.5   THE SCRIPT TO OPEN THE ORDER WINDOW.

```
1:   function complete() {
2:      OrdWin=window.open('complete.html','OrdWin');
3:   }
```

Putting It All Together

You now have all of the components of a basic shopping cart. To put them all together, Listing 23.7 shows the complete `products.html` document with all of its script functions.

LISTING 23.7   THE COMPLETE SHOPPING CART SCRIPT.

```
1:    <HTML>
2:    <HEAD>
3:    <TITLE>Products List</TITLE>
4:    <SCRIPT LANGUAGE="JavaScript">
5:    var items = new Array(10);
6:    var numitems = 0;
7:    function Item(d,c,q) {
8:    this.desc = d;
9:    this.price = c;
10:    this.quantity = q;
11:    }
12:    function additem(desc, price,quantity) {
13:    items[++numitems] = new Item(desc,price,quantity);
14:    displaycart();
15:    }
16:    function displaycart() {
17:        var totalcost=0;
18:        with (parent.cart.document) {
19:            open();
20:            write("<HTML><BODY>");
21:            write("<H1>Shopping Cart</H1><HR>");
22:            if (numitems==0) {
23:                write("No items ordered.");
24:                close();
25:                return;
26:            }
27:            write("<TABLE BORDER=1><FORM NAME='form1'>");
28:            for(i=1;i<=numitems;i++) {
29:                write("<TR><TD>");
30:                write("<INPUT NAME='qty' TYPE='TEXT' SIZE=2 VALUE=");
31:                write(items[i].quantity + ">");
32:                write("<TD>" + items[i].desc);
33:                write("<TD>" + items[i].price);
34:                write("<TD>" + (items[i].price * items[i].quantity));
35:                write("</TR>\n");
36:                totalcost += (items[i].price * items[i].quantity);
37:            }
38:            totalcost = Math.floor(totalcost*100) /100;
39:            write("<TR><TD COLSPAN=3><B>Total Cost:</B>");
40:            write("<TD>" + totalcost);
41:            write("</TABLE>");
42:            write("<INPUT TYPE=BUTTON VALUE='Update'");
43:            write("onClick='parent.products.updatecart();'>");
44:            write("<INPUT TYPE=BUTTON VALUE='Complete Order'");
45:            write("onClick='parent.products.complete();'>");
46:            write("</FORM></HTML>");
47:            close();
48:        }
```

continues

LISTING 23.7   CONTINUED

```
49:    }
50:    function updatecart() {
51:       for (i=1; i<=numitems;i++) {
52:       if (numitems == 1)
53:          items[i].quantity=parent.cart.document.form1.qty.value;
54:       else
55:          items[i].quantity=parent.cart.document.form1.qty[i-1].value;
56:       }
57:       displaycart();
58:    }
59:    function complete() {
60:       OrdWin=window.open('cart_complete.html','OrdWin');
61:    }
62:    </SCRIPT>
63:    </HEAD>
64:    <BODY onLoad="displaycart();">
65:    <IMG SRC="fsclogo.gif" alt="Fictional Software Company"
66:    width=405 height=65><BR>
67:    <H1>Products</H1>
68:    <P>The following products are available online. Click the
69:    ORDER NOW link to order a product.</P>
70:    <P><B>Fictional Word Processor 97</B>: Our greatest word processor
71:    ever, now with more features and a name that only makes it seem two
72:    years old.</P>
73:    <UL>
74:    <LI><B>Price: $399.95</B>
75:    <A HREF="javascript:additem('WP 97', 399.95,1);">
76:    <B>ORDER NOW</B></A>
77:    </UL>
78:    <P><B>Fictional Spreadsheet 97:</B> A powerful spreadsheet with
79:    such innovative features as addition, multiplication, and
80:    division. New to Spreadsheet 97 is a feature that lets you add
81:    a list of numbers together.</P>
82:    <UL>
83:    <LI><B>Price: $199.95</B>
84:    <A HREF="javascript:additem('SP 97', 199.95,1);">
85:    <B>ORDER NOW</B></A>
86:    </UL>
87:    <P><B>Fictional Database 97:</B> A newer, bigger, and slower
88:    version of our popular database. Now so complex you need a
89:    degree to understand it.</P>
90:    <UL>
91:    <LI><B>Price: $499.95</B>
92:    <A HREF="javascript:additem('DB 97', 499.95,1);">
93:    <B>ORDER NOW</B></A>
94:    </UL>
95:    <HR>
96:    </BODY>
97:    </HTML>
```

To test the script, save this document as `products.html` and then load the frameset document from Listing 23.1. Figure 23.1 shows this script in action after a few items have been ordered.

FIGURE 23.1

The shopping cart script in action.

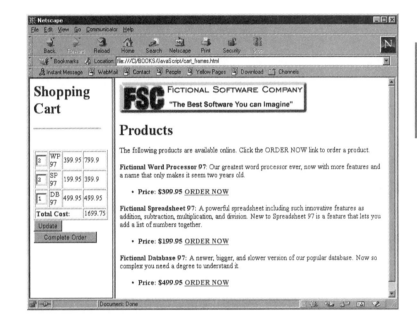

23

Workshop: Creating the Final Order Form

The shopping cart works nicely so far, but there is no way to actually finalize the order. The final missing step is the `complete.html` document, which is opened when the Complete Order button in the shopping cart is clicked.

This document uses a script of its own, included in the body of the document, to display the list of items in the shopping cart one more time. Listing 23.8 shows the order form document.

LISTING 23.8 THE HTML AND SCRIPT FOR THE ORDER FORM.

```
1:    <HTML>
2:    <BODY>
3:    <IMG SRC="fsclogo.gif" width=405 height=65><BR>
4:    <H1>Complete Order</H1>
5:    <HR>
6:    <FORM NAME="form1">
7:    <B>Your Name:</B>
```

continues

LISTING **23.8** CONTINUED

```
8:    <INPUT TYPE="TEXT" NAME="ordername" SIZE=25>
9:    <B>Phone:</B>
10:   <INPUT TYPE="TEXT" NAME="phone" SIZE=18>
11:   <BR>
12:   <B>Shipping Address:</B><BR>
13:   <INPUT TYPE="TEXT" NAME="address1" SIZE=30><BR>
14:   <INPUT TYPE="TEXT" NAME="address2" SIZE=30><BR>
15:   <B>Items Ordered:</B><BR>
16:   <TABLE BORDER=1>
17:   <TR><TD>Quantity <TD>Item
18:   <TD>Unit Cost <TD>Total Cost</TR>
19:   <SCRIPT LANGUAGE="JavaScript1.1">
20:   var numitems = opener.numitems;
21:   var totcost = 0;
22:   for (i=1; i<=numitems; i++) {
23:      document.write("<TR><TD>" + opener.items[i].quantity);
24:      document.write("<TD>" + opener.items[i].desc);
25:      document.write("<TD>" + opener.items[i].price);
26:      cost = opener.items[i].price * opener.items[i].quantity;
27:      cost = Math.round(cost * 100) /100;
28:      totcost += cost;
29:      document.write("<TD>" + cost);
30:      document.write("</TR>\n");
31:      document.write("<INPUT TYPE=HIDDEN NAME='qty" + i + "'");
32:      document.write(" VALUE='" + opener.items[i].quantity + "'>\n");
33:      document.write("<INPUT TYPE=HIDDEN NAME='desc" + i + "'");
34:      document.write(" VALUE='" + opener.items[i].desc + "'>\n");
35:   }
36:   document.write("<TR><TD COLSPAN=3><B>Total Cost:</B>");
37:   document.write("<TD>" + totcost + "</TR>");
38:   </SCRIPT>
39:   </TABLE>
40:   <INPUT TYPE="SUBMIT" VALUE="Submit Order">
41:   </FORM>
42:   </BODY>
43:   </HTML>
```

Here is a breakdown of this document's components:

- Lines 1–6 start the HTML document and the form.
- Lines 7–18 display the beginning of the HTML form.
- Lines 17–38 use a script to display each ordered item and include its description and quantity in a hidden field.
- Lines 39–43 end the form and the HTML document.

Figure 23.2 shows a typical order displayed by this document.

FIGURE 23.2

*The order form docu-
ment in action.*

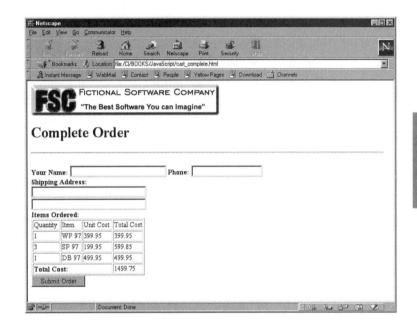

In addition to displaying the order, this script places the quantities and descriptions of the items in hidden form fields. You can change the form's ACTION attribute to send this information by email or send it to a CGI script to finalize the order.

Summary

In this hour, you've applied the techniques you learned in this book to create a JavaScript-based shopping cart application and order form. This is a good example of using JavaScript in business applications.

In the next hour, you will create a decidedly non-business application in JavaScript: a draw poker game.

Q&A

Q Is there a way to store the shopping cart data so that a user can add items on subsequent visits to the page?

A Yes. This can be done with cookies, a browser feature supported by JavaScript. See Appendix A, "Other JavaScript Resources," for more information about this feature.

Q **In the order form script, what does opener mean?**

A This is an object that represents the window that opened the current window, in this
case, the product list frame.

Q **Will this shopping cart script work in Internet Explorer?**

A Some of the features of the script require JavaScript 1.1, but it should work equally
well in Netscape 3.0 and later and Internet Explorer 4.0 and later.

Quiz

1. What's the correct syntax for a script in a frame to refer to a variable in another
   frame?

   a. `document.frames.frame2.varname`

   b. `parent.frame2.varname`

   c. `parent.frame2.document.varname`

2. Which statement clears the cart frame and enables a new document to be written
   to it?

   a. `parent.cart.document.open()`

   b. `parent.cart.open()`

   c. `parent.cart.document.clear()`

3. What happens if you use several elements with the same name in an HTML form?

   a. The form does not display correctly.

   b. The browser suffers an identity crisis.

   c. JavaScript treats them as an array.

Answers

1. b. The correct syntax is `parent.frame2.varname`.

2. a. The statement is `parent.cart.document.open()`.

3. c. If several elements have the same name, JavaScript treats them as an array.

Exercises

If you want to gain more experience with the JavaScript techniques used in this hour, try these exercises:

- Add an action to the order form in Listing 23.8 to send the data to your email address. (This technique is explained in Hour 14, "Getting Data with Forms.")
- As it is, the shopping cart will allow you to order a quantity of 0 for an item. Modify the scripts to remove any item with a quantity of 0 from the shopping cart list and the order form.

23

HOUR 24

Creating a JavaScript Game

Only one more hour to go until you're done with your 24-hour tour of JavaScript. In the final hour, you'll create a JavaScript-based game. This is the longest and most complex script you've dealt with so far.

Hour 24 covers the following topics:

- Creating graphics for the game
- Choosing variables to store data
- Designing the HTML document
- Creating the game program

Planning the Program

In this hour you'll create a JavaScript program that plays a game. It will be a casino-style draw poker game, although it won't cost you a penny to play. In the process you'll learn what it's like to create a complex JavaScript program, complete with graphics, user interaction, and complex calculations.

Creating Graphics

Because this is a card game, you will need graphics for each of the 52 cards in the deck. In case you're not an artist, I've made a set of cards available on this book's Web site at http://www.jsworkshop.com/. (When you look at them, you'll see that I'm not an artist either.)

Five cards will be displayed on the screen at the same time, so I used graphics files with a width of 106 and height of 136. This will allow the game to be played on a 640×480 monitor and should also look good at other resolutions.

One of the main considerations in a program like this is the naming of the graphics files. Although names like Ten of Spades.gif are friendly to users, they would be difficult for the JavaScript interpreter to work with.

To make it easy for the script, I've named the files with the numbers 1-13 (Ace is 1; Jack, Queen, and King are 11, 12, and 13). The file names are simply this number plus a letter representing the suit (c, h, s, or d). As an example, the Jack of Clubs would be 11c.gif.

I've also created a title graphic, a Hold button to be displayed under each dealt card, and Deal and Draw buttons to control the gameplay.

Choosing Variables

The next step in planning the script is to choose the variables that will be used. You can add variables later, but choosing them beforehand helps you plan the way the script will store data.

Listing 24.1 shows the global variable definitions for the draw poker game. The variables include the following:

- score—An integer representing the player's current score. This starts at 100. One point will be bet each time the cards are dealt, and the score will increase based on the poker hand's score.
- dealt—A flag that you'll use to indicate that the cards have been dealt, and the player can now hold or draw cards.
- hand—An array that stores the values of the five cards in the current hand.
- held—An array of flags that indicate whether each card should be held or discarded.
- deck—An array that stores the deck of 52 cards that will be shuffled and dealt from.

24

LISTING 24.1   GLOBAL VARIABLES FOR THE GAME.

```
1:  var score = 100;
2:  var dealt = false;
3:  var hand = new Array(6);
4:  var held = new Array(6);
5:  var deck = new Array(53);
```

To simplify data storage, you will create an object that represents a card. This object will store the card's number, its suit, and a function to calculate the graphics filename to display the card.

LISTING 24.2   THE DEFINITION FOR THE card OBJECT.

```
1:  // Make a filename for an image, given Card object
2:  function fname() {
3:      return this.num + this.suit + ".gif";
4:  }
5:  // Constructor for Card objects
6:  function Card(num,suit) {
7:      this.num = num;
8:      this.suit = suit;
9:      this.fname = fname;
10: }
```

Lines 2–4 define a function that calculates the filename for a card, and lines 6–10 are the definition for the Card object. The deck and hand arrays will store a Card object for each card.

Creating the HTML Document

You should perform one more task before you do any actual scripting: designing the HTML layout for the game. Listing 24.3 shows a basic layout, using an HTML table to align the cards and buttons.

LISTING 24.3   THE HTML DOCUMENT FOR THE GAME.

```
1:  <HTML>
2:  <HEAD>
3:  <TITLE>Draw Poker</TITLE>
4:  </HEAD>
5:  <BODY>
6:  <IMG src="title.gif" width=381 height=81>
7:  <HR>
8:  <FORM NAME="form1">
```

continues

LISTING 24.3 CONTINUED

```
 9:    <TABLE>
10:    <TR>
11:      <TD> <IMG border=0 src="blank.gif" height=136 width=106>
12:      <TD> <IMG border=0 src="blank.gif" height=136 width=106>
13:      <TD> <IMG border=0 src="blank.gif" height=136 width=106>
14:      <TD> <IMG border=0 src="blank.gif" height=136 width=106>
15:      <TD> <IMG border=0 src="blank.gif" height=136 width=106>
16:      <TD> </TD>
17:    </TR>
18:    <TR>
19:      <TD> <A HREF="#" onClick="Hold(1);">
20:          <IMG border=0 src="hold.gif" height=50 width=106></A>
21:      <TD> <A HREF="#" onClick="Hold(2);">
22:          <IMG border=0 src="hold.gif" height=50 width=106></A>
23:      <TD> <A HREF="#" onClick="Hold(3);">
24:          <IMG border=0 src="hold.gif" height=50 width=106></A>
25:      <TD> <A HREF="#" onClick="Hold(4);">
26:          <IMG border=0 src="hold.gif" height=50 width=106></A>
27:      <TD> <A HREF="#" onClick="Hold(5);">
28:          <IMG border=0 src="hold.gif" height=50 width=106></A>
29:    </TR>
30:    <TR>
31:      <TD> <B>Total<BR>Score:</B>
32:          <INPUT TYPE="TEXT" SIZE=6 NAME="total" VALUE="100"></TD>
33:      <TD colspan=2> <B>Current <BR>Hand:</B>
34:          <INPUT TYPE="TEXT" SIZE=20 NAME="message"
35:           VALUE="Press DEAL to begin.">
36:      <TD>
37:      <TD> <A HREF="#" onClick="DealDraw();">
38:          <IMG border=0 src="deal.gif" height=50 width=106></A>
39:    </TR>
40:    </TABLE>
41:    </FORM>
42:    </BODY>
43:    </HTML>
```

Here's a breakdown of the HTML components used in this document:

- Line 9 starts an HTML table, which will line up the elements on the page.

- Lines 10 through 17 define a row of the table that displays the five cards. A blank picture (blank.gif) is used as the source because no cards have been dealt yet.

- Lines 18 through 29 define the second row of the table. This row contains Hold buttons for each card.

- Lines 30 through 38 define the third row. This row includes text fields for the total score and the status of the current hand, as well as the Deal button (which will change into a Draw button after the cards are dealt).

Figure 24.1 shows the HTML document as displayed by Netscape before a game has started.

FIGURE 24.1

The completed HTML layout for the game.

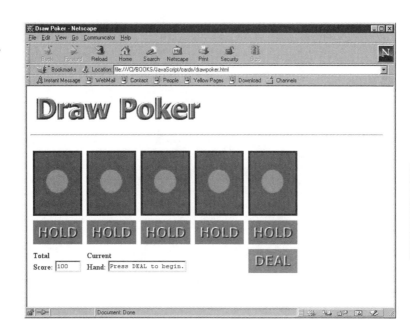

24

Writing the Program

You're now ready to write the actual script to play the game. Because this is a game, the script will be entirely controlled by the user. Each of the functions is called by an event handler in the HTML document.

Handling the Deal/Draw Button

Because the Deal and Draw buttons are the same button, you will need a function that determines which action should be performed. The DealDraw function will be called by the button's event handler:

```
function DealDraw() {
   if (dealt == true) Draw();
   else Deal();
}
```

This function checks whether the cards have been dealt. If they have, it calls the Draw function; otherwise, it calls the Deal function.

Shuffling the Deck

The Deal function deals five cards into the five spaces in your HTML document. To begin, you first need a shuffled deck of cards. Listing 24.4 shows the first half of the Deal function, which fills the deck array with cards and then shuffles them.

LISTING 24.4   THE SCRIPT TO SHUFFLE THE DECK OF CARDS.

```
1:  function Deal() {
2:  // fill the deck (in order, for now)
3:     for (i=1; i<14; i++) {
4:        deck[i] = new Card(i,"c");
5:        deck[i+13] = new Card(i,"h");
6:        deck[i+26] = new Card(i,"s");
7:        deck[i+39] = new Card(i,"d");
8:     }
9:  // shuffle the deck
10:     var n = Math.floor(400 * Math.random() + 500);
11:     for (i=1; i<n; i++) {
12:        card1 = Math.floor(52*Math.random() + 1);
13:        card2 = Math.floor(52*Math.random() + 1);
14:        temp = deck[card2];
15:        deck[card2] = deck[card1];
16:        deck[card1] = temp;
17:     }
```

Here's a breakdown of the actions performed by this function:

- Lines 3–8 fill the deck with cards. To begin with, the cards are in order by number and then by suit.
- Lines 9–17 shuffle the deck. This is accomplished by picking a random number (line 10) and starting a loop based on that number. In each loop iteration, two random cards are chosen (lines 12 and 13) and swapped (lines 14–16).

Dealing the Cards

The second half of the Deal function will actually deal the cards. Listing 24.5 shows the remainder of this function.

LISTING 24.5   THE SCRIPT TO DEAL THE CARDS.

```
1:  // Deal and Display cards
2:     for (i=1; i<6; i++) {
3:        hand[i] = deck[i];
4:        document.images[i].src = hand[i].fname();
5:        document.images[i+5].src = "hold.gif";
```

```
 6:        held[i] = false;
 7:      }
 8:    dealt = true;
 9:    score = score - 1; //deduct one for bet amount
10:    document.form1.total.value = score;
11:    document.images[11].src="draw.gif";
12:    Addscore();
13: }
```

This half includes the following actions:

- Line 2 begins a loop that will range from 1 to 5, using the variable i.
- Line 3 assigns the next card in the deck to the hand.
- Line 4 displays the dealt card.
- Line 5 changes the button below the card to the standard hold.gif. (An alternate version will be loaded when the user presses the button.)
- Line 6 resets the held flag for the current card.
- Line 7 ends the loop.
- Lines 8 and 9 set the dealt flag and subtract the bet from the total score.
- Line 10 displays the score in the text field.
- Line 11 changes the Deal button to the Draw button.
- Line 12 calls the Addscore function to calculate the score so far for the dealt hand. We'll examine this function later.

Holding and Discarding Cards

Next, you will need a function that is called when the user presses the Hold button below a card. Listing 24.6 shows the Hold function.

LISTING 24.6 THE Hold FUNCTION.

```
 1:  //Hold or discard a card
 2:  function Hold(num) {
 3:     if (!dealt) return;
 4:     if (!held[num]) {
 5:        held[num]=true;
 6:        document.images[5+num].src="hold2.gif";
 7:     }
 8:     else {
 9:        held[num]=false;
10:        document.images[5+num].src="hold.gif";
11:     }
12:  }
```

This function accepts a parameter indicating the card to hold. Line 3 returns if the cards have not yet been dealt. Lines 3–12 toggle the held flag for the card and display either a highlighted or a plain version of the Hold button to tell the user the card's status.

Drawing New Cards

Next is the Draw function, which is called when the Draw button is clicked. It draws more cards from the deck to replace the cards that the user wants to discard (those that aren't set to Hold). Listing 24.7 shows the Draw function.

LISTING 24.7   THE SCRIPT TO DRAW NEW CARDS.

```
1:  //Draw new cards
2:  function Draw() {
3:     var curcard = 6;
4:     for (i=1; i<6; i++) {
5:        if (!held[i]) {
6:        hand[i] = deck[curcard++];
7:        document.images[i].src = hand[i].fname();
8:        }
9:     }
10:    dealt = false;
11:    document.images[11].src="deal.gif";
12:    score += Addscore();
13:    document.form1.total.value = score;
14: }
```

Here's how the Draw function works:

- Line 3 sets a local variable called curcard to indicate the next card to be drawn from the deck. Because five cards have already been drawn, it starts at card number 6.

- Lines 4–9 are a loop that checks each card's status in the held array. If the card is not held, it is replaced with the next card from the deck and the image on the page is updated.

- Because this hand is finished, lines 10 and 11 prepare for the next hand. The dealt variable is set back to false, and the Deal button replaces the Draw button.

- Lines 12 and 13 call the Addscore function to calculate the score. Unlike the Deal function, this time the score is added to the total score and redisplayed.

Calculating the Score

Last but not least, the Addscore function calculates the score for the current poker hand. The score is one of the following values, loosely based on the odds of different hands:

- One pair (Jacks or better): 1 point

- Two pair: 2 points

- Three of a kind: 3 points

- Straight: 4 points

- Flush: 5 points

- Full house: 10 points

- Four of a kind: 25 points

- Straight flush: 50 points

- Royal flush: 100 points

Listing 24.8 shows the complete Addscore function.

24

LISTING 24.8   THE SCORE CALCULATION FUNCTION.

```
1:   // Calculate Score
2:   function Addscore() {
3:      var straight = false;
4:      var flush = false;
5:      var pairs = 0;
6:      var three = false;
7:      var tally = new Array(14);
8:   // sorted array for convenience
9:      var nums = new Array(5);
10:     for (i=0; i<5; i++) {
11:        nums[i] = hand[i+1].num;
12:     }
13:     nums.sort(Numsort);
14:  // flush
15:     if (hand[1].suit == hand[2].suit &&
16:         hand[2].suit == hand[3].suit &&
17:         hand[3].suit == hand[4].suit &&
18:         hand[4].suit == hand[5].suit) flush = true;
19:  // straight (Ace low)
20:     if (nums[0] == nums[1] - 1 &&
21:         nums[1] == nums[2] - 1 &&
22:         nums[2] == nums[3] - 1 &&
23:         nums[3] == nums[4] - 1) straight = true;
24:  // straight (Ace high)
25:     if (nums[0] == 1 && nums[1] == 10 && nums[2] == 11
26:         && nums[3] == 12 && nums[4] == 13)
27:         straight = true;
28:  // royal flush, straight flush, straight, flush
29:     if (straight && flush && nums[4] == 13 && nums[0] == 1) {
30:        document.form1.message.value="Royal Flush";
31:        return 100;
```

continues

LISTING 24.8 CONTINUED

```
32:      }
33:      if (straight && flush) {
34:        document.form1.message.value="Straight Flush";
35:        return 50;
36:      }
37:      if (straight) {
38:        document.form1.message.value="Straight";
39:        return 4;
40:      }
41:      if (flush) {
42:        document.form1.message.value="Flush";
43:        return 5;
44:      }
45: // tally array is a count for each card value
46:      for (i=1; i<14; i++) {
47:        tally[i] = 0;
48:      }
49:      for (i=0; i<5; i++) {
50:        tally[nums[i]] += 1;
51:      }
52:      for (i=1; i<14; i++) {
53:        if (tally[i] == 4) {
54:          document.form1.message.value = "Four of a Kind";
55:          return 25;
56:        }
57:        if (tally[i] == 3) three = true;
58:        if (tally[i] == 2) pairs += 1;
59:      }
60:      if (three && pairs == 1) {
61:        document.form1.message.value="Full House";
62:        return 10;
63:      }
64:      if (pairs == 2) {
65:        document.form1.message.value="Two Pair";
66:        return 2;
67:      }
68:      if (three) {
69:        document.form1.message.value="Three of a Kind";
70:        return 3;
71:      }
72:      if (pairs == 1) {
73:        if (tally[1] == 2 || tally[11]==2
74:        || tally[12] == 2 || tally[13]==2) {
75:          document.form1.message.value="Jacks or Better";
76:          return 1;
77:        }
78:      }
79:      document.form1.message.value="No Score";
80:      return 0;
81: }
```

This function includes some complex calculations, but it isn't too difficult to understand. Here's a breakdown of how it works:

- Lines 3–7 initialize variables, including flags for the various types of poker hands.
- Lines 8–13 create the nums array, which stores a sorted version of the list of card values in the hand. This makes it easier to detect some hands (such as straights).
- Lines 14–18 detect a flush (all cards have the same suit).
- Lines 19–27 detect a straight (all cards in a sequence). Because Aces can represent either 1 or 13, straights ending in Ace are checked separately.
- Lines 28–32 detect a royal flush (10, J, Q, K, A) and return the score.
- Lines 33–44 return the scores for straight flush, straight, and flush hands.
- Lines 45–51 create an array called tally. This is used to count the number of cards of each value in the hand.
- Lines 52–71 use the tally array to detect four of a kind, full house, two pair, three of a kind, and pair hands.
- If the previous code detected a pair of cards, lines 72–78 check whether it's a pair of Jacks or better and return the appropriate score.
- If no scoring hand was detected, lines 79 and 80 return from the Addscore function with no score.

Workshop: Putting It All Together

Listing 24.9 shows the complete draw poker game. In case you don't want to type all this yourself, you can download the complete script from this book's Web site at http://www.jsworkshop.com/.

LISTING 24.9 THE COMPLETE DRAW POKER GAME.

```
 1:  <HTML>
 2:  <HEAD>
 3:  <TITLE>Draw Poker</TITLE>
 4:  <SCRIPT LANGUAGE="JavaScript1.1">
 5:  var score = 100;
 6:  var dealt = false;
 7:  var hand = new Array(6);
 8:  var held = new Array(6);
 9:  var deck = new Array(53);
10:  function DealDraw() {
11:      if (dealt == true) Draw();
12:      else Deal();
```

continues

LISTING 24.9 CONTINUED

```
13:  }
14:  function Deal() {
15:  // fill the deck (in order, for now)
16:      for (i=1; i<14; i++) {
17:        deck[i] = new Card(i,"c");
18:        deck[i+13] = new Card(i,"h");
19:        deck[i+26] = new Card(i,"s");
20:        deck[i+39] = new Card(i,"d");
21:      }
22:  // shuffle the deck
23:      var n = Math.floor(400 * Math.random() + 500);
24:      for (i=1; i<n; i++) {
25:        card1 = Math.floor(52*Math.random() + 1);
26:        card2 = Math.floor(52*Math.random() + 1);
27:        temp = deck[card2];
28:        deck[card2] = deck[card1];
29:        deck[card1] = temp;
30:      }
31:  // Deal and Display cards
32:      for (i=1; i<6; i++) {
33:        hand[i] = deck[i];
34:        document.images[i].src = hand[i].fname();
35:        document.images[i+5].src = "hold.gif";
36:        held[i] = false;
37:        }
38:      dealt = true;
39:      score = score - 1; //deduct one for bet amount
40:      document.form1.total.value = score;
41:      document.images[11].src="draw.gif";
42:      Addscore();
43:  }
44:  //Hold or discard a card
45:  function Hold(num) {
46:      if (!dealt) return;
47:      if (!held[num]) {
48:        held[num]=true;
49:        document.images[5+num].src="hold2.gif";
50:      }
51:      else {
52:        held[num]=false;
53:        document.images[5+num].src="hold.gif";
54:      }
55:  }
56:  //Draw new cards
57:  function Draw() {
58:      var curcard = 6;
59:      for (i=1; i<6; i++) {
60:        if (!held[i]) {
61:        hand[i] = deck[curcard++];
```

```
62:            document.images[i].src = hand[i].fname();
63:          }
64:        }
65:        dealt = false;
66:        document.images[11].src="deal.gif";
67:        score += Addscore();
68:        document.form1.total.value = score;
69:    }
70:    // Make a filename for an image, given Card object
71:    function fname() {
72:        return this.num + this.suit + ".gif";
73:    }
74:    // Constructor for Card objects
75:    function Card(num,suit) {
76:        this.num = num;
77:        this.suit = suit;
78:        this.fname = fname;
79:    }
80:    // Numeric sort function
81:    function Numsort(a,b) { return a - b; }
82:    // Calculate Score
83:    function Addscore() {
84:        var straight = false;
85:        var flush = false;
86:        var pairs = 0;
87:        var three = false;
88:        var tally = new Array(14);
89:    // sorted array for convenience
90:        var nums = new Array(5);
91:        for (i=0; i<5; i++) {
92:            nums[i] = hand[i+1].num;
93:        }
94:        nums.sort(Numsort);
95:    // flush
96:        if (hand[1].suit == hand[2].suit &&
97:            hand[2].suit == hand[3].suit &&
98:            hand[3].suit == hand[4].suit &&
99:            hand[4].suit == hand[5].suit) flush = true;
100:   // straight (Ace low)
101:        if (nums[0] == nums[1] - 1 &&
102:            nums[1] == nums[2] - 1 &&
103:            nums[2] == nums[3] - 1 &&
104:            nums[3] == nums[4] - 1) straight = true;
105:   // straight (Ace high)
106:        if (nums[0] == 1 && nums[1] == 10 && nums[2] == 11
107:            && nums[3] == 12 && nums[4] == 13)
108:            straight = true;
109:   // royal flush, straight flush, straight, flush
110:        if (straight && flush && nums[4] == 13 && nums[0] == 1) {
111:            document.form1.message.value="Royal Flush";
112:            return 100;
```

24

continues

LISTING **24.9**   CONTINUED

```
113:        }
114:        if (straight && flush) {
115:          document.form1.message.value="Straight Flush";
116:          return 50;
117:        }
118:        if (straight) {
119:          document.form1.message.value="Straight";
120:          return 4;
121:        }
122:        if (flush) {
123:          document.form1.message.value="Flush";
124:          return 5;
125:        }
126:  // tally array is a count for each card value
127:        for (i=1; i<14; i++) {
128:          tally[i] = 0;
129:        }
130:        for (i=0; i<5; i++) {
131:          tally[nums[i]] += 1;
132:        }
133:
134:        for (i=1; i<14; i++) {
135:          if (tally[i] == 4) {
136:            document.form1.message.value = "Four of a Kind";
137:            return 25;
138:          }
139:          if (tally[i] == 3) three = true;
140:          if (tally[i] == 2) pairs += 1;
141:        }
142:        if (three && pairs == 1) {
143:          document.form1.message.value="Full House";
144:          return 10;
145:        }
146:        if (pairs == 2) {
147:          document.form1.message.value="Two Pair";
148:          return 2;
149:        }
150:        if (three) {
151:          document.form1.message.value="Three of a Kind";
152:          return 3;
153:        }
154:        if (pairs == 1) {
155:          if (tally[1] == 2 || tally[11]==2
156:          || tally[12] == 2 || tally[13]==2) {
157:            document.form1.message.value="Jacks or Better";
158:            return 1;
159:          }
```

```
160:    }
161:    document.form1.message.value="No Score";
162:    return 0;
163: }
164: </SCRIPT>
165: </HEAD>
166: <BODY>
167: <IMG src="title.gif" width=381 height=81>
168: <HR>
169: <FORM NAME="form1">
170: <TABLE>
171: <TR>
172:   <TD> <IMG border=0 src="blank.gif" height=136 width=106>
173:   <TD> <IMG border=0 src="blank.gif" height=136 width=106>
174:   <TD> <IMG border=0 src="blank.gif" height=136 width=106>
175:   <TD> <IMG border=0 src="blank.gif" height=136 width=106>
176:   <TD> <IMG border=0 src="blank.gif" height=136 width=106>
177:   <TD> </TD>
178: </TR>
179: <TR>
180:   <TD> <A HREF="#" onClick="Hold(1);">
181:       <IMG border=0 src="hold.gif" height=50 width=106></A>
182:   <TD> <A HREF="#" onClick="Hold(2);">
183:       <IMG border=0 src="hold.gif" height=50 width=106></A>
184:   <TD> <A HREF="#" onClick="Hold(3);">
185:       <IMG border=0 src="hold.gif" height=50 width=106></A>
186:   <TD> <A HREF="#" onClick="Hold(4);">
187:       <IMG border=0 src="hold.gif" height=50 width=106></A>
188:   <TD> <A HREF="#" onClick="Hold(5);">
189:       <IMG border=0 src="hold.gif" height=50 width=106></A>
190: </TR>
191: <TR>
192:   <TD> <B>Total<BR>Score:</B>
193:       <INPUT TYPE="TEXT" SIZE=6 NAME="total" VALUE="100"></TD>
194:   <TD colspan=2> <B>Current <BR>Hand:</B>
195:       <INPUT TYPE="TEXT" SIZE=20 NAME="message"
196:        VALUE="Press DEAL to begin.">
197:   <TD>
198:   <TD> <A HREF="#" onClick="DealDraw();">
199:       <IMG border=0 src="deal.gif" height=50 width=106></A>
200: </TR>
201: </TABLE>
202: </FORM>
203: </BODY>
204: </HTML>
```

24

Figure 24.2 shows Netscape's display of the script after a game has been in progress for a while. (You'll notice that I'm losing.)

FIGURE 24.2

The complete game in action.

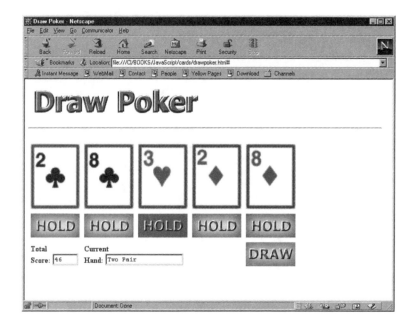

Summary

In this hour, you've created a complete—and hopefully fun—JavaScript application. You've seen how graphics, HTML, and JavaScript can be fitted together to create a complete application.

You've reached the end of this book. I hope you've enjoyed spending 24 hours learning JavaScript and that you'll continue to learn more about it on your own. See this book's Web site at `http://www.jsworkshop.com/` and Appendix A, "Other JavaScript Resources," for some starting points to further your learning.

Q&A

Q Is this about as complex as a JavaScript program can get?

A Not by any means. You can write much more complicated scripts that can encompass several different HTML files.

Q **I thought the images in the `images` array were indexed starting with 0, but the game uses the indices 1-5 to display the cards. How does this work?**

A The game includes a title graphic at the top, which uses the `images[0]` space.

Q **Why use an object to store cards when the filename (such as `10h.gif`) already stores a card's information?**

A Just for convenience. By using an object, you can individually access the card's value and its suit, which are heavily used by the scoring routine.

Quiz

1. Which array can you use to change images in a Web page?

    a. `this`

    b. `document.src`

    c. `document.images`

2. Which of the following is the correct expression for a random integer between 1 and 52?

    a. `Math.random(52)`

    b. `Math.floor(52*Math.random() + 1)`

    c. `Math.floor(52*Math.random())`

3. What are the odds of being dealt a royal flush while playing this game?

    a. 1 in 5,000

    b. 1 in 50,000

    c. 1 in 500,000

Answers

1. c. The `document.images` array can be used to change images on a page.

2. b. Because the `Math.random` method returns a number between 0 and 1, the correct expression is `Math.floor(52*Math.random() + 1)`.

3. c. The odds are about one in half a million, but I didn't really expect you to know that offhand.

24

Exercises

If you want to gain more experience with the techniques you learned in this chapter, try these exercises:

- Modify the draw poker game to allow the player to bet a variable amount instead of one point for each turn, and adjust the scoring accordingly.

- Add text fields to the draw poker display to keep track of the number of wins (hands that returned a score) and losses (hands with no score) and modify the script to update these fields.

- Use the <EMBED> tag and the play method, described in Hour 20, "Working with Multimedia and Plug-Ins," to add sounds to the game.

APPENDIX **A**

Other JavaScript Resources

While you've learned a lot about JavaScript in 24 hours, you still have a lot to learn. If you'd like to move on to advanced features of JavaScript or learn more, the resources listed in this appendix will be helpful.

Other Books

The following books, also from Sams, discuss JavaScript in more detail:

- *Pure JavaScript* by Jason Gilliam et al. ISBN 0-672-31547-5
- *Sams Teach Yourself JavaScript 1.3 in 21 Days* by Arman Danesh. ISBN 1-57521-304-4
- *Dynamic HTML Unleashed* by Rick Darnell et al. ISBN 1-57521-353-2

JavaScript Web Sites

The following Web sites will help you learn more about JavaScript:

- JavaScript Developer Central, part of Netscape's DevEdge site, includes links to a wide variety of JavaScript resources.

  `http://developer.netscape.com/tech/javascript/index.html`

- Netscape's JavaScript Reference is the definitive JavaScript reference.

  `http://developer.netscape.com/docs/manuals/communicator/jsref/index.htm`

- Live Software's JavaScript Resource Center includes links to a number of resources, as well as discussion groups you can participate in.

  `http://www.livesoftware.com/jrc/index.html`

This Book's Web Site

As with everything else on the Internet, JavaScript is constantly changing, and sometimes it's hard for a printed book to keep up. For this reason, I've created a Web site to accompany this book:

`http://www.jsworkshop.com/`

At this site you'll find the following:

- The latest news about JavaScript and the Web in general
- Updated links to other JavaScript pages and resources
- Corrections and clarifications for this book
- Tips and tricks for new JavaScript techniques
- Online versions of the examples in this book, which you can copy and use yourself
- Updated examples showing JavaScript's capabilities
- A chance to communicate with the author and other JavaScript users

Appendix B

Tools for JavaScript Developers

One of the best things about JavaScript is that it requires no specialized tools—all you need to start scripting is a Web browser and a simple text editor. Nonetheless, tools are available that will make scripting easier. Some of these are described in this appendix.

HTML and Text Editors

While they aren't specifically intended for scripting, a wide variety of HTML editors are available. These allow you to easily create Web documents, either by automating the process of entering tags or by presenting you with an environment for directly creating styled text.

HomeSite

HomeSite, from Allaire, is a full-featured HTML editor. It is similar to a text editor, but includes features to automatically add HTML tags and to easily create complicated HTML elements such as tables.

The latest version also includes JavaScript features, such as creating tags automatically and coloring script commands to make them easy to follow.

A demo version of HomeSite is available for download from Allaire's site at

```
http://www.allaire.com/
```

FrontPage

Microsoft FrontPage is a popular WYSIWYG (what you see is what you get) HTML editor that allows you to easily create HTML documents. The latest version, FrontPage 2000, includes a component to create simple scripts automatically.

You can download FrontPage from Microsoft's site at

```
http://www.microsoft.com/frontpage/
```

NetObjects ScriptBuilder

NetObjects ScriptBuilder is a development environment for JavaScript that provides a sophisticated editor and tools to create simple scripts automatically. You can learn more about it from the NetObjects Web site at

```
http://www.netobjects.com/
```

BBEdit

For Macintosh users, BBEdit is a great HTML editor that also includes JavaScript features. You can download BBEdit Lite or purchase the full version from Bare Bones Software's Web site at

```
http://www.bbedit.com/
```

Alpha

Macintosh users should also check out the Alpha text editor. This is a powerful, highly customizable, interactive text editor that emacs power users should feel right at home with. Information and downloads can be found at

```
http://alpha.olm.net/
```

Other Editors

Often a simple text editor is all you need to work on an HTML document or script. Here are some editors that are available for download:

- EditPad, by Jan Goyvaerts, is an enhanced replacement for Windows' Notepad accessory, including extra features such as search and replace. You can download EditPad from `http://www.ping.be/jg/editpad.shtml`.

- TexEdit Plus, by Trans-Tex Software, is a scriptable, styled text editor that fills the gap between Apple's SimpleText and a full-featured word processor. It's fast, efficient, and has a clean, uncluttered interface. It's also great for cleaning up text that is transmitted over the Internet. It can be downloaded from `http://www.near-side.com/trans-tex/software/tex-edit-plus2.4.sit.hqx`.

Netscape's Visual JavaScript

Visual JavaScript is a new graphical tool for JavaScript from Netscape. It allows you to use JavaScript components, which you can download, and customize them for your own use. Visual JavaScript is available from Netscape's site at

`http://www.netscape.com/`

B

APPENDIX C

Glossary

ActiveX A technology developed by Microsoft to allow components to be created, primarily for Windows computers. ActiveX components, or controls, can be embedded in Web pages.

applet A Java program that is designed to be embedded in a Web page.

argument A parameter that is passed to a function when it is called. Arguments are specified within parentheses in the function call.

array A set of variables that can be referred to with the same name and a number, called an index.

Boolean A type of variable that can store only two values: true and false.

concatenate The act of combining two strings into a single, longer string.

conditional A JavaScript statement that performs an action if a particular condition is true, usually using the `if` statement.

decrement To decrease the value of a variable by one. In JavaScript, this can be done with the decrement operator, `++`.

debug The act of finding errors, or bugs, in a program or script.

element   A single member of an array, referred to with an index.

event   A condition, often the result of a user's action, that can be detected by a script.

expression   A combination of variables, constants, and operators that can be evaluated to a single value.

function   A group of JavaScript statements that can be referred to using a function name and arguments.

Hypertext Markup Language (HTML)   The language used in Web documents. JavaScript statements are not HTML, but can be included within an HTML document.

increment   To increase the value of a variable by one. In JavaScript, this is done with the increment operator, - -.

interpreter   The browser component that interprets JavaScript statements and acts on them.

Java   An object-oriented language developed by Sun Microsystems. Java applets can be embedded within a Web page. JavaScript has similar syntax, but is not the same as Java.

JavaScript   A scripting language for Web documents, loosely based on Java's syntax, developed by Netscape. JavaScript is now supported by the most popular browsers.

loop   A set of JavaScript statements that is executed a number of times or until a certain condition is met.

method   A specialized type of function that can be stored in an object and acts on the object's properties.

Navigator   A browser developed by Netscape, and the first to support JavaScript.

object   A type of variable that can store multiple values, called properties, and functions, called methods.

operator   A character used to divide variables or constants used in an expression.

parameter   A variable sent to a function when it is called, also known as an argument.

property   A variable that is stored as part of an object. Each object can have any number of properties.

scope   The part of a JavaScript program that a variable was declared in and is available to.

statement   A single line of a script or program.

string   A group of text characters that can be stored in a variable.

variable   A container, referred to with a name, that can store a number, a string, or an object.

VBScript   A scripting language developed by Microsoft, with syntax based on Visual Basic. VBScript is supported only by Microsoft Internet Explorer.

C

Index

Symbols

! (Not logical operator), 88
!- - tag, 53
!= (is not equal to) conditional operator, 87
< (is less than) conditional operator, 87
<= (is less than or equal to) conditional operator, 87
&& (And logical operator), 87
( ) parentheses, operator precedence, 21
{ } (curly braces), methods, 46
+ (plus sign), statements, 22
+ operator, combining string values, 72
++ operator, 63
+= operator, 63, 73

- - operator, 63
- -> tag, 53
-= operator, 63
/* */ (C-style comments), 54
// (comments), 54
|| (Or logical operator), 87
= (assignment operator), avoiding bugs, 271
= = (equality operator), avoiding bugs, 271
== (is equal to) conditional operator, 87
> (is greater than) conditional operator, 87
>= (is greater than or equal to) conditional operator, 87
; (semicolon), ending statements, 21

A

<A NAME> tag, 126
accessing array elements, 78
ACTION parameter, <FORM> tag, 176
action property, 177
ActiveX, 13
  controls, 13
  defined, 335
  JavaScript, compared, 13
adding
  items to shopping carts, 300
  properties and methods, existing objects, 138
  scripts
    features, 26-27
    HTML document listing, 9
    statements, 20-21
    Web pages, 9-10, 22-23

S

SAMS
Teach Yourself
in 24 Hours

When you only have time for the answers™

Sams Teach Yourself in 24 Hours *gets you the results you want—fast! Work through 24 proven 1-hour lessons and learn everything you need to know to get up to speed quickly. It has the answers you need at the price you can afford.*

Sams Teach Yourself Java 2 in 24 Hours

Rogers Cadenhead
0-672-31630-7
$19.99 US/$28.95 CAN

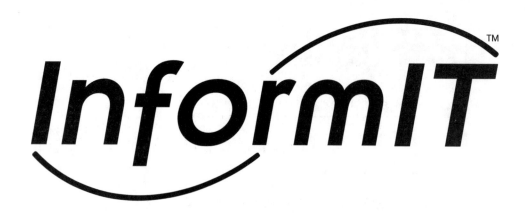